3 64 W9-AQA-392

How New Is the
"New Employment Contract"?

How New Is the "New Employment Contract"?

Evidence from North American Pay Practices

David I. Levine
Dale Belman
Gary Charness
Erica L. Groshen
and
K.C. O'Shaughnessy

2002

W.E. Upjohn Institute for Employment Research
Kalamazoo, Michigan

Dedicated with love to
V.E.,
A.T.W.,
W.A.R.,
C.W.B.,
and
L.S.O.

Contents

List of Figures   ix

List of Tables   x

Acknowledgments   xiii

1 **Introduction**   1
   The Old Employment Contract   2
   The New(?) Employment Contract   3
   The Data   4
   Overview of Results   6

2 **Theories of Internal Labor Markets**   9
   What is an Internal Labor Market?   10
   Institutionalist Approaches to Understanding   13
      Internal Labor Markets
   Institutionalist Hypotheses of Changing Internal Labor Markets   15
   Economic Theories of Internal Labor Markets   25
   Overview   40
   Why Study Internal Labor Markets and their Evolution?   41
   Notes   42

3 **Changes in Internal Labor Markets**   45
   Career Length: Tenure and Displacement   46
   Employee Attitudes   48
   Relation of Internal and External Markets   50
   Pay Practices   51
   Employee Benefits as Risk-Sharing Mechanisms   56
   Work Organization   57
   Sectoral shifts   59
   Discussion   60
   Notes   60

4 **Wage Structures at Large and Small Employers**   63
   Methods: Decomposing Changes in the Size-Wage Gap   63
   Results   67
   Background: Has the Employer Size Declined   67
      for the Typical Employee?
   Are Wage Structures at Large and Nearby   78
      Small Employers Converging?

Summary   83
Notes   84

5 **Changes in Wage Structures within and between Employers**   85
   The Data   85
   Methods   87
   Results   94
   Trends in Total Variation   94
   Persistence of Wage Components   103
   Notes   108

6 **Job Characteristics, Skills, and Wages**   111
   The Data   111
   Results with the 1986 Hay Data   112
   Results with the Indiana/Japan Data   118
   Results over Time in the Hay Data   126
   Conclusion   128
   Notes   128

7 **Changes in Attitudes toward Pay Flexibility**   129
   The Data   129
   Hypotheses   130
   When are Layoffs Acceptable?   138
   Justice Theory Hypotheses   140
   Results   145
   Conclusion   150
   Notes   150

8 **Conclusions**   153
   Predictions and Study Results   153
   Have Institutions and Wage Structures Weakened? 156
   Study Results in Terms of Theory   161
   Implications of this Research   167
   Limitations and Future Research   176
   Note   178

Appendix A: An Illustrative Model of Human Capital Theory   179

Appendix B: The Current Population Survey   183

Appendix C: The Cleveland Community Salary Survey   199

Appendix D: How Representative is the Community Salary Survey?   205

Appendix E: Did Deregulation or Growing Imports   211
         Weaken Wage Structures?

Appendix F: The Hay Data   215

Appendix G: The Indiana/Japan Data   225

Appendix H: The Survey Questions Concerning Layoffs   227

Appendix I: Complete Results of Layoff Questions   231

Reference List   233

The Authors   247

Cited Author Index   249

Subject Index   255

About the Institute   263

Figures

5.1   Standard Deviation of CSS Wage Components over Time   95
5.2   Changing Returns on Skill   98
5.3   Covariance of Employer and Occupational Effects over Time   100
5.4   Occupation, Employer and Internal Structure   104
        Wage Differentials Autocorrelations by Length of
        Time between Observations
5.5   Occupation Autocorrelations over Time   106
5.6   Employer Autocorrelations over Time   106
5.7   Internal Structure Autocorrelations over Time   107

6.1   Decomposing Inequality   116
6.2   Standard Deviation of Establishment Effects with   127
        and without Job Characteristics
6.3   Changes in Inequity (Hay data, 1986–92)   127

8.1   The Size-Wage Gap   157

Tables

1.1   The Five Data Sets   5

2.1   Summary of Hypotheses   39

3.1   Use of Incentive Plans in Large U.S. Employers: 1987–1996   54

4.1   Distribution of Employment by Firm Size   67
4.2   Industry Proportions of Employment by Firm Size   68
4.3   Firm Size Effects on Wages: 1979–1993   70
4.4   Decomposing Changes in the Size-Wage Gap   71
4.5   Sorting of High- and Low-Wage Business Service   76
        Occupations by Industry
4.6   Are Large and Small Firm Regional Effects Converging?   80
4.7   Effects of Local Labor Market Conditions on Wages   81
4.8   Correlation of Large- and Small-Firm Estimated Coefficients   83
        within a Region

5.1   Characteristics of the CSS Data Set, 1956–96   88
5.2   Occupation Winners and Losers, 1974–1990   96
5.3   Wage Dispersion within CSS Job Cells during   102
        the 1980s and 1990s

6.1   Predicting Base Wages   114
6.2   Predicting Base Pay Plus Bonus   117
6.3   The Determinants of Wages in Indiana and   119
        Japan: Baseline Model
6.4   The Determinants of Wages in Indiana and Japan: 121
        Model with Job

7.1   Responses to Pay Cut Questions in Canada and Silicon Valley   131
7.2   Effects of Justifications in Canada and Silicon Valley   135
7.3   Aggregated Results When Pay Cuts Are Fair   137
7.4   How Does the Source of the Shock Affect the Fairness   146
        of Layoffs?
7.5   How Do Employer Reactions Affect the Fairness of Layoffs?   147
7.6   How Does CEO Compensation Affect the Fairness of Layoffs? 149
7.7   Do Employee Characteristics Affect the Fairness of Layoffs?   149

8.1   Summary of Hypotheses   173

B.1 Coefficients and Gap in Large- and Small-Firm   185
    Coefficients, 1979–1993

B.2 The Gap in Means of Characteristics, 1979–1993   187

B.3 Are Returns at Large and Small Firms Converging?   190

B.4 Are Employee Characteristics at Large and Small   192
    Firms Converging?

B.5 Are Returns Rising for Characteristics Common   194
    at Large Firms?

B.6 Do Employees at Large Firms Increasingly Have   196
    Characteristics Large Firms Reward Well?

C.1 Occupations in the Cleveland Community Salary Survey   201
    (1955–96)

D.1 Comparison of Weekly Earnings in the 1995 CSS with the   206
    1995 CPS Outgoing Rotation File

D.2 Comparisons of CSS and Matched Compustat Employer   208

E.1 The Effect of Deregulation on Measures of Industrial   212
    Labor Markets

E.2 The Effect of Foreign Competition on Measures   213
    of Internal Labor Markets

F.1 Summary Statistics of Hay Data   220

F.2 Hay Skill Points   220

F.3 Base Pay   220

F.4 Total Compensation (Base Pay + Bonus)   221

F.5 Industry Breakdown of Respondents   221

F.6 Functional Breakdown of Respondents   222

Acknowledgments

This book emphasizes the collaborative nature of research. David Levine co-authored each chapter. Erica Groshen led the analysis of the Cleveland Salary Survey, Dale Belman the Current Population Survey, and K.C. O'Shaughnessy and Peter Cappelli the Hay data. Gary Charness led the Fairness Survey design, collection, and analysis. O'Shaughnessy also co-authored Chapter 3.

We received many helpful comments from Toshi Akutsu, George Baker, Ben Campbell, Knut Gerlach, Mark Gilkey, Rafael Gomez, Christoph Kohler, Doug Kruse, Adriana Kugler, Jonathan Leonard, Daniel Levine, Georgina Moreno, David Neumark, Trond Peterson, James Rebitzer, Steve Raphael, Chad Slawner, George Strauss, Joseph Tracy, Jimmy Torrez, and Robert Valletta. Students in the University of California, Berkeley, business administration class on the changing employment contract provided helpful comments. Referees at several journals and at the W.E. Upjohn Institute were quite helpful, as was our monitor at the Upjohn Institute, Kevin Hollenbeck.

Comments from seminar or conference participants at the Society of Labor Economists, University of California, Berkeley, University of California, San Diego, University of Southern California, Harvard University, the Russell Sage Institute, the Federal Reserve Bank of New York, the W.E. Upjohn Institute, and the American Social Science Association are gratefully acknowledged.

Danny Kahneman, James Lincoln, The Hay Group, and the Federal Reserve Bank of Cleveland were all extremely generous in sharing their data. We appreciate the excellent research assistance of Libby Bishop, Amanda Moses, Dana Rapoport, and Kren Schiele.

We thank the Upjohn Institute for its support. In addition, we also thank the Clausen Center for International Economics (Charness and Levine), the Economic Policy Institute (Belman), and the Institute of Industrial Relations at U.C. Berkeley (Levine), which provided additional financial support.

The views expressed are those of the authors and do not necessarily reflect the views of the Federal Reserve Bank of New York or the Federal Reserve system. Any errors or omissions are the responsibility of the authors.

1
Introduction

During the 1990s, the media announced the death of the "old" employment contract that promised to exchange hard work for employment security. In its place, the media proclaimed the birth of a new implicit contract based more on market forces: *Fortune* wrote of "the end of traditional notions of corporate loyalty" (Kiechel 1987); *Training* described "a dwindling sense of job security among middle managers and professionals" (Lee 1987); while *Executive Excellence* explained there had been a "dramatic breakdown of [the] tacit agreement [to] exchange of hard work and loyalty for security" (Cashman and Feldman 1995). In short, these and many other sources explained that employers no longer reward employees' loyalty to the company with loyalty and employment security from the company; instead, employers now reward each employee's skills as valued by the labor market this year.

So far, the evidence of any large-scale shift from the old to the new model is suggestive, but not conclusive. For example, there has been a decline in job stability for prime-aged men (Farber, Haltiwanger, and Abraham 1997). At the same time, average tenure has not declined much (e.g., Farber 1995; Neumark, Polsky, and Hansen 2000). On the one hand, employees report lower average perceptions of job security and believe employers are less loyal than they used to be (Cappelli et al. 1997). On the other hand, Americans did not report lower trust in their employer in 1997 than in 1989 (Kruse and Blasi 1998, pp. 22–23). Several prominent large employers such as IBM and Kodak have weakened their commitment to long-term employment, and human resource executives at many large employers report a shift from the stereotypical old employment contract to the new (Hackett 1996). At the same time, commitments for long-term employment never covered more than a few percent of the workforce (Foulkes 1980). (These dimensions of the old and new employment contract are reviewed in more detail in Chapter 3.)

The employment contract involves the terms of an exchange: quantities of employees' time for a certain price (that is, the wage). Past research on the employment contract has emphasized rigidities in the quantity side of the employment relationship, looking for changes in the distribution of job tenure and of rates of displacement. This study focuses on rigidities in the price side, with a focus on whether wage structures are more "flexible." There are many possible dimensions of wage flexibility, and we examine a number of them.

THE OLD EMPLOYMENT CONTRACT

In 1971, Doeringer and Piore published an influential account of how wages are set at large U.S. employers. The internal labor markets they described had a number of wage rigidities. These rigidities, in turn, were due to a range of causes such as long-term commitments between workers and employers, defined career paths, limited ports of entry, and institutions of pay determination such as job evaluation. Most directly, the desire to satisfy norms of constant relative pay kept relative wages rigid. Among the important rigidities they cited were that larger firms paid higher wages; large employers paid similar workers similar wages, even when the employees were in regions with quite different local labor markets; and relative pay between occupations did not vary much over time.

Internal labor markets largely tied wages to job titles and, in most cases, did not rely much on performance evaluation or other forms of incentive pay to determine pay levels within a detailed occupation at an employer. That is, high performance might lead to a promotion, but usually would not increase pay much at the current job title.

Theories of internal labor markets were related to theories of segmented (or "balkanized") labor markets (Kerr 1954) in that they assumed barriers to entry slowed or halted the operation of market forces. Employees who were hired by firms with high ability to pay (for example, larger firms with oligopoly power in the product market) earned above-market wages. These high wages were supported in part because the limited entry ports and traditional patterns of hiring excluded women and minorities from most jobs at high-wage employers.

THE NEW(?) EMPLOYMENT CONTRACT

Each facet of the old employment contract becomes a testable hypothesis for changes in the employment contract. For example, assume the old employment contract had large differences in pay depending on the employer (for similar employees). The new contract should then have less variance of pay among employers. Assume the old employment contract had distinctive internal labor market wage structures that differed among employers. Then the new contract should have all employers paying more-similar relative wages across occupations. Moreover, deviations from the market average in both wage levels and internal wage structures should largely reflect accidents and measurement error, not policy. Thus, both distinctive employer wage levels and within-employer wage patterns should have become less persistent. We examine these hypotheses in the Cleveland Salary Survey, a survey of employers' internal wage structures dating back to 1955 (see Chapter 4).

If the old contract had little pay variation within a job title, the new contract should have more reliance on merit pay and bonuses (although perhaps lower variation due to seniority). We examine this hypothesis in the Cleveland Salary Survey and in the Hay Survey, a survey by the nation's largest compensation consultant.

If the old employment contract had large differences in pay depending on employer size and the old contract has declined, the new contract should have a smaller size-wage effect. Moreover, the distinctive pay patterns (such as higher returns to education) at larger employers should have eroded. Finally, wages at large firms should be more responsive to local labor markets. We examine these hypotheses using the 1979 and 1993 Current Population Surveys, nationally representative samples of the population (see Chapter 5).

The old contract's rigidities were motivated in part by people's perceptions of what is fair. If the new contract has become widely accepted, people will be more accepting of pay flexibility. Conversely, limits on acceptance of pay flexibility may have limited the spread of any new contract. Thus, we also examine changes in attitudes toward pay cuts (see Chapter 6). Separate from an analysis of changes in the contract, we also examine when people perceive layoffs as being fair.

We compare responses with models of traditional and new employment contracts.

Complementing and often building on this descriptive theory of wage determination, economists have developed a number of theories that attempt to explain the observed wage differentials and related institutions (Chapter 2 reviews these theories at more length). Human capital theory suggests that high-wage firms hire more capable workers. The theory of compensating differences argues that undesirable nonpecuniary characteristics of some jobs lead to high wages. Efficiency wage theory argues that high-wage firms paid above-market wages to increase effort, reduce turnover, and achieve other benefits. Rent-sharing theories suggest that wage differentials are due to employers' market power in the product market. Finally, incentive theorists say that variations on the theme of piece rates increase effort and productivity and, thus, wages.

In general, the predictions of human capital theory differ from theories of declining rigidities along most of these dimensions. Human capital theory posits that wage differentials proxy for skills. Unexplained wage differentials, such as those between employers in general or between large and small employers in particular, are assumed to be due to unmeasured skills. Moreover, a number of studies have found that the returns to skills have risen from the 1970s to the 1990s. Thus, wage variation among employers and between large and small employers should have increased. Moreover, good measures of skills should be increasingly useful in predicting wage differentials both within and between employers. We test these hypotheses with the Hay data set, which includes a remarkably good measure of skills and responsibility, the Cleveland Salary Survey, and a pair of data sets collected in Indiana and in Japan in the early 1980s.

THE DATA

A unique aspect of this study is the many sources of data examined, a total of five in all. Table 1.1 briefly describes the five data sets; Chapter 4 contains more detail.

Table 1.1 The Five Data Sets

Data set	Dimensions	Distinctive features
Current Population Survey with Benefits Supplements	Roughly 60,000 people per year in 1979 and in 1993	Nationally representative sample of employees; information on employer size and benefits
Hay Consulting Group	Over 50,000 managers and professionals at 39 firms in 1986 and 1992	A measure of skill and responsibility that correlates 0.80 with wages
Cleveland Salary Survey	Roughly 80 staff occupations at 80 employers per year, 1955–95	Survey with the longest time period with wage structures; occupations explain 80% of wage differences
Indiana/Japan data set	2000 employees at 48 manufacturing establishments in the U.S.A. and 38 in Japan in 1982–83	Measures of training, skill, autonomy, and responsibility
Fairness Survey	Several hundred Canadians in 1985, and 950 Canadians and 1059 U.S. residents in 1997–98	Updating and extension of quasi-experimental survey of fairness in the employment relationship by Kahneman, Knetsch, and Thaler (1986)

It is difficult to study wage structures within enterprises because public data sources do not have information on multiple employees per employer. Thus, in addition to the standard Current Population Survey, we analyze two proprietary data sets (Hay and Cleveland Salary Survey), a unique data set with information on employers and employees in both the United States and Japan, and a survey on fairness in employment relations that was collected specifically for this study. Of the five data sets, three have data on the wages of employees and employers (Hay, CSS, and Indiana/Japan). Among the few sets with employee/employer data, even fewer are longitudinal. In this study, two of the data sets are longitudinal (Hay and CSS) and a further two are repeated cross sections (Current Population Survey and the portion of the Fairness Survey concerning pay cuts).

Three of the data sets contain distinctive measures of skills and working conditions. For example, in addition to standard controls such as age and education, the Indiana/Japan data sets also include multiple measures of job characteristics such as autonomy and complexity. The CSS includes a complete set of detailed occupation codes. These occupation controls explain several times the variation of wages than do standard human capital and demographics controls. For the Hay data set, we have a unique measure of skill and responsibility that is constructed from a detailed job evaluation. This measure correlates more highly with wages than any other skill or responsibility measure we know.

The topics of the book follow the data sets fairly well: that is, we use the CPS to examine whether large and small employers have become more similar to each other. We then look at the Cleveland and Hay data sets for changes among large employers. Thus, each chapter largely presents results from a single data set. At the same time, some substantive issues can be addressed by using multiple data sets. In such cases, results from other data sets may be presented, with a reference to a later chapter's description of the data.

OVERVIEW OF RESULTS

The contributions of the study are several. First, we document in quite novel data sets the rising overall inequality in wages that others have observed. Importantly, we decompose the rising overall inequality into rising inequality within an employer and rising inequality for similar workers at different employers (Hay and CSS). This decomposition has not been carried out with such detailed microdata or for such a long time span.

We also document the rising returns on skill that others have found. Two of our data sets (Hay and CSS) contain extremely good measures of skills and responsibility. Thus, if rising returns on skill are the main change in the labor market, we should see a particular pattern of changes in returns within and among employers as well as among occupations. For example, the rising inequality among occupations appears highly related to the years of education normally needed by that occupation (CSS) and to the Hay points allocated to the job (Hay). In contrast, rising returns to skills do not explain rising inequality among employers (Hay), in contrast to the predictions of human capital theory.

We also test whether shocks to product markets (deregulation and rising imports) or to labor markets (local unemployment rates and local wage rates) affect the level of wages paid by large employers or the rigidities over time and space at large employers. To our surprise, we found little evidence that these factors affect either wage levels or rigidities.

The use of multiple data sets permits us to replicate some results and use multiple data sets to fill in gaps in each alone. As an example of replication, the cross-sectional analysis of whether job characteristics explain why some employers pay high or low wages is carried out in both the Hay and the Indiana/Japan data sets. As an example of complementary analyses, the CSS and Hay data sets permit us to investigate changes in pay practices at large employers. The CPS data set provides a complementary analysis of how pay practices at large and small employers are diverging.

While most existing studies of changes in the employment relationship emphasize changes in job tenure and displacement (the "quantity" side of the employment relationship), we present data on the structure of wages (the "price" side). We complement the data on wages with an attitude survey that examines when people feel layoffs and pay cuts are fair. Importantly, the questions on pay cuts repeat many questions that Kahneman, Knetsch, and Thaler (1986) asked in the mid 1980s, so it is possible to look for changes over time in the perceived fairness of wage flexibility.

In short, the book contributes a description of changing wage structures over four decades. We relate these changes to economic and other theories of wages and careers, and we use these facts and theories to understand the changing employment relationship at large employers in the United States. The result will be a better understanding of what internal labor markets have been and the extent to which they still exist or have been superseded by a "new employment contract." Our results also shed light on human capital and other explanations of internal labor markets.

2
Theories of Internal Labor Markets

Economists typically assume that the market sets wages. In fact, for most employees in the United States, the wage structure determined by their employer's human resource department largely determines their wages, at least in the short run. The administrative design of wage structures and of other aspects of the employment relationship leads to what is known as an internal labor market (to contrast it with the external labor market of textbook economics). Just as wages differ between an external and an internal labor market, job length differs between a classic spot labor market and an internal labor market. Internal labor markets typically have long-term employment relationships, with many employees' careers lasting decades within a single employer.

We first give several overlapping definitions of an internal labor market and provide a brief introduction to the theories of why internal labor markets exist. These theories overlap extensively, so the divisions between the theories are always somewhat artificial. Correspondingly, the theories' predictions often also overlap.

We start with an institutionalist description of internal labor markets. (We refer here to institutionalist labor economics, not new institutionalist theories of economics, sociology, etc.) This historical and descriptive approach is well summed up in Doeringer and Piore's seminal book (1971). The insights in this literature drew on and helped contribute to the economic theories of labor markets: human capital, compensating differences, efficiency wages, and rent-sharing. Each theory has a number of unobservable factors; thus, almost any prediction of one approach can be rephrased to be consistent with another. Nevertheless, due to their distinctive methods and sometimes distinct hypotheses, we treat the institutionalist approach and its several neoclassical alternatives separately.

The original research in this volume focuses largely on one component of an internal labor market: the structure of wages, particularly those in large U.S. employers. If internal labor markets are declining, then we should see changes in the structure of wages inside firms as well as increased acceptance in employees' attitudes towards flexibility of wages. If, however, internal labor markets are not in decline but instead are evolving, then it is important to understand how wages are structured in these new internal labor markets. This chapter formulates the specific hypotheses from each theory that are examined in Chapter 4 through Chapter 7.

WHAT IS AN INTERNAL LABOR MARKET?

The study of internal labor markets has its roots in the institutional labor economics of the 1940s and 1950s (e.g., Lester 1948; Kerr 1954; Dunlop 1957; Livernash 1957). These researchers studied labor market anomalies appearing in the wages and employment conditions of many workers in large organizations. This stream of descriptive research led to Doeringer and Piore's seminal analysis of internal labor markets and their accompanying wage rigidities in large U.S. employers in the late 1960s.

The key distinction that defines an internal labor market is that the wage-setting and job-allocation decisions inside the organization are buffered from the external market. Thus, internal labor market wages are not always equal to external market wages, and employees experience long tenures with a single organization. All descriptions of internal labor markets have a common core of long tenure, some employer-specific skills, procedures that increase perceptions of fairness (as opposed to pure managerial discretion), and some kind of rules-based wage setting.[1]

This definition of internal labor markets is quite encompassing and it is interesting to discuss specific examples that have appeared in the literature. As is appropriate for the historical approach of institutional-ist theories, each description is specific to a time and labor market sector.

For example, Doeringer and Piore studied largely blue-collar manufacturing jobs at the end of the 1960s in the United States. The internal labor markets they described included long-term commitments between employers and employees, defined career paths, limited ports of entry for each career path, wages tied to job (rather than personal) characteristics, and pay structures that exhibit rigidities across occupations and time.

Internal labor markets, as described by Doeringer and Piore, placed high emphasis on custom and history. For example, Doeringer and Piore (as well as standard compensation textbooks today) described a system of pay determination based on job evaluations and wage surveys that institutionalized rigid relative pay between occupations. (Levine [1993b] provided more recent evidence of the persistence of many of these practices.) Specifically, managers and human resource specialists (sometimes in consultation with unions) analyzed and wrote job descriptions for each job title. In the job evaluation process, they then scored these job descriptions along a number of dimensions such as skill and working conditions, yielding a total point count or pay grade for each job title. Compensation departments then examined several wage surveys to determine the average wage changes for broad occupational groups (such as professionals and managers vs. clerical). Because broad occupational groups receive identical percentage increases in pay ranges over time, relative wages among occupations remained largely rigid.

Because most large employers performed their own job evaluations with idiosyncratic weights on different skills and other job attributes, each employer had a distinctive internal wage structure that rewarded some groups of jobs more heavily than their counterparts in the external market. Doeringer and Piore reported that procedural justice, job rights, and protection from layoffs based on seniority contributed to the long tenures of individuals with employers. They showed how limited points of entry into and exit from the internal labor market result in careers buffered from external labor markets.

Working in this tradition, Cappelli et al. (1997) emphasized the importance of the stability of internal labor market jobs in creating incentives for both employees and employers to invest in firm-specific skills. Their analysis suggests that some low-skill jobs acted as ports of entry into job ladders. New hires into these positions then went through training and development, primarily on the job. The defined job ladders were based on seniority and minimum skills qualification. Work was organized by scientific management principles of specialization leading to a functional organizational structure and centralized decision making. The job security evolving from this system was seniority-based for blue-collar workers and essentially lifetime employment for white-collar workers.

Other researchers, such as Osterman (1984), have described alternative combinations of management policies that make up internal labor markets different than those described by Doeringer and Piore. In a more recent example, Brown et al. (1997, p. 10) contrasted U.S. and Japanese ideal-type internal labor markets. The U.S. unionized systems they studied emphasized rigid, highly-specialized job classifications, adversarial labor relations, and minimal training. These workplaces also tended to have some long-term security based on seniority, rigid wages, and little employee involvement. In contrast, Brown et al. presented the Japanese model with lifetime employment, seniority-based wage structures, career job ladders based on skill attainment, on-the-job skill accumulation, and the flexible assignment of labor. The Japanese system required employment stability so that both labor and management would invest in training and involvement. Volatile product markets and publicly granted income security both could reduce the incentives for workers to commit.

While Japanese high-skill workplaces allocated jobs based on skills and seniority, the U.S. version of the skill-intensive system for blue-collar workers had employees bid for jobs that employers posted. Japanese high-skill workplaces also based pay on skills and seniority, while U.S. high-skill employers largely tied pay to jobs.

Thus, some very different descriptions of "internal labor markets" demonstrate the breadth of definitions of the phrase. They are all internal labor markets in that the wages and work practices often diverge sharply from those of a spot market; at the same time, they can also diverge widely from each other.

Other scholars have also examined the testable implications of the theory of internal labor markets. For example, Baker, Gibbs, and Holmstrom (1994) found that labor market conditions at time of hire affect employees' wages for many years (for an opposing view, see Beaudry and DiNardo 1991). Lazear (1995) found that the observable characteristics of job incumbents do little to help predict which jobs are part of long career ladders.

INSTITUTIONALIST APPROACHES TO UNDERSTANDING
INTERNAL LABOR MARKETS

The more inductive and institutionalist approaches to the study of internal labor markets emphasize how many aspects of these institutions can promote perceptions of procedural justice and—if historical relative wages become accepted as fair—distributive justice (Doeringer and Piore 1971). Internal labor markets provide structure for the implicit contract between employers and employees. Through the use of long job tenures and promotion from within, employees are encouraged to view their relationship with the organization as a fair agreement. This fair agreement is based on employees building firm-specific skills in return for protection from the vagaries of the external labor market. Changes in the perception of this implicit contract, including notions of fairness, would signal changes in the functioning of internal labor markets.

Sociologists who analyze workplaces have long claimed that employees' productivity depends on their perception of the underlying social contract with the employer, as well as on narrowly economic concerns (Barnard 1962; Blau 1964; Gouldner 1954). Recently, economists have also begun to focus on the implications of this view. Milgrom and Roberts (1992) pointed out that "the employment contract is typically quite imprecise"; Williamson (1975) spoke of "atmosphere"; and Simon (1991) noted that people in organizations do all sorts of things without receiving any specific reward. Akerlof (1982), Akerlof and Yellen (1990), and Levine (1991b) presented models of work behavior that incorporate social factors such as perception of fair treatment. Rousseau (1995) provided an overview of psychological approaches to the employment contract.

When the social contract, atmosphere, and loyalty matter, then perceptions of fairness can matter as well. A dissatisfied worker may deliberately restrict output or even resort to sabotage. "In simple English, if people do not get what they think they deserve, they get angry" (Akerlof and Yellen 1990, pp. 260–261). On the other hand, an employee who feels he or she receives a fair deal is more likely to perform above any minimum requirements.

Recent evidence supports the view that nonpecuniary considerations affect productivity. Levine (1993b) showed that in simulations, compensation executives make decisions as if they believe fairness matters. For example, executives did not give lower relative or nominal wage increases when unemployment was high. Moreover, in interviews, the executives justified their decisions on fairness grounds.

Rabin (1993) surveyed the literature more broadly and suggested that reciprocity is an important norm in determining fairness—people do not usually believe it is fair when one person responds to gentle actions with harsh actions. Experimental evidence also supports this reasoning. Fehr, Kirchsteiger, and Riedl (1993) and Fehr et al. (1998) found that employees respond to higher (above-market) wages with higher effort, even in an environment where their reputation does not matter. Charness (1998) found that reciprocity is a significant factor in the level of costly effort an employee chooses. Specifically, work effort by "employees" in a laboratory experiment was more sensitive to wages when these are chosen by an "employer" than when they are chosen randomly or by an external entity.

While the experiments mentioned above related to observable work effort, it is likely that in the real world, most employees have more discretion to react in terms of extra-role behavior such as "organizational citizenship behavior" (Organ 1988). Organizational citizenship behavior involves behavior that is above and beyond the call of duty, is discretionary, and not rewarded by an organization's formal reward structure. A number of studies have found that such behavior is higher when employees perceive more fairness, especially when they perceive more procedural justice (e.g., Farh, Podsakoff, and Organ 1990; Konovsky and Pugh 1994; Moorman 1991). Other studies provide fairly consistent evidence that organizational citizenship behavior contributes to organizational performance (e.g., MacKenzie, Podsakoff, and Fetter 1991; Podsakoff, Ahearne, and MacKenzie 1997). The implication is that organizations have an incentive to maintain what employees perceive to be a fair employment contract.

The literature on the employment contract (and on procedural justice more generally) emphasizes that not just the level of pay, but also the causes and processes for changing it can affect employees' reactions (Lind and Tyler 1988; Leventhal 1976). Among other factors, theories of procedural justice emphasize that most respondents consider procedures more fair if the decision maker treats the respondent with respect, has no vested interest in a decision that is harmful to the respondent, and has limited choice in making a decision.

The latter factor implies that changes in the economic context can affect the sense of entitlement. For example, Kahneman, Knetsch, and Thaler (1986) found that economic shocks that reduce profits justify lower wages, but that increases in market power do not. While 77 percent of respondents consider it unfair for a company that has been making money to reduce wages by 5 percent (even if it could easily replace workers with others at the lower wage), 68 percent thought that this wage reduction was acceptable if the company were losing money. More generally, Shore and Tetrick (1994, p. 104) summed up the research on violations of perceived employment contracts by noting the importance of how employees assess responsibility for unmet obligations:

> If an organization appears to break the psychological contract voluntarily, judgments of injustice may be greater than when the organization is not held fully responsible. For example, a psychological contract representing organizational obligations of job security in exchange for employee obligations to be loyal, which is broken (e.g., when an employee is fired or part of a layoff) may be viewed as only a partially broken contract if an economic downturn caused the organization to be unable to fulfill the obligation. In addition, when the organization claims that they cannot completely fulfill a contract, but attempts to partially do so (e.g., early voluntary retirement rather than a layoff), this voluntary attempt may lessen perceptions of a violation.

INSTITUTIONALIST HYPOTHESES OF CHANGING INTERNAL LABOR MARKETS

According to numerous authors (e.g., Hackett 1996, Kanter 1987; and contributors to the special issue of the *Academy of Management Executive* 1996), the old employment contract for core employees at large employers had the following provisions: 1) We expect loyalty from our core mid-level employees, and we provide loyalty in return.

2) If you work hard and receive satisfactory performance ratings, your job is secure. (We might take exception if the financial health of the company is threatened.)

At a small number of large and visible employers (most notably IBM, but also AT&T, Hewlett-Packard, and a few dozen others [Foulkes 1980]), this contract was both generations old and supplemented with provisions that managers and professionals would agree to move or be retrained.

Many authors have expressed the view that we are in the midst of a major shift away from internal labor markets and toward a new employment paradigm characterized by greater employee mobility and diminished ties between employer and employee. For example, the *Academy of Management Executive* (1996) recently devoted a special issue to the new employment contract and its effect on careers. The new contract is said to be particularly prevalent in the professional and technical areas. In contrast to the old contract, the new employment contract has the following provisions: 1) The work you do will be interesting, and you will learn new skills while you are here. 2) Your employability will be high, although perhaps not at this employer. We work on great projects, but as each project ends, it is up to you to find a new place for yourself within the company—otherwise, you must find a new place for yourself outside the company.

The first paragraph of Chapter 1 listed several typical examples of claims of changes in the new employment contract. These and many other articles identify less stable and more market-related compensation patterns as a key part of the new employment relation (e.g., Cappelli 1995; Kanter 1987; Manicatide and Pennell 1992; and Stiles et al. 1997).

Understanding changes in internal labor markets requires an understanding of how perceptions of the implicit contract between employers and employees have changed. Cappelli (1999) stressed that the employment contract has become more market-like. A contract that produced long-term job security and skills training in return for loyalty and commitment is being replaced, many suggest, by a contract which purchases skills for the time period that they are useful, thus encouraging skill acquisition designed to promote employability. If, as we stated above, the common denominator of internal labor markets is that they provided a buffer between employees and the labor market, then changes in the contract to be more market-like will be apparent in the observed wages and career paths of employees. Thus, if internal labor markets are in decline, we should expect to observe a decline in job tenures. We should also see pay structures that respond more to the market and are less rigid.

The hypothesis of declining rigidities is well described by James Annable, a prominent business economist. Annable (1997) observed that historically "explicit and implicit contracts evolved over time guaranteeing . . . established wage differentials." In contrast to this historical pattern, he explained that internal relativities have become less rigid; now "managers are increasingly willing to change wage differentials, especially to isolate skill groups that are in short supply." Moreover, between-company relative wages have also become less rigid: "Companies are breaking away from formal and informal cost-of-living arrangements as annual wage increases give way to performance awards, often linked to the corporation's equity price."

If, as Annable and others in the business press claim, these institutional forces have eroded, then the wage structures described by Doeringer and Piore should have weakened between 1980 and 1996. That is,

Inst 1:   The mean wage employers pay for similar employees and the internal wage structures (relative wages) they pay have become more similar from the 1970s to the 1990s. At the same time, the persistence of both forms of wage structures has declined.[2]

The internal labor market defined above (see pp. 10–12) is an ideal type; at the same time, actual internal labor markets varied greatly. The majority of workers were not in a rigid internal labor market when Doeringer and Piore's study was published (1971), so there is no reason to expect a majority to be in such workplaces today. Thus, changes in a single element of classic internal labor markets may not be symptomatic of a decline in internal labor markets; instead, the shift in management practices may be evidence of a shift from the type of internal labor market used by one set of firms toward the internal labor market type used by another set of firms.

At the same time, other institutional changes may have led to offsetting effects. Changes in comparisons that compensation professionals use to establish pay systems can also increase inequality among employers. Consider, for example, the extreme case in which employers have set pay in line with a wage survey based on other firms' pay levels. If this institutional pay-setting arrangement breaks down, then inequality among employers may rise (Levine 1995). To see this effect most clearly, consider a union that maintains perfect pattern bargaining, i.e., equal wages across employers for similar work. If the pattern breaks down, we have the hypothesis

Inst 1′: Inequality between firms (for similar workers and jobs) has risen.

Employer Size and Internal Labor Markets

The descriptive model of internal labor markets stresses that these labor market institutions are concentrated among large employers (Doeringer and Piore 1971). Internal labor markets are likely to be more common in large enterprises for several reasons. First, the efficiency advantages of internal labor markets are due in large part to replacing idiosyncratic bargaining with agreed-on rules (Williamson 1975). Such rules are more important when each employee is not dealing with the owner–manager. The creation and maintenance of these systems of rules requires substantial fixed costs. As such, they are proportionately less expensive for larger firms. Foulkes (1980) estimated that human resource systems associated with internal labor markets were not cost-effective in establishments of fewer than 500 employees. Opportunities for internal advancement, a concomitant of internal labor markets, also presupposes a firm with a sufficient number of positions to make such advancement a reasonable possibility.

In addition, internal labor markets presume a long-term relationship between the employee and employer; only enterprises of a certain size can plausibly commit to being in business five or more years in the future. Valletta (2000) and Bertrand (1999) formally modeled how implicit long-term contracts that provide insurance or incentives to employees can depend on employers' ability to pay.

Technologically, small employers tend to have multiskilled employees performing a number of roles. The institutionalized wage structures associated with classic internal labor markets cannot arise until the division of labor has become detailed enough to make a formal structure fairly stable over time and employees.

Many aspects of internal labor markets are based on customs and norms; large employers have more incentive to obey norms because their reputation is more valuable. For small employers, reneging on a single employee can raise profits substantially, while for a large employer, it is more likely that the sanctions from remaining and future employees make such reneging unprofitable. Finally, large employers also tend to have more rents and quasi-rents at risk if the workers unionize, making union avoidance a more important consideration.

Although we emphasize that relatively few small employers have internal labor markets, small employers do not all need to pay spot market wages or only provide short-term jobs. Many small employers participate in structured labor markets such as occupationally based markets (for example, in unionized construction). Other small enterprises provide long-term jobs with family ties, not economic ties, while others may create long-term ties with partnership agreements and other mechanisms.

Have the levels of wages at large and small firms converged?

To the extent the returns to size is due to union threat, to employees capturing a share of (now-diminished) product market rents, and to fairness and other more institutional forces that have declined, we have the hypothesis

Inst 2: The returns to size have declined.

Have the structures of wages at large and small firms converged?

Internal labor market theory implies that primary-sector employers paid higher returns to skill and tenure (Dickens and Lang 1985). In our analysis of the size-wage effect, we contrast the labor market in 1979 with that of 1993, where the former period is presumably a time of stronger internal labor markets. If segmented labor market theory is correct, the interaction of education × size and tenure × size should both be positive in 1979. If internal labor markets and labor market dualism have declined, we have

Inst 3a: The returns to education and tenure at large and small
employers have converged.

This hypothesis also arises if size is a weaker correlate of sector
over time. More generally, if internal labor markets have declined, we
should see

Inst 3b: The returns at small and large firms are converging.

Katz and Krueger (1991, Table 4) found mixed results on a related
set of comparisons over a shorter time period: although returns to education were larger in large firms than in small firms in both 1979 and
1988, the size differential declined. In contrast, the returns to experience widened between large and small firms over this time period.

Are local labor markets increasingly important for large employers?

Wages are often set by institutional forces as well as by labor markets. For example, outside of Alaska, the federal government often
pays identical nominal wages to each employee with the same job title,
regardless of location (Katz and Krueger 1991). In addition, unions
such as the United Steel Workers of America often insist that large
employers pay identical wages for identical job titles, regardless of
region. For example, the central issue of the steel strike of 1959, one of
the longer and larger strikes in U.S. history, was whether the pay scale
at southern mills would be brought up to that of the balance of the
country.

Although these are extreme cases, they indicate how large employers (especially if they have rents or quasi-rents) can insulate their
employees from the local labor market. A key question is whether such
insulation occurs in nongovernmental and nonunion settings. We
examine whether other large employers used to have such insulation
but have less in the 1990s. We look for convergence both in means and
in structures between large employers and nearby small employers.
Our methods loosely follow those of Katz and Krueger (1991), who
examined the relationship between government wages and local labor
markets.

If internal labor markets have become less important, then we have
the hypothesis

Inst 4:   The correlation between average wages in a local labor market and large-company wages has risen from 1979 to 1993.

A related test examines not the wage levels but the structure of wage differentials at large and small employers in a region. For example, it might be that the returns to education at large and small firms differed in the early period but not in the later one. To do this analysis for many employee characteristics, we need to summarize all the many coefficients in the large-firm wage equation and in the small-firm wage equation.

We estimated a separate wage equation for each of the nine census regions for each size class, large and small. We then estimated the wage each individual in the region would receive if paid according to the estimated coefficients for large firms, and then as if paid using the coefficients for small firms. We then correlated these predicted wages for the entire sample. If the predicted wages from the two equations in a region are highly correlated, then large and small employers in the region reward the same characteristics. The hypothesis of declining rigidities implies just this convergence

Inst 5:   The correlation of predicted wages using coefficients estimated at a region's large and small employers has increased from 1979 to 1993.

Fairness, Internal Labor Markets, and Sorting

Fairness theories, in which low-wage employees compare themselves with those in the same firm, can also lead to increased sorting when inequality rises in the market. If many employees perform wage comparisons within the employer, then as wage inequalities widen, it becomes increasingly costly to keep high- and low-wage employees in the same company (Cowherd and Levine 1992). The result can be increased outsourcing and thus increased sorting.

This hypothesis is also consistent with fairness theories suggesting that it is costly for enterprises to have both high- and low-wage employees. (Akerlof and Yellen [1990] and Levine [1991b] surveyed evidence for the existence of such costs.) Consider the case where fairness norms are constant over time and reduce productivity at the margin when inequality within the firm is large. In this situation, when inequality rises in the labor market, low-wage companies have an incentive to outsource high-wage occupations such as lawyers and accountants. Conversely, high-wage companies have an incentive to outsource low-wage occupations such as security guards and janitors. These fairness motivations for outsourcing lead to

Inst 6a: High-wage (low-wage) industries have reduced their relative employment intensity of low-wage (high-wage) business services.

Segmented labor market theories stress that access to primary market jobs was often restricted to men, to whites, and to prime-age workers. People of color, women, and youth were more likely to be relegated into the secondary sector. The threat of litigation under Title VII of the Civil Rights Act is also greater at larger employers (Leonard 1996). This threat gives an additional reason why large employers have increased their female and minority (particularly black and Hispanic) employment. If internal labor markets and segmented labor markets have declined, or if the threat of litigation has increased largely at large employers, we should see

Inst 6b: The relation between employer size and employee demographics has weakened.

Fairness and the Employment Contract

Given that perceptions of fairness may matter, what evidence exists concerning community standards of fairness in the employment relationship? In the mid 1980s, Kahneman, Knetsch, and Thaler (1986) conducted a series of quasi-experiments to investigate perceptions of fair treatment in Vancouver and Toronto, outlining the circumstances under which respondents felt that pay cuts were or were not likely to be accepted by employees. One result was that reductions in wages due to slack labor markets were considered unfair for current employees much more frequently than identical cuts in pay for new employees. Another result indicated that pay cuts during times of unemployment were usually perceived as unfair unless the employer was also losing money.

If a new employment contract has both spread and become accepted, we should see that community standards of fairness have changed. If the typical employment contract has, in fact, undergone important changes to more closely resemble the results in the external labor market, then more employees should report that they perceive employer behavior that mimics the market as "fair" in the late 1990s than in the mid 1980s. For example, employees should be more willing to judge pay cuts in times of excess labor supply as fair.

In her widely cited book *Psychological Contracts in Organizations*, Rousseau (1995) used this reasoning to identify trends in the employment contract. She used the same method that we did, adopting the Kahneman, Knetsch, and Thaler questions about when pay cuts are fair. Importantly, her more recent sample was U.S. executives and managers; Kahneman, Knetsch, and Thaler's results were from a representative phone sample of two Canadian cities. Rousseau claimed that from the 1980s to the 1990s, typical answers shifted so that pay cuts were more often perceived as fair (p. 213). Given that both Rousseau's research and that of Gorman and Kehr (1992) found differences based on the occupation and industry of the respondents, these prior results emphasize the need to make comparisons using a sample comparable to that of Kahneman, Knetsch, and Thaler.

We conducted our study in the same two Canadian cities surveyed by Kahneman, Knetsch, and Thaler: Vancouver and Toronto. One test is whether there is a change over time. Greater public acceptance of pay cuts due to the infusion of the new employment contract would lead to

Inst 7:   Pay cuts are considered more fair in 1997 than in the mid 1980s.

It is possible that the employment relation has not changed that much for most employees (as suggested by the relative stability of average tenure, noted above). It is also possible that at many companies, managers have changed the implicit employment contract they offer but that employees do not accept the new contract as fair. That is, norms of fair behavior may be lagging behind the behavior that is common. Either of these possibilities leads to

Inst 7′:   Pay cuts are not considered more fair in 1997 than in the mid 80s.

Current research results on this hypothesis are conflicting. Consistent with the view that companies have changed the contract they offer, Kruse and Blasi (1998, p. 22) presented survey evidence that in 1995, the majority of Americans believed employers were less loyal to employees than they were 10 years before. At the same time, separate surveys did not find that Americans have lower trust in their employer in 1997 than in 1989 (Kruse and Blasi 1998, pp. 22–23).

Although the labor market institutions and culture are quite similar, it is possible that the stability of attitudes we find in Canada has not been matched in the United States. For most of this century, Canada has been associated with a stronger welfare state, a more active government, and lower legitimacy for market forces (Lipset 1990; Card and Freeman 1993). Silicon Valley, California, in contrast, is an unusual region with a history of low unemployment and high mobility among skilled engineers. Moreover, the rhetoric of the new employment contract was clearly annunciated by some Silicon Valley employers such as Apple Computers (e.g., Sculley 1987, pp. 92–99). These differences led us to

> Inst 8a: Pay cuts are perceived as more fair in Silicon Valley than in Canada.

We chose Silicon Valley with the expectation that respondents there are probably more accepting of the new employment contract than would be the typical U.S. respondent. Thus, the tests below provide a one-sided test for U.S.–Canadian differences; even if respondents in Silicon Valley are more accepting of the new contract than respondents in Vancouver and Toronto, most of the United States may hold attitudes more similar to those of Canadians.[3]

It is likely that attitudes toward the fairness of employment policies change more slowly than technology and organizational form; that is, customs and norms matter largely because they change relatively slowly. If there is a lag between when employers would like to introduce a new implicit contract and when most employees accept the new terms as fair, implementation of new organizational contracts and new organizational forms can be slowed. From a managerial perspective, many traditional internal labor market policies may still be useful (at least until any transition is complete).

ECONOMIC THEORIES OF INTERNAL LABOR MARKETS

Given the merits of the market in creating incentives and allocating resources, an important question for the study of organizations is why they exist at all (Coase 1937). This classic question reappears within the discussion of why internal labor markets might exist.

For the first decade after Doeringer and Piore's classic work, economists had few models for incorporating their insights about internal labor markets into mainstream theory. Today, the situation is reversed. Various features of internal labor markets have been modeled as serving a range of functions. Internal labor markets can help provide incentives via tournaments for promotions (Lazear and Rosen 1981), via delayed compensation (Lazear 1981; Becker and Stigler 1974), via threats of dismissal or other efficiency wage effects (Shapiro and Stiglitz 1984; Levine 1992, 1993a), or via enhancing employees' perceptions of fairness (Akerlof 1984). The stability inherent within internal labor markets can provide valuable insurance to employees (Baily 1974; Bertrand 1999) and can attract employees with characteristics such as stability (Salop and Salop 1976).

Where rents or quasi-rents exist, internal labor markets can alleviate problems of collusion (Milgrom and Roberts 1990) or bargaining (Williamson 1975) between employees and managers. Conversely, the high wages and job stability of internal labor markets can act to share rents between workers and owners (Groshen 1991a; Carruth and Oswald 1989). Moreover, internal labor markets can help improve productivity by encouraging senior employees to train junior employees and by motivating employees to acquire firm-specific human capital (Becker 1975), particularly when employees and employers might both be concerned about the other reneging on any agreement to pay for the training (Malcomson 1997).

We group the theories into five overlapping bundles: 1) human capital theory, 2) compensating differences, 3) efficiency wage, 4) rent-sharing and conflict theories, and 5) incentive theories. We discuss several testable implications for each theory of internal labor markets and for how each theory can be consistent with the decline described in the business press. (Other divisions of the theories are possible. The first two theories are traditional neoclassical, while the latter three grow out of agency theoretic versions of neoclassical theory. Sociological forces are stressed in institutionalist theories, fairness versions of efficiency wages, and some forms of rent-sharing and conflict theories.)

Human Capital Theory

Human capital theory is the predominant model that economists use for explaining the level and changes of wages. This theory posits that high-wage establishments (or high-wage occupations within an establishment) employ workers with higher levels of ability than low-wage establishments and occupations.

Consistent with the theory of general human capital, high-wage industries and employers typically hire employees with above-average observable skills such as education and experience. At the same time, observable skills typically leave most of the between-industry and between-employer wage gap unexplained. Two approaches have been used to study the role of ability in explaining establishment and industry effects: longitudinal studies of job changes and adding better measures of ability to the wage equation.

The first approach controls for individual differences by examining wage changes for an individual who changes jobs. Examining only job changers can lead to problems of self-selection and of very high measurement error due to misclassification of industry. Examining displaced workers, for whom job changes are presumably involuntary, and correcting for misclassification rates leaves industry effects largely unexplained (Krueger and Summers 1988).

Increasing the quality of the measures of ability is the second approach to examine whether establishment and industry effects are due to human capital that is unobserved in most wage equations. Examples include IQ and vocational ability test scores (Blackburn and Neumark 1992), family background measures such as parents' occupations and education (Blackburn and Neumark 1992), and extremely detailed occupation controls (Groshen 1991b). In these studies, the controls have little effect on the estimated industry or establishment effects. In Blackburn and Neumark, for example, the standard deviation of industry effects fell from 13.5 percent to 12.3 percent when measures of cognitive ability (test scores) were added to the equation, while the industry effects estimated with few controls had correlations of approximately 0.90 with the industry effects estimated with extensive controls for individual characteristics. In contrast, Abowd, Kramarz, and Margolis (1999) found that controlling for wages at an employee's past job greatly reduced the differences that employers paid for apparently similar employees. These results are not completely convincing because their model does not account for the endogeneity of employee mobility.

When skills are specific to an employer, the theory of human capital can predict many of the features of internal labor markets, such as long-term employment relationships and large wage declines after employee displacement. These theories overlap with efficiency wage theories, in which employers pay trained workers above-market wages to reduce turnover. The important difference is that the theory of firm-specific human capital posits that starting wages are bid down in the competition for these high post-training wages.

Human capital theory and employer wage effects

Human capital theory posits that high-wage employers have employees with high general and firm-specific skills. The work presented in this book is complementary to previous studies on industry and employer wage effects. The previous studies largely investigated whether the characteristics of workers (not their jobs) explain industry or establishment effects; here, we investigate whether the characteristics of jobs (not individual workers) explain establishment effects and internal wage structures.

Appendix A (p. 179) presents an illustrative model in which wage differences are determined solely by differences in skill requirements. In the model, employers differ in their average skills, and thus, employers differ in their average wages. That is, when estimating a model with employer-specific dummies, the standard deviation of the employer wage effects is large. Assume that a good (but imperfect) measure of skills exists; for example, in the 1986 Hay data set, the measure of skill is correlated 0.80 with wages. In this situation we have

HumCap 1: Wage inequality among firms is substantially smaller when controlling for skills than when not controlling for skills.

Human capital theory and changes in wage structures

Human capital theory also offers explanations about changes in wage levels and changes in employer wage effects that are based on returns to skill. Let us assume that the sorting of skills across firms is constant (as shown below, this fact holds approximately in the Hay and Cleveland data sets). If firms differ in their initial complements of skills and returns to skill have increased over time, then we have

HumCap 2: Wage inequality between firms has increased at the same pace as returns to skills increased.

Other researchers have used the converse argument to conclude that rising inequality among employers is due to higher returns to skill. For example, Davis and Haltiwanger (1991, pp. 156–157) estimated a rising correlation between establishment size and wages within manufacturing between 1967 and 1983. They interpreted this result as consistent with a size-wage effect that results from a relationship between unmeasured skills and size coupled with rising returns to skill.

To the extent that employer size proxies for unobserved skills and the returns to skill have risen, human capital theory provides the opposite hypothesis from institutionalist theory of declining differences (Inst 2), i.e.,

HumCap 3: The returns to size have risen.

As in the data set examined by Davis and Haltiwanger, inequality between firms rose over time in the data set we examine. Human capital theory suggests that most of the rise in between-firm inequality should be eliminated if one can control for skill requirements with an accurate measure of skills. Empirically, we have

HumCap 4: The increase in inequality among employers is much smaller when controlling for skill than when not controlling for skill.

Other theories of wage determination suggest additional reasons why between-firm inequality may have risen. For example, inequality among employers (measured perhaps by the standard deviation of firm effects) will also rise if employers increase their reliance on company-wide profit sharing.

Other developments may reduce inequality among employers. If wage levels above the market level were largely due to the ability of some employers to pay more (as in rent-sharing, bargaining, and some fairness theories), then increased competition from imports, deregulation, and other product market shifts should reduce wage inequality among employers by driving down the "rich" employers' ability to pay above-market wages. This pressure is reinforced if the increase in product market competition is greater for companies whose employees have the highest bargaining power and would therefore be more able to secure higher wages. (Bertrand [1999] provides indirect support for this proposition.) More generally, compensation practices such as internally consistent wage structures (as described in prescriptive compensation textbooks and in Levine 1993b) will lead to some inequality among employers. If, as the business press claims, these institutional forces have eroded, this should reduce inequality among employers.

Sorting and skills

Kremer and Maskin (1995) showed that under fairly general conditions, a model that is rich enough to create sorting by skills will also find that shocks that raise the returns to human capital also increase sorting. Given the evidence presented here and elsewhere that returns to skills have increased, we have

HumCap 5a: The correlation between being a high-wage employer and being an employer that employs many high-wage occupations has increased.

If we also assume that the size-wage effect is due to unobserved skill and that returns to skills have risen, the Kremer and Maskin model leads to

HumCap 5b: The characteristics of employees at large and small employers have diverged.

Size and returns to employee characteristics

As noted above, human capital theory implies that the high wages paid in large firms are due to their employees' higher skills. When returns to skill rose in the economy, then human capital theory suggests

HumCap 6:   Returns to characteristics common at large firms have risen.

Although we do not have room to outline all of them here, Belman and Levine (2001) show how many of the predictions of human capital theory concerning the size of employers approximate those of the institutionalist approach if technological change both increases demand for highly skilled workers and has been most rapid in smaller workplaces. Substantial evidence supports the hypothesis that technological change is biased in favor of highly skilled workers, and it is possible that microcomputers have permitted smaller employers to benefit from technology that was generally available at large employers in the 1960s and 1970s.

The Theory of Compensating Differences

The theory of compensating differences suggests that apparently high wages at an employer or job are merely due to unobserved characteristics of the workplace that make the job less desirable. Compensating differences may plausibly explain many of the observed industry effects on wages. For example, teachers (who enjoy summer vacations) receive relatively low pay, while miners (who have dangerous jobs) receive relatively high pay.

In spite of these successes, past research on the effects of working conditions on wages have been mixed at best. Brown (1980) and Killingsworth (1990), for example, surveyed studies that augmented the standard wage equations with measures of undesirable work conditions; the coefficients were rarely both positive and significant. Krueger and Summers (1988, pp. 273–274) added measures of 10 job characteristics (e.g., whether the job was hazardous, whether work conditions were pleasant) to a wage equation. Adding these variables did not substantially alter the measured inter-industry wage differentials.

The research Brown (1980) and Killingsworth (1990) reviewed typically augmented wage equations with job characteristics typical of a worker's occupation, as coded by the U.S. Department of Labor or as calculated from a separate data source. Our study uses the job characteristics actually experienced by the worker, a procedure that should reduce measurement error.

If the high wages are caused by either general human capital or by compensating differences, then quit rates should be uncorrelated with wages (after controlling for observable measures of skills and working conditions). Numerous past researchers have found that firms and industries that pay high wages (controlling for observable characteristics) have lower quit rates (e.g., Akerlof, Rose, and Yellen 1988; Freeman 1980; Levine 1993a). The negative relationship between pay and quits implies that firms are not merely rewarding workers for good skills or for bad working conditions.

The theory of compensating differences posits that jobs with high wages have unmeasured undesirable working conditions. Thus,

> CompDiff 1: Inequality among employers is substantially lower in equations with extensive controls for relevant working conditions than in equations with no such controls.

To the extent that the same set of observable job characteristics may measure both high skill and poor working conditions, this hypothesis will often yield the same predictions as the first hypothesis for human capital theory.

The theory of compensating differences suggests that higher average bonus payments should be (on average) largely offset by lower base pay because employees are ultimately interested in the risk-adjusted level of total compensation. If employers differ for some reason in the average size of the bonuses they pay, then competitive labor markets work to equalize total compensation. This reasoning suggests

> CompDiff 2: Total pay (base + bonus) should be more equal across firms than is base pay.

The data are biased against supporting this hypothesis to the extent that bonuses are more transitory than base wages. In that case, the variance of average total pay at a firm is increased by the transitory bonus, but the compensating difference should be paid based on the long-run average of the expected bonus.

The Efficiency Wage Theory

The efficiency wage hypothesis states that when the productivity of apparently similar workers depends upon their wages, firms set wages to minimize unit labor costs. Higher wages are hypothesized to bring a variety of benefits to the employer, such as increased effort and unmeasured human capital, as well as lower turnover rates and recruitment costs. Katz (1987) and Levine (1992) surveyed this literature. Several tests of efficiency wage theories directly examined these outcomes (e.g., Levine 1992, 1993a; Cappelli and Chauvin 1991).

Other researchers have argued by the process of elimination that persistent establishment and industry effects that do not appear correlated with worker ability or working conditions are indirect evidence of efficiency wages (Dickens and Katz 1987; Krueger and Summers 1988; Groshen 1991a). This source of evidence remains indirect unless it can be shown that high-wage industries and establishments actually have the characteristics that lead to high efficiency wages.

Dickens and Katz (1987) found that industries with a high capital/labor ratio tend to pay higher wages. This result is consistent with the efficiency wage prediction that workers whose shirking can cause the most harm will be paid an efficiency wage. It is also consistent with rent-sharing theories, as employers with much capital at risk have high quasi-rents that employees can try to capture.

Efficiency wages are more likely to be paid in jobs that have high turnover costs and are difficult to monitor. Thus, controlling for job characteristics that are correlated with turnover costs and monitoring difficulty should increase the explanatory power of the regression and should lower the standard deviation of plant and industry effects. Jobs with high levels of training, high levels of complexity, and high levels of autonomy should have higher wages.[4] Thus, just as with unmeasured human capital theory, efficiency wage theories predict

EffWage 1: Inequality among employers is substantially lower in equations with extensive controls for relevant working conditions than in equations with no such controls.

The Hay data set contains information on several dimensions of a job, such as the know-how needed to perform the job. A second dimension, "accountability," measures roughly the discretion held by an employee times the effect the jobholder can have on outcomes times the dollar magnitude of the outcomes. That is, accountability measures how many dollars a firm can lose if an employee provides low effort. Importantly, this is quite close to the measure that efficiency wage theories posit lead to high wages (Shapiro and Stiglitz 1984).

The know-how and accountability dimensions are highly collinear; nevertheless, they usually both contribute independently to predicting wages. Human capital theory suggests they should both be important for wages, with the accountability dimension largely picking up skills omitted from the "know-how" factor. Efficiency wage theories stress that

EffWage 2: The accountability factor has large incremental value in predicting wages after controlling for the know-how factor.

The Rent-Sharing and Bargaining Theories

Theories of rent-sharing, conflict (Marglin 1974), bargaining (Dow 1993), and insider-outsider relationships (Lindbeck and Snower 1986) posit that worker bargaining power and the size of the rents and quasi-rents to be divided affect compensation. These theories overlap with theories of fairness, as employees may feel resentful if prosperous employers do not share the rent. These theories also overlap efficiency wage theories when one of the employer's benefits of setting high wages is avoiding unions (Dickens 1986).

Rent-sharing and bargaining theories of internal labor markets assume that some employers have high rents and purchase their workers' cooperation with relatively high wages. Moreover, such employers have incentives to maintain rigid wage structures to reduce employee bargaining and influence with their supervisors (Milgrom and Roberts 1990; Williamson 1975). In addition, high-wage employers should find it easier to maintain a rigid internal wage structure (Reynolds 1951) that helps insure employees against downturns (Bertrand 1999) and provides incentives based on long-term contracts (Valletta 2000). In either case, employers with high ability to pay are less likely to go out of business soon; thus, their promises are more credible. Because employees give more credence to their promises, such employers are also more likely to make robust promises and long-term implicit contracts.

Most studies find that increased ability to pay (as measured by past high profits per employee, product-market innovations, or declining costs of inputs) is correlated with higher wages (e.g., Blanchflower, Oswald, and Sanfey 1996 and Carruth and Oswald 1989; but also see Groshen 1990).

Other studies examine how changes in the environment can affect aspects of internal labor markets besides wage levels. For example, Bertrand (1999) studied the hypothesis that internal labor markets exist in part to insure employees' earnings. In that case, employees choose that future earnings stay near the earnings at the time of hire instead of bearing the risk of adjusting earnings to future labor market conditions. In such a model, earnings depend on the labor market at the time of hire and, if insurance is complete, later changes in labor market conditions have little effect on current wages.

In Bertrand's model, insurance is not perfect because employers sometimes refuse to or are unable to pay the agreed-on wages in bad times. For example, manufacturing industries that import from countries whose exchange rate has weakened relative to the dollar (an unfavorable exchange rate shock for the domestic employer) will have a higher probability of going bankrupt and, thus, will have lower ability to keep implicit promises to insure employees' wages against fluctuations in local labor market conditions. Consistent with this theory, Bertrand found that in industries that face an unfavorable exchange rate shock, wages are more closely related to current unemployment in the state than are wages in other industries. Moreover, in such industries, wages are less closely related to unemployment at the time the job began.

Importantly, Bertrand did not find these effects for industries with rising import levels. She hypothesized that after demand for an industry's output declines, an industry with strong internal labor markets will have high wages relative to the spot market wage. These high wages, in turn, may induce imports, leading to reverse causality.

Rent-sharing theories as explanations for changes over time

Rent-sharing theories posit that high wages are due to the combination of employers' ability to pay and employees' bargaining power. The management press often sounds as if it is clear that globalization and deregulation have systematically increased competition and reduced product-market rents and employers' ability to pay.[5] The increased turmoil and lower ability to pay, in turn, implies companies are less able to make and keep commitments to employees.

It is not clear that economy-wide profits have declined or that product-market turmoil has increased. (The cases of deregulated industries or those facing rapidly rising import competition are discussed in the next section.) The very high stock market values of the late 1990s suggest that the marginal investor considered profits both high and likely to keep rising.

Even if employers' ability to pay has not on average declined, the employees' share of the rents may have declined. For example, the threat of unionization has declined in most sectors, which may reduce employees' bargaining power. Moreover, in some cases, new workplace practices may largely reduce, not increase, employees' bargaining power (Parker 1985). Such reductions in bargaining power will reduce a group of employees' idiosyncratic wage payments. If bargaining power led wages to diverge from the market, reduced bargaining power should reduce such divergences of an employer's wage level or structure diverging from the market. In our data, this effect implies

> Bargaining 1: Employer and internal structure differentials are smaller and less persistent in the 1990s than in earlier decades.

There is substantial evidence that in many workplaces, changes in work organization have raised skill demands and task variety (Ichniowski et al. 1996). Although the evidence is murkier, some analysts claim that these changes are pervasive, and that these changes increase employees' bargaining power (e.g., Lindbeck and Snower 1996; Snower 1998). Snower argued that what he refers to as the Organizational Revolution "tends to give more scope for earnings to be determined by factors that cannot be captured within the conventional supply-demand framework." Instead, efficiency wage effects are more important as turnover costs rise and as managers find it more difficult to monitor employee effort. Moreover, employees' bargaining power rises due to the higher turnover costs and the increased need for more inter-worker cooperation. Helper, Levine, and Bendoly (forthcoming) provided evidence that at U.S. automobile suppliers, changes in work organization that increased employee involvement were correlated with slightly higher wages.

It is difficult to disentangle whether wages at a workplace with more employee involvement are due to higher general skill (human capital theory); higher turnover costs (efficiency wages and insider-outsider theory); or more difficulty monitoring (efficiency wages and insider-outsider theory). Nevertheless, with additional assumptions, there are observable differences among the theories. The pace of organizational change has been quite uneven among employers (Levine 1995). Moreover, within an employer, usually only a subset of jobs are changed by new workplace practices (Lawler, Mohrman, and Ledford 1995). Thus, if new workplace practices increase employees' wages and appear in only a subset of occupations, then we have

> Bargaining 1′: Employers' internal wage structures have diverged from 1980 to 1995.

Deregulation and globalization

As noted above, it is unclear if ability to pay has declined on average. At the same time, industries subject to deregulation or facing rising foreign competition have experienced above-average declines in ability to pay. Substantial evidence suggests that increased product-market competition due to increased international trade (Abowd and Lemieux 1993) and deregulation in trucking (Belzer 1995), airlines (Card 1996), and telecommunications (see review in Fortin and Lemieux 1997) lowered the level of wages in the most affected industries. Importantly, these studies almost exclusively found effects in unionized settings.

If between-firm gaps in compensation were due to the sharing of product-market rents, then the decline of such rents should (in most cases) have reduced between-firm wage inequality.[6] More generally, if product-market rents have declined, companies are less able to make and keep commitments to employees; thus, we should see weaker internal labor markets. To the extent that employee wage levels and employer wage rigidities were enhanced by the earlier product-market rents, we have

Bargaining 2:   Employer and internal structure differentials have declined most rapidly and become least persistent in the 1990s relative to earlier decades in industries subject to deregulation or rising foreign competition.

Organizational change and employer size

The organizational innovations that have decreased the division of labor and enhanced frontline employees' decision-making power (discussed on p. xx) have been more prevalent in larger organizations (Lawler, Mohrman, and Ledford 1995). Many organizational changes are focused on codifying employees' tacit knowledge. This knowledge had the possibility of conferring some bargaining power onto employees, because such knowledge made them difficult to replace. We see that many organizational changes are concentrated at large employers. If these changes reduce employees' bargaining power on average (Parker 1985), and the changes are concentrated at large employers, the relative wages of large employers should decline. In short,

Bargaining 3:   The size-wage effect has decreased.

Moreover, the division of labor was more intense in large organizations, while smaller workplaces typically always had implicit job rotation and multitasking. Thus, new work organizations with more integrated task groupings imply a greater change of work organization at large than at small workplaces. Finally, early successful adapters of new workplace practices will increase their market share. If their employment grows, then (all else being equal) successful adapters will be more likely to appear in the large size category. All of these forces lead to

Bargaining 3′:   The size-wage effect has increased.

Bargaining and sorting

If larger firms are forced to pay high wages due to employee bargaining power, then the employers will hire employees with high levels of both observed and unobserved skills. In this setting, a reduction in the relative bargaining power of employees at large firms should both reduce the size-wage effect and reduce the sorting of employees by firm size. Intuitively, Wal-Mart is less selective than IBM. These forces imply

> Bargaining 4: Sorting of observed skills by employer size has changed in the same direction as the size-wage effect.

The Incentive Theories

Economic theories posit that monetary incentives (among others) can increase performance. At the same time, "You get what you pay for." Thus, when it is difficult to measure all dimensions of performance, incentive plans may motivate only the behaviors that are measured and not the ones that are valuable to employers. This result has two important implications. First, incentives that are narrowly focused on one or two measurable dimensions of performance (e.g., units of output) reward employees who provide low performance on harder-to-measure dimensions of performance such as quality. Second, individual-level incentives reward employees who provide low performance on harder-to-measure dimensions of performance that affect the entire work group (e.g., cooperation with colleagues or training new employees). At the same time, group-level incentives are usually subject to free-rider problems. (Levine and Shaw [2000] reviewed theories and evidence on the effects of incentive pay.)

Many of the descriptive pieces noted above also claim that pay for performance has increased from the 1970s to the 1990s. These articles typically mentioned both individual-based merit pay and bonuses as well as bonuses based on organizational performance such as gain sharing or profit sharing. An increased role for individual-level merit pay implies

> Incentives 1: Pay variation among employees with the same job title at a single employer has increased.

Annable (1997) (and many others) suggested that many employers are increasing their connection between pay and firm-specific productivity or profitability. This effect implies

> Incentives 2: Pay variation among employers has increased.

Table 2.1 Summary of Hypotheses

Observable	Hypotheses
Wage inequality between firms in the 1970s	Was substantially smaller when controlling for skills and working conditions than when not controlling for skills: HumCap 1, EffWage 1, CompDiff 1
Wage inequality between firms over time	Declined: Inst 1, Bargaining 1 Increased: HumCap 2, Inst 1', Bargaining 1', Incentives 2 Is higher (lower) when looking at base pay + bonus: Incentives 3 (CompDiff 2)
Change in wage inequality between firms over time controlling for job characteristics	Risen: HumCap 2 Much smaller rise with controls: HumCap 4 Risen: Incentives 2
Persistence of employer wage effects	Declined: Inst 1, Bargaining 1 Increased: Bargaining 1'
Size and persistence of employer wage effects in sectors with declining ability to pay	Declined: Bargaining 2
Compensation levels at large and small employers	Converged: Inst 2, Bargaining 3 Diverged: HumCap 3: Bargaining 3'
Returns paid for employee characteristics at large and small employers	The returns of education and tenure in large and small employers have converged: Inst 3a Converged overall: Inst 3b
Employees characteristics at large and small firms	Converged due to breakdown of ILM: Inst 6b Converged due to lower employee rents at large firms: Bargaining 4 High-wage (low-wage) industries have reduced their relative employment intensity of low-wage (high-wage) business services: Inst 6a Diverged due to rising skill demands: HumCap 5
Returns to characteristics common at large firms	Risen: HumCap 6
Wage levels at large and nearby small employers	Converged: Inst 4

(continued)

Table 2.1 (continued)

Observable	Hypotheses
Returns paid for employee characteristics at large and nearby small employers	Converged: Inst 5
Attitudes toward pay cuts and layoffs	More accepting in 1990s than 1980s (data only for pay cuts): Inst 7 More accepting in Silicon Valley than Canada: Inst 8a, b

NOTE: Unless otherwise noted, "Inst" hypotheses refer to institutionalist predictions when labor market rigidities decline, and "HumCap" hypotheses refer to human capital theory predictions when returns to general skills increase.

To the extent that individual bonuses reflect company performance (for example, due to profit sharing), we have

Incentives 3:   Between-company inequality is higher with total pay than with base pay.

Increases in pay tied to the performance of a team or subunit within the organization (for example, via gain-sharing for a single division or department) will increase the short-run variability of pay within an organization. These forms of subunit compensation imply

Incentives 4:   Internal wage structure has increased in variability.

OVERVIEW

In addition to summarizing the many hypotheses, Table 2.1 also highlights two features of social science theories. First, the theories often overlap. For example, almost all theories suggest that controlling for job characteristics should reduce inequality among employers for apparently identical employees (HumCap 1, EffWage 1, CompDiff 1). The theories differ on whether the job characteristics proxy for skills, difficulty in monitoring, or undesirable working conditions, but not on the role they will play in reducing the variability of the estimated employer wage effects.

Second, one variant of a theory can predict a wage differential rise, while another variant of the same theory can predict its decline. For example, assume new work practices are most common at large firms. If these work practices reduce employee bargaining power (as posited by Parker 1985), then the size-wage gap should decline (Bargaining 3). If these work practices raise employee bargaining power (as posited by Lindbeck and Snower 1996), then the size-wage gap should rise (Bargaining 3′). Thus, the correlation we will report will support or fail to support variations of some important theories, but it cannot decisively test any general theory.

WHY STUDY INTERNAL LABOR MARKETS AND THEIR EVOLUTION?

Internal labor markets and employer wage structures are important for several reasons. First, the observation that the organization of work has undergone a dramatic change over the last 15 or so years is well accepted in the business press and corporate hallways, but the evidence has not convinced all academics. As Cappelli (1999, p. 113) suggested: "While I have yet to meet a manager who believes that this change has not stood his or her world on its head, I meet plenty of labor economists studying the aggregate workforce who are not sure what exactly has changed." Studying changes in internal labor markets, then may be a means to connecting theories of organization with the experiences of those employed in organizations.

Second, the large firms and government agencies that historically administered formal wage structures remain an important part of the U.S. labor market. The share of total nonfarm employees that work for government or for employers with more than 1,000 employees is large (52 percent in 1992) and has remained almost constant over the last 20 years.[7] Third, understanding these structures is also key to understanding whether rising pay inequality stems more from increasing variation for people who remain at a single employer or for those who changed jobs (Gottschalk and Moffitt 1994). Finally, the careers of individuals are largely dependent on the actions of the organizations to which they belong. Changes in the structure of the employment relationship affect the choices available to individuals as they attempt to meet their career goals. Without any long-term assurances of employment, individuals may choose to avoid making investments in firm-specific skills and choose to concentrate on marketable skills instead.

Notes

1. In models with full information, long tenure can be facilitated by flexible wages. Conversely, in models with compensating differences (discussed below), employment security can permit employers to hire employees at lower wages. Thus, although long job length and rigid wages need not be found together, in fact they usually are—leading to the anomalies (from the traditional neoclassical economic perspective) that led to the development of the theory of internal labor market.
2. This chapter presents the many hypotheses that are tested in this book. We label these hypotheses with abbreviations of the underlying theories or frameworks: "Inst" for institutional framework; "HumCap" for human capital; "CompDiff" for compensating differences; "EffWage" for efficiency wages; "Bargaining" for rent-sharing and bargaining theories; and "Incentives" for incentive theories. We have disaggregated some hypotheses into parts, and so we have added an "a" or "b" to the label. Finally, in some cases theoretical justification is presented for opposing hypotheses; in these cases, we add a prime (′) to the label.
3. Conversely, Francophone Quebec has a very different history and somewhat different culture than the rest of Canada. In many studies, respondents in Quebec often are less accepting of the market and are more different from U.S. respondents than are Anglophone Canadians (Lipset 1990). Thus, any findings of U.S.–Canadian similarity may not generalize to Quebec.
4. At a given level of desired product quality, jobs with more autonomy and lower levels of monitoring should be paid a higher wage to ensure high effort. If a firm would like to ensure high quality, it may both monitor intensely and pay high wages.
5. A June 1999 search of Lexis-Nexis on the phrase "increasingly competitive" within three words of the word "market" yielded 360 examples from the general business press in the two years preceding the search. Searches over longer time periods identified over 1,000 documents.

    Old organizations with classic internal labor markets may face declining ability to pay if competitors have invented new organizational systems that produce the similar output without expensive commitments to workers. In this case, the new contract between employers and employees is not the result of a decline in protected markets but is itself an innovative form of organization that threatens established internal labor markets.
6. However, Lawrence and Lawrence (1985) provided evidence and theory that increased product-market competition need not reduce bargained wages. They noted that as competition rises, some employers will quit making investments. In

that case, employees can bargain for the value of the current capital stock, a source of quasi-rents they would have to leave for the employer if the employer were still investing.

7. This calculation combines data on the private-sector employers with more than 1,000 employees from the Bureau of the Census's Enterprise Statistics with data from the Bureau of Labor Statistics on government and total nonfarm employment.

3

Changes in Internal Labor Markets
A Survey

As noted in Chapter 1, many articles assure readers that careers have changed dramatically in the United States. The authors of these articles typically explain that rigidities of wages and of employment are much less common than a generation ago. This survey reviews the mixed evidence for these assertions.[1]

A discussion of changes in careers and declines in internal labor markets is complicated because internal labor markets have many dimensions and because no single definition of "internal labor market" exists. Moreover, internal labor markets have always been heterogeneous. Given this heterogeneity, conclusions regarding the decline of internal labor markets are difficult to draw.

As we discuss the changing elements of a classic internal labor market, the following conclusions appear justifiable. On the one hand, it is difficult to say in some overall sense that internal labor markets are declining. The evidence of any large-scale shift from the old to the new model is suggestive but not conclusive. On the other hand, internal labor markets are clearly changing, although it is not evident that the pace of change has increased. Moreover, as Jacoby (1999) pointed out, institutions have tended to look more market-like during periods of relative political and economic stability. Thus, any movement toward more market-like wage-setting and employment allocation may be more representative of movement in the pendulum between markets and institutions than of the disappearance of the institutions.

Internal labor markets have many components, ranging from job stability to perceptions of job security to wage rigidity to employee attitudes and beliefs. Thus, more examination of the gap between internal labor markets and the external market is an important step toward understanding whether they are disappearing or just changing form. This chapter reviews how each of the main components of an internal labor market has evolved in recent decades.

It is important to understand changes in internal labor markets because they are important institutions in creating or constraining inequality, insecurity about earnings and employment, and opportunities for skill enhancement and career mobility.

CAREER LENGTH: TENURE AND DISPLACEMENT

Diminishing job tenures are often presented as the primary evidence of the decline of internal labor markets. Early attempts to verify the notion that downsizing during the 1980s resulted in a decline in job tenure instead found that throughout the 1980s there was overall stability in job tenures (Farber 1995; Diebold, Neumark, and Polsky 1997; Swinnerton and Wial 1996; Jaeger and Stevens 1999; Neumark 2000 reviews this evidence). There were small declines in job tenure for older males and for less-educated males, which were matched by increases in tenure for older females and more-educated females (Farber, Haltiwanger, and Abraham 1997). More recent work, using data from the early 1990s, has shown a fairly dramatic decline in job tenure among the most experienced workers (Farber, Haltiwanger, and Abraham 1997; Neumark, Polsky, and Hansen 2000), which is fairly consistent with declining internal labor markets. To the contrary, though, Allen, Clark, and Schieber (2000) reported increasing job tenure among a sample of employees from 51 large employers. The percentage of employees with 10 or more years of employment with these firms actually increased during the 1990s.

Consistent with declining internal labor markets, it could be that job tenure remains fairly stable while more job changes are involuntary (layoffs and dismissals) instead of voluntary quits. However, Farber, Haltiwanger, and Abraham (1997) pointed out that displacement rates for experienced workers have not changed appreciably. Thus, we see no rise in displacement to accompany the declines in tenure for senior employees. There is, however, some evidence that job displacement by reason of a job being abolished has increased over time. There has also been an increase in job displacement for more educated (Boisjoly, Duncan, and Smeeding 1998), male (Medoff 1993), and white-collar workers (Gardner 1995). Thus, while overall displacement rates are relatively unchanged, there is some evidence pointing to higher displacement rates for those employees (such as middle-aged men with a college education) thought most likely to work in internal labor markets.

The changes in tenure rates that occurred for males in the 1990s,[2], if they do in fact reveal a trend, occurred later than the suggested causes of tenure declines. If foreign competition was driving the changes, why did these changes not appear until the mid 1990s? If corporate downsizing was the cause, why again did it not reduce tenure until the mid 1990s? If declining tenure is part of a decline in internal labor markets, why do we not see it most evident in large firms, which are the most likely to use internal labor markets? Thus, if tenure has declined, it is not clear that the connection to declining internal labor markets is direct.

The increased use of temporary workers has also been presented as an exemplar of declining tenure. For example, there has been an 11 percent annual growth in employment in the temporary services industry. Further, it has been suggested that the growth of temporary employment has been concentrated in firms associated with internal labor markets; for example, large firms (over 1000 employees) are more likely to use temporary workers. Segal and Sullivan (1995) estimated that between 1991 and 1993 temporary jobs in manufacturing grew enough to offset half of the decline in permanent manufacturing jobs.

Increases in temporary workers, however, are not necessarily evidence of the decline of internal labor markets. First, temporary workers are still a small part of the workforce, suggesting that far more workers have some significant attachment to their organizations. Although the percentage of workers in contingent situations (broadly defined) may be as much as 25 or 30 percent of the labor force (Belous 1989), only perhaps 2 percent of the labor force are temporary workers (Segal and Sullivan 1997). Second, the increases in the use of temporary employment may provide a buffer for workers in the internal labor market. This buffering function is, in fact, a trademark of the Japanese internal labor market.

In summary, the evidence of changes in the durability of relationships between employers and employees is mixed. Evidence suggestive of changes includes declines in tenure and increases in displacement rates for older white males (the stereotypical beneficiaries of the classic internal labor market) coupled with the rapid growth in temporary employment. At the same time, the average job tenure of women is increasing, displacement rates for white-collar workers are still quite modest, and temporary workers are still a very small portion of the labor force.

Still, even if tenure (and probably promotion from within) have not changed much, the careers of individuals may have shifted from old-style internal labor markets with well-defined career paths to new style ones where the paths are less defined. Consistent with this thought, Towers Perrin reported that 94 percent of respondents agree that it is their responsibility to remain employable by continually learning new job skills (*Business Wire,* September 16, 1997). On the one hand, we do not know if this percentage has increased over time. On the other hand, this high level of agreement with a major dimension of the new contract is consistent, there being some change in the stability of skills and job ladders, even if there is little decrease in job stability while at the same time the career protection provided by internal labor markets may be on the decline.

EMPLOYEE ATTITUDES

Classic internal labor markets maintained rigidities in wages and employment partly to maintain an implicit contract with employees. Thus, if internal labor markets are in decline, employees' loyalty to and trust in their employers should also have declined.

Such a decline appeared in some data sets and in some responses. The S.R.A. Corporation attitude studies measure the satisfaction and commitment of employees. The results were fairly stable from the 1950s until the mid 1980s, when they began a steep decline (Cappelli 1999). The Mayflower Group reported a similar reduction in employee loyalty during the mid 1980s; a Ganz-Wiley survey also found a decline in employee attitudes between 1985 and 1996, particularly among older employees; surveys from Hay Associates found the same during the 1980s (Cappelli 1999).

Other survey evidence suggests that employee loyalty has not declined. Sibson and Co. (LeBlanc and Mulvey 1998) reported 80 percent of employees were committed to their companies; that level is sufficiently high to preclude massive previous declines. Looking at short-term changes, Aon Consulting's commitment index was approximately the same in 1998 as it was in 1995 when they began surveying employees. A Shell Oil Co./Peter Hart Research survey reported 72 percent of people prefer the security of long-term employment with a single employer, suggesting a continuing interest in committed careers by employees.

Satisfaction similarly does not appear to be adrift. Watson Wyatt found that 65 percent of workers were satisfied with their jobs in 1995. This rate was virtually unchanged from the 1987 value of 64 percent (Reinemer 1995). Over a shorter period, Towers Perrin reported that in 1997, 72 percent of workers were satisfied with their jobs, an improvement from 58 percent in 1995.

An indirect form of evidence for a change over time is changes among cohorts. If a new employment model is now widespread, most analysts predict it will be most accepted by younger employees. A 1999 survey by Interim Services and Louis Harris and Associates found that age was essentially uncorrelated with acceptance of the new workplace model, which they measured as desiring pay for performance and not minding job-hopping.

To the extent that loyalty, commitment, and/or satisfaction declined, some of the decline is probably the result of the downsizing and restructuring that many firms encountered during the mid to late 1980s. The annual American Management Association survey on downsizing routinely found almost half of the responding firms reporting a downsizing event in the previous year (Greenberg 1998). The suggestion is that employees reacted to the uncertainty in their organizations by reducing their commitment and loyalty. Evidence from the General Social Survey (a repeated cross section of a random sample of U.S. workers) shows that workers' perception of job stability did decline during the 1990s (Aaronson and Sullivan 1998).

Case studies also relate downsizing to reduced loyalty. Luthans and Sommer (1999) found a decline in commitment, satisfaction, and trust related to the downsizing of a healthcare organization. Batt's (1996) case study of a downsized telecommunications firm showed decreased loyalty. An internal survey revealed that 92 percent of managers believed that job security had declined and 89 percent believed that opportunities for promotion had declined.

There is a question of whether or not the change in attitudes is permanent. Allen et al. (1995) found some evidence that declines in workers' attitudes immediately following downsizing are followed by a trend upward in the years that follow. There is also some suggestion that procedural justice has an impact on the attitudes of workers who survive a layoff. Seemingly consistent with this idea is the fact that satisfaction in the Defense Department remained fairly consistent over the 1980s even in the face of rather dramatic downsizing (Steel and Rentsch 1997). Perhaps the perceived fairness of the downsizing in the Defense Department was related to the procedural justice, i.e., employees knew the downsizing was due to structural changes in the economy, not to the choices of managers who were uncaring. If such causality held, it would imply that organizations can periodically downsize without declines in employees' attitudes and that an adjusted internal labor market which encourages commitment and loyalty is possible even with the knowledge that downsizing is part of the agreement.

Interestingly, the number of HR executives reporting a shift away from the old high-loyalty contract is far greater than the number working at employers that ever had reputations for implicitly promising job security. That is, many HR managers report a shift to a low-security model in the 1990s (Hackett 1996), but few reported employment security guarantees (even implicit ones) in the 1970s (Foulkes 1980). Thus, even if employee reports of perceived employment security are low, that does not imply that these perceptions are lower than those of a generation earlier.

RELATION OF INTERNAL AND EXTERNAL MARKETS

Internal labor markets produce wage rigidities that protect employees from product market shocks. Baker and Holmstrom (1995) pointed out that in internal labor markets demotions are rare and nominal wages are downwardly rigid. Baker, Gibbs, and Holmstrom (1994) also found that wage rates at hire influence wage rates many years later, suggesting a variance from market wages.[3] Evidence of a closer connection between external and internal market wages would be evidence of declining internal labor markets.

The mainstream media story suggests a two-part decline in internal labor markets. In the first stage, largely during the 1980s, formerly stable employers laid off workers who previously would have been protected. Thus, the loss of firm-specific skills and returns to tenure for displaced workers should have spiked at that time. By the 1990s, the story goes, the new contract was largely in place. Thus, we should observe a decline in the premium paid for firm-specific human capital. Such a reduction could lead to lower earnings losses after displacement.

In fact, the data are inconsistent. Rose (1995) reported that the displacement penalty declined in the 1980s versus the 1970s, while Polsky (1998) reported that the consequences of involuntary job loss worsened. Farber (1993) found no difference in postdisplacement losses in 1990–1991 compared with 1982–1983.

Below (Chapters 5 and 6) we show that the variance and persistence over time of employer wage effects appear to be fairly stable. Moreover, the relationship between large company wages and local labor market wages has not changed substantially from the 1980s to the 1990s (Chapter 4). These results suggest that internal labor markets have not radically dissolved.

PAY PRACTICES

The pay-setting practices of traditional internal labor markets include tying wages to jobs. Movement away from wages rigidly attached to jobs and toward wages tied to individuals or toward wages that vary according to individual, group, or organizational performance would be consistent with declining internal labor markets. There are three elements of change in compensation schemes that reflect declining internal labor markets (at least in theory if not in practice). The first element includes methods to decrease the role of job in determining wages. The second is an increase in the variability of an individual's pay directly connected to their performance. The third is greater variability of an individual's pay connected to the performance of the organization or group. A review of the recent management literature found increased use of all three elements.

Some firms are moving away from wages tied to jobs through efforts to set up groups of jobs in the same broad pay range (broadbanding). Nearly one-third of 3,400 companies surveyed by New York–based William M. Mercer are broadbanding at least some of their pay plans (Poe and Courter 1995). An American Compensation Association survey in 1995 showed 20 percent of firms planning to introduce broadbanding and 16 percent having introduced it during the prior 12 months (Lissy and Morgenstern 1995). A Hay survey showed 25 percent of 277 firms had implemented broadbanding for at least one group of employees by 1996 (*IRS Employment Review* 1996). A survey by Hewitt Associates reports that broadbanding is most often attempted by large organizations (median sales $1.6 billion in their survey) and in organizations that claim to rely more on market wage survey data to set wages for individuals than with their traditional systems (Wagner and Jones 1994). Thus, it appears that broadbanding is favored by firms that more typify the traditional internal labor market, and broadbanding results in pay to individuals that is more representative of external market wages for that individual.

Contrary evidence to the decline story is provided by a survey by the Industrial Society, which found that the proportion of organizations with formal job evaluation schemes has increased significantly over the last five years (*IRS Employment Review* 1997). Although it appears that the job evaluation being practiced today is different from earlier forms, job evaluation remains contradictory to broadbanding.

Variable Individual Pay

Firms are reporting the adoption of pay plans that increasingly use variable bonuses for individuals. From 1992 to 1996, the share of Fortune 1000 companies offering performance bonuses to middle managers and professional employees rose from 56 percent to 64 percent, according to a survey by Buck Consultants. At the same time, the percentage of firms offering bonuses to clerical and support employees grew from 26 percent to 35 percent (Block and Lagasse 1997).

Variable Group-Based Pay

The amount of compensation that varies with firm performance has changed in kind if not in amount. While firms have increased the use of stock options, the use of profit sharing has actually declined recently.

A survey from Coopers and Lybrand found that 20 percent of the respondents provided a tax-qualified deferred profit-sharing plan in 1998, down from 22 percent in a comparable 1995 survey. The prevalence of these plans increases with company size, with 30 percent of the respondents with 10,000 or more employees reporting a profit-sharing plan (Hansen 1998).

The use of group incentive or variable pay schemes has grown rapidly in the United States over the past 50 years. While in 1945 there were only 2,113 profit sharing plans operating in the United States, by 1991 this figure was 490,000, with more than one-quarter of them including immediate cash payments. With respect to employee stock ownership programs (ESOPs), Blasi and Kruse (1991) projected that by the year 2000, more than one-quarter of the publicly traded firms on the New York, American, and over-the-counter stock exchanges will be more than 15 percent owned by their employees (Nalbantian and Schotter 1997). According to the National Center for Employee Ownership, 11,000 companies had ESOPs in 1999, up from 9,000 in 1990.

An increasing number of firms are using gain sharing and other group-based performance plans. Under these plans, the pay of groups of employees varies with the performance of the group (thus looking less like internal labor market–type wages), but pay does not vary within the group (thus maintaining internal labor market–type features). O'Dell and McAdams (1987) found that 13 percent of firms responding to their survey had some form of gain sharing in place.

The set of surveys collected by the Center for Effective Organization at the University of Southern California provides one of the only repeated data sets on a wide array of incentive pay practices (Lawler, Mohrman, and Ledford 1998, Table 5.1); these data are summarized in Table 3.1. The sample is of the Fortune 500 Industrials and Fortune 500 Service employers (with the service employers stratified by broad industry group). Thus, compared with the economy as a whole, the sample overrepresents manufacturing and only covers large employers.

Table 3.1 Use of Incentive Plans in Large U.S. Employers: 1987–1996

Pay plan	Mean % of employees covered by this incentive
Individual incentives	
1987	20.3
1990	27.0
1993	27.7
1996	34.3
Work-group or team incentives	
1990	15.3
1993	21.0
1996	25.8
Gain sharing	
1987	5.5
1990	7.3
1993	11.6
1996	13.3
Profit sharing	
1987	34.8
1990	36.2
1993	37.4
1996	43.4
Employee stock ownership plan	
1987	45.2
1990	48.4
1993	52.4
1996	52.6
Stock option plan	
1993	23.6
1996	28.5
Nonmonetary recognition awards for performance	
1990	47.8
1993	55.1
1996	58.8

SOURCE: Data from Lawler, Mohrman, and Ledford (1998), Table 5.1.

Moreover, the response rate has been about 40 percent per year, with a different mix of respondents each year. Responses are from a single respondent per company. The data for each form of incentive are seven categories of employment coverage by that pay plan; for example, whether profit sharing covers nobody, 1–20 percent of the workforce, 21–40 percent, and so forth.

With these cautions in mind, the trends in the data are clear. Between 1987 and 1996, the use of incentive pay rose rapidly. The rise was present for incentives based on all organizational levels, ranging from individual to team to company-wide. For example, individual incentives covered 20 percent of the workforce in 1987 but more than one-third in 1996. The proportion of the workforce eligible for gain sharing more than doubled, rising from less than 6 percent of the work-force in 1987 to over 13 percent in 1996. Work group or team incentives also grew rapidly, rising from 15 percent in 1990 to 26 percent in 1996. ESOP and profit sharing plans start from a higher base, each covering more than one-third of employees in 1987, but they also rose almost 1 percentage point per year.

The value of stock options held by employees doubled from the late 1980s to the late 1990s (Rock 1998; *Investor Relations Business* 1999). Some of this increase was due to the unexpectedly strong rise in the stock market, but some was due to an increase in option grants. Most options were given to top executives; the blocks of shares owned or controlled by senior managers doubled between 1989 and 1999 to 13.2 percent of total shares (*The Economist* 1999). At the same time, more companies were giving option grants to employees other than top executives (Gilles 1999). Hewitt Associates reported that by 1997, about half of the Fortune 200 companies gave some stock options to employees below the senior management level (Martin 1998). Some prominent employers such as Starbucks and Levi Strauss made stock options available even to frontline employees.

Summary of Changes in Pay Plans

That firms are using broadbanding, bonuses, and stock options suggests that internal labor markets are in decline but is not convincing. Instead, the proof needs to be that wages are closer to market wages. For example, if wages are less tied to jobs, then we should observe an increase in the variance of wages within jobs in firms. But, the analyses in Chapter 5 will suggest that inequality among workers with the same job title at the same employer grew very little in the 1980s and 1990s. In addition, if internal labor markets are in decline, then we ought to observe less downward wage rigidity. However, Campbell and Kamlani (1997) found that firms still rely on wage rigidity to reduce white-collar turnover and fulfill their implicit contracts with lower-level workers.

In summary, firms are using a greater variety of elements in their compensation schemes, and on the surface, some of these elements should result in wages that appear more market-like. The evidence, however, does not yet show the wages of employees in large firms fluctuating with the vagaries of the external market.

EMPLOYEE BENEFITS AS RISK-SHARING MECHANISMS

In addition to any changes in pay policies, employees in internal labor markets face more risk due to changes in pensions, health insurance, and social insurance. Companies are replacing defined-benefit pension plans with defined-contribution plans. Defined-contribution plans have lower risk of pension loss after job turnover before vesting. Nevertheless, on average, the move to defined-contribution plans shifts inflation and asset market risk to the employee. Surprisingly, the increased portability of defined-contribution plans is not associated with increases in the frequency of job changes (Gustman and Steinmeier 1995).

Health insurance plans are increasingly requiring copayments and deductibles. The goal is largely to cut costs by improving incentives, but the effect is shifting some risk to employees. More importantly, caps on payouts (such as no more than $100,000 for injury) can greatly increase the risk employees bear.

The expected value of social insurance is also declining. Few young people expect Social Security or Medicare to be there for them, especially not at current benefit levels. Eighty-three percent of 18- to 34-year-olds surveyed by the Luntz Research Company (www.third-mil.org/surveys; accessed September 1999) believe that the government has made promises to their generation that it will not be able to meet. More respondents believe that UFOs exist than believe that Social Security will exist by the time they retire.

WORK ORGANIZATION

Work is organized within internal labor markets in ways that buffer employees from the external market. For example, in the companies Doeringer and Piore studied, rigid job ladders led some jobs to be filled only from within the organization.

Two somewhat distinct changes in work organization inside large firms have affected internal labor markets. First, downsizing and restructuring has led to less predictable and often less stable careers. Second, the move toward Japanese-style work organization, including flexible manufacturing and empowered work teams, suggests an evolution of the internal labor market. That is, employers using these workplace practices still rely on long careers and pay distinct from the spot market, but the institutions they use to create these conditions are quite distinct from those in traditional U.S. internal labor markets (Brown et al. 1997).

Widespread downsizing and restructuring have directly changed the employment contract by reducing the perceived job security of employees. Moreover, as firms restructured and downsized, they removed more managerial jobs, flattening the hierarchy (Cappelli and O'Shaughnessy 1995). The flattening removed some of the steps of the job ladder. This change in the organization of work makes the employment relationship closer to arm's length. For example, Batt (1996) showed fairly dramatic changes at a telecommunications firm; delayering and downsizing reduced job security and increased job mobility. As another example, the number of managers at Porsche declined by 38 percent when they reduced the number of layers of management from six to four (Womack, Jones, and Roos 1990).

The second type of change in work organization is symptomatic of a movement toward a form of internal labor markets based on a subset of Japanese management practices (Osterman 1995). In this system (often called a high-performance work system), flexible manufacturing and team-based work are used to improve flexibility and horizontal information flows (Aoki 1988; Levine 1995; Ichniowski et al. 1996). Flexible manufacturing and work teams require that the joint investment in skills by the employer and employee increase. Therefore, as in the Japanese model being copied, long-term relationships between the company and its workers are necessary. For at least the core employees, long-term protection from the fluctuations in the external environment is the result. The high-performance work system appears to be a mutated form of the traditional internal labor market instead of a market-like substitute for the internal labor market. Broader skills reduce the number of job classifications and reduce the length of job ladders. These changes affect job ladders, ports of entry, and skill development.

Clear ports of entry, defined as key jobs that provide organizational entry and exit, were an important component of the internal labor markets described by Doeringer and Piore (1971). It is not clear, however, whether or not ports of entry were in place in the majority of organizations in the economy. Both Lazear (1992) and Baker, Gibbs, and Holmstrom (1994) found little evidence of ports of entry. Although these two studies only investigated two companies, they suggest that the evidence showing that ports of entry no longer exist is not balanced by evidence that they ever existed for many firms.

Given the weak evidence for the prevalence of job ladders with defined ports of entry, it is difficult to measure changes in the role of job ladders. However, the rise of worker participation and self-managing work teams may reduce the role of job ladders. First, if work teams are self-managing, there will be less need for supervisors, thus removing a step from the ladder. Second, high-performance work teams generally result in enriched jobs and reduced job classifications, further removing steps and distributing some of the low skill activities such as housekeeping to all jobs. This removes entry-level positions that historically may have been ports of entry. Furthermore, if some of the low-skill jobs are outsourced or turned into temporary positions, then the available number of ports of entry further declines.

Osterman (1994) found that 55 percent of establishments use teams. Similarly, Lawler, Mohrman, and Ledford (1995) found increased use from 1987 to 1993 of high-performance work practices, including the use of quality circles, job enrichment, and self-managed work teams. In contrast, Kruse and Blasi (1998) reported that only 10 percent of firms are adopting a broad set of high-performance work practices. Furthermore, the trend in adoptions was flat between 1994 and 1997. Reports that the "new paradigm" of work is spreading widely is not borne out in the National Employer survey that Kruse and Blasi analyzed.

SECTORAL SHIFTS

Part of the perceived decline in internal labor markets can be attributed to employment shifts from sectors of the economy more favorable to internal labor markets toward more external-market-oriented sectors. For example, the shift toward temporary work increases the number of jobs outside the traditional internal labor market. Still, temporary workers are only a very small part of the economy (perhaps 2 percent). The decline in employment in manufacturing should also affect the number of employees covered by internal labor markets. Davis, Haltiwanger, and Schuh (1996) showed an average annual decline of 1.2 percent in manufacturing employment over the years 1973–1988. This should result in the appearance of a decline in internal labor markets because fewer workers are in internal labor market–type jobs. However, at the same time, some firms outside of manufacturing are beginning to look more like internal labor market firms. For example, the 910,000 employees of Wal-Mart seem to be buffered from the external market in ways similar to the traditional internal labor market, particularly as compared to the "mom-and-pop" stores they displaced.

On the one hand, most employers with internal labor markets contracted out some business services. On the other hand, some business services increasingly provided by internal labor market–type employers. Information technology providers such as EDS and Cisco Systems are handling programming and software maintenance activities traditionally handled in-house, thus, moving jobs from the client firm to the contractor (Duffy 1999).

DISCUSSION

One conclusion suggested by the evidence in this chapter is that the "demise of the Great American Job is greatly exaggerated" (Farber 1995). While most jobs do not last that long, the prevalence of long-term jobs has not undergone a sea change; nor have other elements of internal labor markets (ranging from stable pay to employee attitudes) undergone dramatic changes.

The reasons for the gap between common perceptions of rapid change and data that show modest evolution are many. First, internal labor markets were never homogenous. Organizations pieced together internal structures that contained many of the elements detailed by Doeringer and Piore, yet rarely (if ever) contained all of the elements. Moreover, the unionized blue-collar internal labor markets that Doeringer and Piore described never covered that many U.S. employees, even though most employees worked in some form of internal labor market.

The evidence does seem to show that elements of internal labor markets are changing. First, pay practices have evolved. Firms are using more pay at risk and more pay based on skills. Second, there is some evidence, though mixed, that the long-term connections between employees and employers is changing. It may be that the lifetime jobs at AT&T and GM were replaced by long-term jobs at Wal-Mart and Microsoft, but the lifetime jobs at Wal-Mart and Microsoft were not being guaranteed (even in some vague sense) by the employer. Third, there is some evidence that employees' loyalty to their employer has declined. Whether these declines are related to the waves of downsizing and press coverage of the downsizing is a lingering question.

The following chapters present original evidence on changes in wage structures and attitudes toward pay rigidities and employment security. As such, they will shed light on many of the unresolved issues concerning the extent of decay of internal labor markets.

Notes

1. We build on the reviews of this topic in Jacoby (1999), Cappelli (1999), and Kruse and Blasi (1998).

2. Farber, Haltiwanger, and Abraham (1997) found declines in the 20- and 30-year tenure rates for males; Jaeger and Stevens (1999) found declines in tenure rates for males over 30 years of age with 10 years of tenure with the current company.

3. The institutionalist explanation of why initial wages affect future wages is that wage changes are usually expressed in percentage change terms, not absolute terms. More neoclassical theorists posit that a risk-sharing contract is also consistent with these facts (Malcomson 1997).

4
Wage Structures at Large and Small Employers

In this chapter,[1] we examine the hypotheses concerning changes in the employer size-wage gap.[2] If returns to skills have risen in ways uncorrelated with employer size, then human capital theory suggests that both employees' characteristics and their compensation should have diverged between large and small employers. In contrast, if the size-wage gap was due to employer rigidities and institutions that have weakened over time, employee characteristics and the compensation of employees at large and at small employers should have converged. (These hypotheses are set out in detail in Chapter 2.) The following two chapters extend the analyses of human capital and institutionalist theories by examining changes in pay structures among large employers.

We first discuss our method for decomposing changes in the size-wage gap. We next present background evidence on changes in size distribution of employers and changes in the total size-wage gap. We then decompose the changes into four components: changes in the characteristics of employees at large firms, changes in rewards for those characteristics, and two other components. Finally, we examine whether large employers today have wage levels and returns more similar to those of small employers in their regions.

METHODS: DECOMPOSING CHANGES
IN THE SIZE-WAGE GAP

Changes in the size-wage gap are not just a matter of overall returns to size. There may be differences in how large and small firms reward the characteristics of employees and in the characteristics of the labor forces of large and small companies. Just as a Oaxaca decomposition provides considerably more information than indicator variable models about differences in the structure of wages between different racial, gender, or sectoral groupings, we can learn considerably more about how the size-wage gap has changed over this period through a decomposition of the structure of wages over time and firm size. Because this decomposition is more complex than the typical Oaxaca, we lay out both our approach and the interpretation of the components of the decomposition.

We model the logarithm of the wage as a function of demographic and human capital factors, occupation, and location, as well as employer size. We estimate separate wage equations in each year (1979 and 1993) for large and for small firms:

$$w_{it}^{L} = x_{ti}^{L} b_{t}^{L} + e_{ti}^{L}$$

and

$$w_{ti}^{S} = x_{ti}^{S} b_{t}^{S} + e_{it}^{S}.$$

In these equations, w_{ti} is the ln(wage) for person i, x_{ti} is the vector of characteristics for person i, b_t is the vector of coefficients, and e_{ti}^{L} is the error for person i in the year t at a large firm. The superscripts L and S refer to large and small employers, and the subscript t refers to the year 1979 or 1993.

Subtraction across years and size classes yields the change in the average size-wage gap: $(W_{93}^{L} - W_{93}^{S}) - (W_{79}^{L} - W_{79}^{S})$. For notational simplicity, let W_t and X_t refer to the mean wage and characteristics of the size categories in a year. Also, we define the change in the large vs. small gap in mean characteristics as

$$\Delta(X \text{ gap}) = (X_{93}^{L} - X_{79}^{L}) - (X_{93}^{S} - X_{79}^{S})$$
$$= (X_{93}^{L} - X_{93}^{S}) - (X_{79}^{L} - X_{79}^{S})$$

and define the change in the large/small gap in coefficients as

$$\Delta(B \text{ gap}) = (b_{93}^{L} - b_{93}^{S}) - (b_{79}^{L} - b_{79}^{S}).$$

Manipulation of the estimated equations permits us to rewrite the change in the size-wage gap as four components, each of which has a meaning. Specifically, the change in the size-wage gap can be rewritten as the sum of the four components:

(4.1) $(W_{93}^L - W_{93}^S) - (W_{79}^L - W_{79}^S) = \Delta(B \text{ gap}) X_t^S + \Delta(X \text{ gap}) b_t^S$
$$+ (X_t^L - X_t^S)(b_{93}^L - b_{79}^L)$$
$$+ (b_t^L - b_t^S)(X_{93}^L - X_{79}^L).$$

The subscript t can refer to either 1979 or 1993, yielding two slightly different decompositions. We discuss both decompositions below; the results were always similar.[3] This decomposition is framed in terms of small-firm characteristics coefficients in the second part of the first two terms. The results were similar using large-firm characteristics as the base. We discuss each component of this decomposition in turn.

Have Returns at Large and Small Firms Converged?

The term $\Delta(B \text{ gap}) X_t^S$ measures the changing difference in coefficients between large and small employers. X_t^S, the mean characteristics of small-firm employees in year t, weights the change in the coefficients gap, aggregating the changes of the individual coefficients into a single measure. If this term is negative, the large- and small-firm coefficients have converged.

The hypothesis of declining differences (Inst 3b) posited that returns at small and large firms are converging. In this decomposition, this prediction implies $\Delta(B \text{ gap}) X_t^S < 0$.

Are Employee Characteristics at Large and Small Firms Converging?

The term $\Delta(X \text{ gap}) b_t^S$ measures the changing gap in characteristics between large and small employers. Here, the b_t^S term is a weight which allows us to aggregate the change in the characteristics gap into a single measure. If this measure is negative, then large- and small-firm characteristics have converged, as predicted by the human capital theory's implication of increased sorting (HumCap 5b), but not by the institutionalist theory of convergence (Inst 6b).

Are Returns Rising for Characteristics Common at Large Firms?

The term $(X_t^L - X_t^S)(b_{93}^L - b_{79}^L)$ measures the effect of changing coefficients on the characteristics particularly common at large firms. The first element, the weights used to aggregate the coefficients, is the difference between the characteristics of large and small firms. The second element of this term is the change in large firms' returns to characteristics between 1979 and 1993. If the overall term is negative, returns to characteristics particularly common to large firms have declined.

The point may be illustrated using education as an example. Large firms had higher average educational levels than small firms in 1979, so the first element is positive. Given that returns to education rose throughout the economy, the second element is also positive. Thus, a constant level of sorting by education, coupled with rising returns to education, widens the gap between large- and small-firm wages.

If large firms sorted on higher skills and the returns to skills rose in the economy, then human capital theory suggests returns to characteristics common at large firms should have risen in accordance with hypothesis HumCap 6: $(X_t^L - X_t^S)(b_{93}^L - b_{79}^L) > 0$.

Do Employees at Large Firms Increasingly Have the Characteristics Large Firms Reward Well?

The term $(b_t^L - b_t^S)(X_{93}^L - X_{79}^L)$ measures whether the characteristics at large firms have become more concentrated in areas where large firms pay above-average returns. The first, the weighting component, measures the eexcess returns provided by large firms, relative to small firms, in year t. The second component is the change in the mean characteristics of large firms between 1979 and 1993. If this term is negative, then large firms hire fewer employees with the characteristics such firms pay particularly well. For example, in 1979, large firms paid higher returns to education than did small firms. If the average education levels at large employers rose, this term will increase. We have no hypothesis for this term.

A final methodological note is that when we correlate fixed effects or estimated coefficients, we correct the correlation for the fact that the coefficients are estimated.

RESULTS

We first examine the distribution of employment at large and small firms and examine the size-wage effect. We then examine the relationship between wages at large and small employers in a region.

BACKGROUND: HAS THE EMPLOYER SIZE DECLINED FOR THE TYPICAL EMPLOYEE?

The proportion of employment at large employers rose between 1979 and 1993 (Table 4.1). Large employers (over 1000 employees) employed 41 percent of the sample in 1979, rising to 45 percent in 1993. This increase was matched by declining employment in small (under 100) employers from 40 percent to 34 percent of the sample. The employment share of middle-sized firms has remained stable. These results are not related to shifts between sectors; results were similar when we control for industry shifts by using 1979 industry weights. (A rising share of employment at large employers provides only weak evidence in the debate on whether small employers create disproportionately many jobs because the population of employers in the "large" category changes over time [Davis, Haltiwanger, and Schuh 1996].)

This pattern is mirrored within all of the 12 major industries included in this study except the mining and the durable goods industries (Table 4.2). The rise in the prevalence of large employers is most apparent in retail trade, where employment at large firms went from 31.3 percent to 46.5 percent of employees between 1979 and 1993, and

Table 4.1 Distribution of Employment by Firm Size (%)

Firm size (no. of employees)	1979	1993	1993 (1979 industry weights)
Less than 100	39.6	34.2	32.9
100–999	19.7	20.9	20.6
1,000 or more	40.8	45.0	44.1

Table 4.2 Industry Proportions of Employment by Firm Size

	1979		1993	
Industry	# obs.	Distribution of employment	# obs.	Distribution of employment
Mining	165		113	
1,000 plus		0.694		0.479
100–999		0.173		0.277
Under 100		0.133		0.244
Construction	758		612	
1,000 plus		0.101		0.106
100–999		0.171		0.157
Under 100		0.728		0.737
Nondurables	1,418		1,198	
1,000 plus		0.532		0.514
100–999		0.240		0.233
Under 100		0.227		0.240
Durable goods	2,364		1,597	
1,000 plus		0.652		0.567
100–999		0.177		0.234
Under 100		0.172		0.199
Transportation	535		576	
1,000 plus		0.523		0.569
100–999		0.339		0.132
Under 100		0.138		0.299
Communications	243		204	
1,000 plus		0.806		0.789
100–999		0.075		0.101
Under 100		0.118		0.110
Utilities	160		152	
1,000 plus		0.774		0.721
100–999		0.124		0.147
Under 100		0.102		0.131
Wholesale trade	645		625	
1,000 plus		0.249		0.284
100–999		0.246		0.248
Under 100		0.505		0.468
Retail trade	2,396		2,494	
1,000 plus		0.313		0.465
100–999		0.123		0.118
Under 100		0.565		0.417

Table 4.2 (continued)

		1979		1993
Industry	# obs.	Distribution of employment	# obs.	Distribution of employment
Finance, insurance, etc.	916		1,020	
1,000 plus		0.430		0.524
100–999		0.187		0.189
Under 100		0.384		0.288
Service industries	428		536	
1,000 plus		0.187		0.323
100–999		0.113		0.176
Under 100		0.700		0.501
Professional services	1,767		2,488	
1,000 plus		0.228		0.327
100–999		0.264		0.252
Under 100		0.509		0.421

in service industries (other than business services), where employment at large firms rose from 18.7 percent to 32.3 percent.

Internal labor markets have not declined in the sense of fewer employees being employed in large firms. Any decline in such institutional structures must then be found in the manner in which employees are treated.

Has the Size-Wage Effect Declined?

Another indicator of decline in internal labor markets would be a decline in the relative wages at large firms. Idson and Oi (1999) reported the size-wage elasticity in manufacturing doubled between 1977 and 1982, then remained constant at least through 1992. We extend their analysis to the nonmanufacturing sectors of the economy. In this section, we take an initial look at the evidence by considering 1) the difference between the mean wages paid by large and small firms in 1979 and 1993 and 2) the difference conditional on employee characteristics (age and its square, education, and indicator variables for marital status, union membership, race, gender, residence in a metropolitan area, and 11 major occupations).

The real wage at middle- and large-sized firms declined between 1979 and 1993, while small firms' wages have remained constant (Table 4.3). While the real wage at small firms remained around

$10.20 per hour (in 1993 dollars), the wage at middle-sized firms fell by 50 cents per hour, from $12.57 to $12.05, and the wage at large firms declined from $14.61 to $13.34, more than a dollar an hour. This corresponds to a decline in the large-firm wage advantage of 9.6 ln points between 1979 and 1993, or 31 percent of the 0.36 ln point advantage at large employers.

The decline in the large-firm wage advantage is more modest in the regression analysis but still remains substantial, having fallen by about one quarter between 1979 and 1993. The premium for working at a medium-sized (100–999 employees) firm instead of at a small employer is 7.5 percent in the 1993 regression, which is noticeably less than the 10.7 percent in 1979. Similarly, the premium for working at a large employer (at least 1000 employees) is 14.2 percent in 1993, which is also less than the 18.5 percent in 1979. Both declines are statistically significant.[4] Our initial analysis, then, supports the view of the institutionalists: wages at large firms are becoming more like those at small firms. The results on the size distribution of employment and the size-wage gap are similar if we look at establishment size instead of employer size (Belman and Levine 2001).

Table 4.3 Firm Size Effects on Wages: 1979–1993[a]

Firm size (employees)	1979	1993
Real wage (1993 dollars)		
Less than 100 employees	$10.19	$10.24
100–999 employees	$12.57	$12.05
(gap in ln[wage] over small-firm wage)	(0.210)	(0.163)
1,000 or more employees	$14.61	$13.34
(gap in ln[wage] over small-firm wage)	(0.360)	(0.264)
Regression estimates of firm effects on ln(wage)		
100–999	0.107	0.075
	$(11.1)^b$	(7.9)
1,000 or more	0.185	0.142
	(23.1)	(18.1)

[a] Control variables are listed in Appendix B, Table B.1. Small employers (< 100) are the omitted category. Deflation uses the CPI-U-X1.

[b] t-Statistics in parentheses.

Decomposing sources of wage changes

The decomposition from Equation 4.1 permits us to understand whether the changing wage patterns at large and small employers are due to sorting or to changes in sector-specific returns to characteristics. Estimates of regression coefficients by firm size and year are in Appendix B, Table B.1, and mean characteristics by firm size are in Table B.2. The specification of the model follows that used in prior models reported in this chapter, except that the age, education, and tenure variables have been recentered on their means and a quadratic term for age has been added (age^2).

Table 4.4 summarizes the decomposition. The returns to large firms declined by between 9.6 and 13.2 percentage points between

Table 4.4 Decomposing Changes in the Size-Wage Gap[a]

Component	Term from Equation 4.1	Size-wage gap (pct. pts.)		% of gap	
		1979 wt.	1993 wt.	1979 wt.	1993 wt.
Overall change in size-wage gap		−9.6	−13.2	100.0	100.0
Term A: Have returns at large and small firms converged?	$\Delta(B\ gap)X_t^S$	−7.5	−8.4	−78.1	−63.6
Term B: Are employee characteristics at large and small firms converging?	$\Delta(X\ gap)b_t^S$	−12.5	−12.2	−130.2	−92.4
Term C: Are returns rising for characteristics common at large firms?	$(X_t^L - X_t^S) \times$ $(b_{93}^L - b_{79}^L)$	8.2	7.2	85.4	54.5
Term D: Do employees at large firms increasingly have the characteristics large firms reward well?	$(b_t^L - b_t^S) \times$ $(X_{93}^L - X_{79}^L)$	2.22	0.06	23.1	0.5

[a] Medium-sized employers are omitted from this analysis. Mean characteristics and coefficients by size class and year are presented in Tables B.1 and B.2.

1979 and 1993, depending on whether 1979 or 1993 weights are used. The decline was caused by convergence in returns at large and small firms (the gap between B_L and B_S declined between 1979 and 1993; $\Delta[B$ gap$]X_t^S$ in Equation 4.1) and by a decline in the gap in characteristics of large and small firms ($\Delta[X$ gap$]b_t^S$). Using the 1979 base, the former accounted for 78 percent and the latter for 130 percent of the 9.6 percentage point decline in the large-firm wage; using a 1993 base, the components accounted for 64 percent and 92 percent, respectively. These trends were partially counterbalanced by improvements in the returns to characteristics common at large firms over time (term C) and improvements in the characteristics of large firms between 1979 and 1993 (term D). The former increased the gap between large and small wages by between 85 percent (1979 base) and 54 percent (1993 base), the latter by between 23 percent and 0.5 percent.

Have returns at large and small firms converged?

Overall, the decomposition indicates that the returns have converged between large and small employers. Using the 1979 base, the converging coefficients knocked out 7.5 percentage points of the size-wage effect, almost half of the 18.5 percent advantage estimated in Table 4.4.

Appendix Table B.3 indicates which coefficients converged. The first three columns, for 1979, show the small-firm variable means for 1979, the change in the large/small gap in coefficients between 1979 and 1993, and the product of the first two columns. For example, the returns to education rose at both large and small firms from 1979 to 1993, but it rose fastest in small firms. Thus, the gap in returns to a year of education in large and small firms declined by 1.44 percentage points between 1979 and 1993. The effect of this convergence in returns to education was to reduce the overall size-wage gap by 0.16 percentage points.

No single relative return of large versus small firms changed substantially. The largest single change between 1979 and 1993 is the decline in the gap between the intercepts of 20.1 percentage points (Table B.2). After allowing for the effect of the intercept, the balance of the shift in the gap is a positive 12.6 percent (or 11.7 percent for the 1993 weights). Given how we measured the variables, the intercept indicates the effect of changing returns to firm size for male employees with mean education, age, and tenure living in the West, working as laborers and employed in retail trade.

The allocation of the effect of the change in the coefficient gap between the intercept and other coefficients varies depending on the chosen omitted category for occupation, region, sex, and industry. Due to the (arbitrary) selection of base category, virtually any change in the omitted category reduces the size of the change in the gap of the large- and small-firm intercepts over time. Nevertheless, the intercepts converged for any choice of base category. These changes suggest that large firms are paying less simply because they are large (the convergence of the intercepts), while increasing their payments for particular employee characteristics.

In the simplest human capital model, both the observed characteristics and the size-wage effect on the intercept measure human capital, with the intercept capturing large firms' higher unobserved human capital. In such a model, if returns to observable skill have increased, then so should returns to unobservable skill as captured by the intercept. (This result is repeating the insight that the size-wage effect should have risen overall if size is correlated with unobserved skills whose returns have risen.) In fact, the relative returns to characteristics and on the intercept have diverged. This set of results is more consistent with a decline in institutionalist pressures that formerly led to a size-wage effect, coupled with rising returns to skill due to factors such as changes in trade or technology.

Turning to specific coefficients, the most notable decline in the coefficient gap is a 1.4 percentage point decline in the large firm education advantage and a small decline in large-firm returns to job tenure of 1–2 years (Table B.3). In contrast, large firms' excess returns rose for age, being female, living in the Northeast, Midwest, or South, being employed as a precision production operative (craft worker), and working in nondurables manufacturing (Table B.3). The change in relative returns is not significant for most individual coefficients; at the same time, many more shifts are positive than negative. These positive shifts substantially outweigh the negative, creating an overall effect of a rising gap between large and small firms (Table B.3). Only the declining gap in intercepts leads to converging coefficients.

Are employees' characteristics at large and small firms converging?

In 1979, employees of large firms were older (mean age 36.5 years, against 35.4 years at small firms) and more educated (12.7 years of education versus 11.9; see Table B.2). Employees at large firms were far more likely to be in a union (33.9 percent versus 9.5 percent) and had almost twice the tenure (8.9 years versus 4.5) of small-firm employees.

We measure the total effect of changing relative characteristics by weighting characteristics by the coefficients on the Equation 4.1, term $\Delta(X \text{ gap})b^S$. If the weighted sum is negative, then characteristics are on average converging. On average, the characteristics of employees at large and small firms converged between 1979 and 1993. This convergence would have overpredicted the decline in the size-wage effect, reducing it by 12.2 ln(wage) points (Table 4.4). This calculation is presented for each variable in Table B.2 ("Difference" column).

Most notably, the percentage of unionized workers at large firms declined from 33.9 percent to 19.2 percent; this decline of 14.7 percentage points was considerably larger than the corresponding decline from 9.5 percent to 4.8 percent at small firms. At the same time that the absolute gap declined, the ratio of union membership at large versus small firms actually increased.

The characteristics that relate most closely to human capital theory are age, tenure, and education. None exhibited the increases in sorting predicted by Kremer and Maskin's version of human capital theory coupled with rising returns to skill (HumCap 5). The gap in age between large and small firms fell from 1.2 years to 0.5 years between 1979 and 1993, the difference in education fell slightly, from 0.8 to 0.7 years (Table B.2), but the change was in the opposite direction of that predicted by Kremer and Maskin. Mean tenure was almost constant at large employers, declining from 8.8 to 8.5 years—well within the sampling error—but it rose from 4.5 to 4.9 years at small employers. (Relatively small changes in levels and patterns of tenure during this time period have been found in the CPS by other researchers such as Diebold, Neumark, and Polsky [1997].)

Overall, convergence in factors closely associated with human capital reduced the gap in wages between large and small firms, although the effects were small. The change in age reduced the gap by 0.3 to 0.4 percentage points, that in tenure reduced the gap by 0.7 to 0.9 percentage points, and the declining gap in education reduced the wage gap by between 0.3 and 0.5 percentage points (Table B.4).

Shifts in occupation and sectoral distribution of employment also influenced the size-wage gap. Although there were only modest changes in the occupational and sectoral distribution of employment in small firms, large firms underwent some large shifts. The most notable was the decline in the proportion of employees in large firms employed in the durable goods industries from 32.4 percent in 1979 to 18.2 percent in 1993 (Table B.2). Durable goods are a high-wage sector for both large- and small-firm employees. Thus, the decline in employment in durable goods in large firms reduced the large-firm wage advantage by between 2.8 and 3.8 percentage points.

Small firms remained about 50 percent female through the 1979–1993 period, but large firms increased from 35 percent to 46 percent female. Given the lower wages of women, this convergence lowered the size-wage effect by about 2 percentage points.

In contrast with most characteristics, employment of black workers has diverged. Even in 1979, employees at large companies were more likely to be black (8.2 percent) than their counterparts in small companies (7.9 percent). This gap has increased substantially in recent years, from 0.3 percent higher to 5.1 percent higher than at small firms (Table B.2). Because the wages of black workers are lower than those of other racial groups, the increasing proportion of blacks at large firms causes a decline in the size-wage gap of about 4 percent.

Thus, these results are consistent with declining barriers to female and minority employment at large firms (consistent with hypothesis Inst 6b). At the same time, as others have found (e.g., Holzer 1998), the 1979 results did not show the lower percentage of blacks at large employers that theories of segmented labor markets predicted. (See Holzer [1998] for more analysis of the lower representation of blacks in smaller establishments.)

In short, with the exception of race, the mean characteristics of employees at large and small employers have either remained constant or converged between 1979 and 1993. These results provide no support for hypothesis HumCap 5b that sorting of worker skills by employer size has increased.

Sorting and outsourcing

As returns to skill rise, high- and low-wage occupations pay wages that are increasingly different from the median pay at a firm. Hypothesis Inst 6 predicts that high-wage industries are particularly likely to outsource low-wage business services such as food service and janitorial work, while low-wage industries are particularly likely to outsource high-wage services such as accounting and law.

Table 4.5 presents the fraction of each industry's employment in high- and low-wage service occupations that are commonly outsourced. In 1979, low-wage industries had a higher concentration of low-wage service occupations, as expected. That is, low-wage industries employed 3 percent low-wage business services, while high-wage industries employed only 1.2 percent low-wage business services. The usage of high-wage business services was more alike (1.9 percent ver-

Table 4.5 Sorting of High- and Low-Wage Business Service Occupations by Industry

Occupations commonly outsourced	1979			1993		
	Low-wage industry	High-wage industry	Total	Low-wage industry	High-wage industry	Total
Low-wage business services (%)	3.0 (1.2)	1.2 (1.2)	2.0 (0.9)	2.4 (1.3)	1.1 (1.3)	1.7 (0.9)
High-wage business services (%)	1.9 (1.3)	1.6 (1.2)	1.8 (0.9)	2.6 (1.8)	1.5 (1.3)	2.0 (0.9)
Ratio of % low-wage to (% low + % high)	0.61	0.43	0.53	0.48	0.42	0.46

NOTE: High-wage business services include accountants, architects, lawyers, nurses, social and recreation workers, social scientists, editors and reporters, photographers, and public relations specialists. The low-wage services include food service workers, protective service workers, and cleaning services such as janitors. Middle-wage occupations are the residual group, which excludes employees who do not report an occupation. High-wage industries are mining, construction, durable manufacturing, transportation, utilities (including communications), and wholesale trade. The low-wage industries are nondurable manufacturing, retail trade, and finance, insurance, and real estate. Service industries, eating and drinking places, and the public sector are excluded from these calculations. Standard errors for the estimates are in parentheses.

sus 1.6 percent). These results in 1979 are consistent with fairness theories, along with the hypothesis that some industries had high average skill demands that caused a concentration of high-wage occupations and a high industry wage effect.

The point of the table is the difference-in-differences test examining if low-wage industries reduced their relative employment of high-wage business services between 1979 and 1993. These results provide no evidence of increased sorting. To the contrary, low-wage industries had a declining concentration of low-wage service occupations (although the change was not statistically significant), while the proportion was constant in high-wage industries. Different classifications of occupations as "high-wage (or low-wage) services likely to be contracted out" changed the levels of the figures, but under no classification scheme did we see the pattern of increased outsourcing predicted by fairness theories. In short, these results provide no evidence for hypothesis Inst 6a.

Are returns rising for characteristics common at large firms?

If large employers specialize in high-skill workers (relative to small firms) and returns to skill have risen (relative to returns in 1979), we should see rising returns to characteristics that are common at large firms. Formally, this theory implies that the term $(X_t^L - X_t^S)(b_{93}^L - b_{79}^L)$ from Equation 4.1 is positive. For example, the combination of rising returns to education (regardless of employer size) coupled with higher average education at large firms should have increased the gap between large- and small-firm wages.

Overall, rising returns for characteristics common at large firms have widened the wage gap by between 8.2 (1979 weights) and 7.2 (1993 weights) percentage points (Table 4.4). This result supports hypothesis HumCap 6 that large firms specialize in high-skill workers and that returns to these skills have increased.

Most specific characteristics with rising returns showed the same pattern. Returns to education at large firms rose by 1.4 percent and widened the gap by 1.1 percentage points, and returns to job tenure increased by 0.6 percent and widened the gap by 2.7 percentage points. Returns also rose substantially for being a union member and being employed in nondurable goods production (where large firms are overrepresented). The largest decline in returns was in construction, where returns fell by 14.5 percent. However, as large firms are underrepresented in construction, the net effect of declining returns was to widen the size-wage gap by 1.4 percentage points.

Do employees at large firms increasingly have the characteristics large firms reward well?

Finally, large employers might have become more- or less-intensive employers of employees whose characteristics they pay particularly well. In fact, this effect is small, accounting for between +0.1 and +2.2 percentage points of the larger size-wage gap. This effect is driven by declining unionization of large-firm employees, coupled with the higher returns to unionization at large employers.

Summary of How the Size-Wage Gap Has Changed

Overall, these results lead to three conclusions. First, the gap in returns by firm size has diminished between 1979 and 1993. Second, the characteristics of employees at large and small firms have also converged over this period. Finally, this convergence is offset in part because the economy has experienced rising returns to characteristics such as education that are prevalent at large employers.

ARE WAGE STRUCTURES AT LARGE AND NEARBY SMALL EMPLOYERS CONVERGING?

In this section, we examine two dimensions of the relationship between wages at large employers and those at nearby small employers. We first consider the relation of the mean wage at large and small employers in a state. We then examine the entire structure of wages within the nine census regions (that is, the occupational wage structure and returns to age, education, and tenure at the large and small employers in each region).

Are Wage Levels Converging within Regions?

When internal labor markets are powerful, large employers can pay nationally based patterns that do not follow local wage patterns closely.

Conversely, if internal wage structures are becoming less important, a region's wage level at small employers should be more useful in predicting wages at large employers (hypothesis Inst 4). To test this hypothesis, we ran separate wage regressions for large and small firms for each of the CPS samples. In addition to the typical variables included in these models, we added regional indicator variables. Estimated regional effects were then correlated across firm size categories. (As before, small firms are defined as firms with fewer than 100 employees, large employers are those with 1,000 or more employees.)

The size of the sample and the geographic coding used in the CPS requires that we analyze regions that are larger than most local labor markets. We begin by examining states. The small number of observations for several states necessitated removing 10 states to produce a matched sample, and our final sample was 41 states (including the District of Columbia).

In 1979, the correlation of the small-firm dummy and the large-firm dummy for the 41 matched states was 58 percent (Table 4.6). The estimated correlation in 1993 rose to 64 percent, but the difference was not statistically significant.

States are imperfect proxies for regional labor markets, and it is possible that the lack of statistically significant convergence is due to excessive aggregation. There are sufficient observations to repeat this exercise after breaking out some of the larger metropolitan areas, and we reran our regressions redefining the relevant labor market as the SMSA where possible. In states with these large metropolitan areas, we defined the remainder of the state as one labor market. The result was 73 regional labor markets for which data exist in both time periods. The correlation of large- and small-firm effects by region is 50.8 percent in 1979 and declines to 43.2 percent in 1993. This decline is not statistically significant and the direction of the change is not consistent, with large firms' wages becoming more like those of nearby small firms. (The weight in these correlations is 1 per state or SMSA.)

To guard against the possibility that firms in large metropolitan areas behaved differently than those outside of such areas, we reran the regressions separately on metropolitan and nonmetropolitan residents. For residents outside of large metropolitan areas, the correlation of region dummies of large employers and of small employers declined slightly from 56 to 39 percent (change not significant). For metropoli-

Table 4.6 Are Large and Small Firm Regional Effects Converging?

Jurisdictions	1979 (%)	1993 (%)	t-Statistic for difference of ρ
Matched states (41 states)			
ρ(large, small)	58.1	63.8	0.5
	(7.8)	(7.9)	
σ(large)	10.5	11.4	
σ(small)	13.6	13.3	
Matched states and cities (73 regions)			
ρ(large, small)	50.8	43.2	−0.92
	(5.9)	(5.8)	
σ(large)	12.5	12.4	
σ(small)	12.6	13.7	
Breaking out metropolitan and nonmetropolitan areas			
Matched states[a]			
ρ(large, small)	55.7	39.3	−1.42
	(8.2)	(8.1)	
σ(large)	13.3	11.4	
σ(small)	14.5	14.2	
Matched cities (35 SMSAs)			
ρ(large, small)	49.4	44.3	−0.4
	(8.2)	(8.2)	
σ(large)	10.9	14.3	
σ(small)	9.8	13.8	

NOTE: Values in parentheses are the standard error of the correlation.
[a] The rural and smaller metro areas from 38 states or state agglomerations.

tan residents, the correlation of region dummies of large employers and of small employers fell from 49 to 44 percent (again, change not significant). Both of the statistically insignificant changes move in the opposite direction of convergence.

The bottom line is that we do not support hypothesis Inst 4 that the wage levels of large employers (adjusted for employee characteristics) came to resemble those of small employers in a region.

We repeated this analysis using the Hay data. We restricted the sample to professionals and first-line supervisors, which are the occupational groups with the closest connection to local labor markets. There were over 10,000 supervisors and professionals in each year. If the compensation structures of firms over time resemble internal labor markets less and their wage-setting mechanisms are more closely tied to external labor market forces, we should see a stronger relationship between wages and local market characteristics over time.

We calculated the percentage difference between the mean wage for each job at each company location and the overall mean wage for that job across the company and regressed it on local market wages and unemployment. Local labor market conditions were not significant predictors of wage differentials in 1986 (Table 4.7). The coefficient on local wages rose from 0.11 in 1986 to 0.21 by 1992 and gained significance, but the change was not statistically significant. Given the idiosyncratic nature of these data, the lack of a statistically significant increase can only be considered suggestive; nevertheless, these results do not suggest that local labor markets are increasingly important for large employers.[5]

Are Returns to Characteristics Converging within Regions?

Although we find no evidence that large- and small-firm wage levels have converged overall by region, it remains possible that at least

Table 4.7 Effects of Local Labor Market Conditions on Wages

Variable	1986	1992
Local unemployment rate	0.050	–0.051
	(0.072)	(–0.055)
Local wages	0.112	0.205
	(0.125)	(0.062)
R^2	0.000	0.002
F statistic	0.94	6.49
n	10,548	11,502

NOTE: Sample is professionals and first-line supervisors. The dependent variable is mean wage per job for each location/mean wage per job across the company. Standard errors are in parentheses.

some elements of wage structure have converged. To examine this issue, we estimated separate large- and small-firm equations for each of the nine census regions:

$$w_{jrst} = X_{jrst} \cdot b_{rst} + e_{jrst},$$

where r = region, t = 1979 or 1993, s = size class (large or small), and j is the sample in that region in that size classification that year.

For each person in the nation that year, we predicted a wage using the estimated coefficients from a region-specific wage equation for each size class ($\hat{b}_{rst}$):

$$\hat{w}_{irst} = X_{it} \cdot \hat{b}_{rst},$$

where i is an index for each person in the nationwide sample that year. The 1979 predictions use the 1979 sample, while the 1993 predictions use the 1993 sample. We correlated the predicted wages using large- and small-firm coefficients by region between 1979 and 1993, $\mathrm{corr}(\hat{w}_{irt,\mathrm{large}} \hat{w}_{irt,\mathrm{small}})$.

Similar to our prior results, there is no evidence of convergence in the wages of large and small employers by region. The correlation of predicted wages is 0.91 in 1979 and 0.89 in 1993. The change is not statistically significant, nor is it in the correct direction to be consistent with convergence.

Turning to specific characteristics, our estimates provide little or no evidence of increasing similarity in returns to characteristics by region between 1979 and 1993 (Table 4.8). Using nine census regions, we find that the coefficients of large firms in a region and the coefficients of small firms in that region were basically uncorrelated for each of the characteristics we examined; that is, regions with high returns for tenure (for example) at large firms did not pay high returns to tenure at small firms.

Sample sizes for each firm size class were modest within region, so some estimated coefficients were implausibly large or small. Thus, we redid the analysis using rank correlations that are not affected by outliers. The correlation between coefficients at large and small employers were not consistently positive and were never different from zero at a level that was statistically significant. These results are consistent with

Table 4.8 Correlation of Large- and Small-Firm Estimated Coefficients within a Region

Variable	1979	1993
Education	0.44	0.21
Age	0.41	−0.64*
Tenure	0.07	−0.34
Married	−0.59	0.51**
Union member	0.02	−0.33
Black	0.21	0.08
Female	−0.11	−0.09
Metropolitan	−0.53	−0.11
Nine occupation categories/region	0.29	0.27
Nine industries/region	0.33	0.38

NOTE: Estimated coefficients come from separate wage equations estimated in each region each year for each employer size class. The sample sizes for the correlations of coefficients is nine regions. Age, education, and tenure have means subtracted. The regressions included squared terms and dummies for tenure < 1 year and tenure 1–2 years. ** = Significantly different from 1979 values in a 5% two-tailed test; * = significantly different from 1979 values in a 10% two-tailed test.

the hypothesis that the labor markets of large and small employers were largely distinct in 1979 and remained largely distinct in 1993, in contrast to hypothesis Inst 4.

SUMMARY

The compensation practices of large and small employers are at least as different in 1993 as in 1979. The wage gap has probably declined; the correlation of large and small employers' regional wage effects has not lessened; the occupational wage structures of large and small employers within a region have not converged; the large-firm advantage in terms of returns to education has increased; and the large-firm advantage in the prevalence of benefits such as pensions has widened as well. In short, the distinctive nature of large-firm employment remains at least as strong in 1993 as in 1979.

In contrast, the characteristics of employees at large and small firms have converged on average. The gaps in tenure, age, and proportion female have all narrowed, while the gap in the proportion unionized has narrowed in absolute terms while widening in relative terms. An exception is the employment of blacks; the proportion of blacks employed was higher at large firms than at small firms in 1979, and the gap widened further by 1993.

Notes

1. This chapter is drawn from Belman and Levine (2001).
2. The size-wage gap is the gap between large firms (more than 1,000 employees) and small firms (fewer than 100 employees).
3. It is also possible to decompose these effects using large-firm characteristics in place of the characteristics of small firms.
4. This reduction in the size-wage gap was partly offset by an increase in the rising gap in pension coverage between large and small employers. Pension coverage at large employers declined by 8 percentage points, from 80 percent to 72 percent of employees from 1979 to 1993, while coverage at small firms declined by 11 percentage points, from 34 percent to 23 percent over the same period. It is unlikely that this change fully offset the decline in the size-wage gap.
5. The nature of the large firms in our sample restricts the breadth of the jobs included in this analysis. For many of the corporate administrative jobs, for example, there is only one location. Thus, the jobs included in this analysis are skewed towards jobs that are more naturally geographically dispersed, such as sales jobs. Our measures of local wages and unemployment may also be reducing the predictive power of our model. We use Bureau of Labor Statistics Standard Metropolitan Area data for our measures of unemployment and wages, and these data may be less representative of the managerial labor market that is relevant for these analyses.

5

Changes in Wage Structures within and between Employers

This chapter discusses data on employer wage structures from 1956 through 1996.[1] The data were gathered in the annual Community Salary Survey (CSS) conducted by the Federal Reserve Bank of Cleveland personnel department, which covers employers in Cleveland, Cincinnati, and Pittsburgh. Our analysis permits us to examine how pay variation between and within employers has evolved over a long time period.

Because the analysis in this chapter relies on salary survey data, it differs in approach from studies that use household surveys. Household data is most naturally directed at identifying how measures of skills (e.g., education) and various demographic measures (such as age and race) correlate with wages. Such regressions typically explain 20–30 percent of the variation of wages (see Chapter 4).

Our alternative approach offers complementary insight into the structure of wages within and between firms. Our employer wage survey is a census of individuals working in selected occupations at selected employers. Thus, unlike a household survey, the CSS permits us to investigate wage variations within and between occupations and employers (Groshen 1996). Salary surveys such as the CSS currently offer the only longitudinal microdata on wages that include both detailed occupation and employer identity in formation. The limitations of our analysis are discussed in Appendix C.

THE DATA

The Bank's personnel department chooses participants in each city to be representative of large employers in the area. The industries included vary widely; the main criterion used is whether the local employer has a large number of occupations that match the descriptions in the survey. Once they join, most employers continue to participate for several decades. On average, about 80 employers are represented in any given year.

Each employer judges which establishments to include in the survey. Some employers include all branches in the metropolitan area, while others report wages for only a single facility. We use the intentionally vague term *employer* to mean the employing firm, establishment, division, or collection of local establishments for which the participant reports wages. This ambiguity is useful, as it makes it likely that (as intended) the participant's unit has wage and personnel policies that are administered uniformly.

In the CSS, we use detailed occupational codes to measure human capital. In predicting wages, the R^2 yielded by occupation alone in the CSS is typically two to three times that yielded by the demographic, education, and broad (1-digit) occupation controls typically found in household data (such as from the Current Population Survey). Moreover, in the CSS, the returns to working in an occupation that typically requires more education has risen about as rapidly as the economy-wide rise in the returns to education.

The surveyed occupations (see Appendix C, Table C.1) are in the categories of office, maintenance, technical, supervisory, and professional personnel. These are the occupations for which external markets are most developed, since they are needed in all industries. Production jobs, which would be specific to a single industry, are not covered. Many jobs are further divided into a number of grade levels, reflecting responsibilities and required experience. Job descriptions for each are at least two paragraphs long.

In many companies, the wage structure determined by the job evaluations is most important for jobs that do not have a clear reference group in the market. In fact, job evaluation is often recommended specifically to help set wages when market wages are difficult to observe. Because our data include only occupations with a clear market, our tests for the importance of wage structures may understate the true extent to which internal wage structures are rigid.

For the years before 1980, each observation gives the median or mean salary of all employees of a given job title in a given year. After 1980, each observation in the original data set gives the salary of an individual employed in a surveyed occupation by a surveyed employer. Cash bonuses are included as salary, but fringe benefits are not.

The first three data columns of Table 5.1 describe the dimensions of the data set. Variation in the number of employers and occupations is due to occasional missing data, to changes in employer participation over time, and to decisions by the Federal Reserve Bank of Cleveland to change the survey's coverage. The CSS covers between 43 and 100 occupations each year; each employer reports wages for an average of 28 of these. The number of employers per year ranges from 41 to 99. Employers have an average of seven incumbents in each job title (this measure is only available in the 1980s and 1990s).

Employers in the CSS that also list employment in the Compustat database have median employment of 10,250. This figure includes all part-time and seasonal employees, as well as all employees of both domestic and foreign consolidated subsidiaries; roughly one quarter are unionized.

CSS employers are not a random sample. However, Appendix D summarizes a number of tests showing that the CSS wages are similar to those found in the Current Population Survey and that the publicly traded participants in the CSS behaved similarly to the Compustat firm in the same industry closest in size. The CSS, at best, reflects changes in pay practices at large employers. Thus, these findings are complementary to those using the CPS (Chapter 4), which compares large and small employers.

METHODS

A high-wage employee may earn a high wage because she is in a high-wage occupation, because she is at a high-wage employer, because her employer pays more than most do for her occupation, or because she earns a lot within her job title at this employer. We decompose the variance of wages into these several factors. Because high-wage occupations are disproportionately found at high-wage employers (controlling for occupation), we also have a covariance term that measures this sorting effect. This section describes how we measure these components and characterize their size over time.

Table 5.1 Characteristics of the CSS Data Set, 1956–96

Year	Job cells	Occupations	Employers	Total sample	Rolling sample (smoothed)
		Total number of		Std. dev. ln(wage) among job cells[a]	
1956	1,473	44	77	0.314	0.304
1957	1,737	47	87	0.310	0.300
1958	1,737	43	88	0.299	0.297
1959	1,749	43	88	0.296	0.297
1960	1,749	43	87	0.303	0.298
1961	1,993	50	96	0.305	0.302
1962	1,978	53	94	0.311	0.304
1963	2,122	53	99	0.313	0.308
1964	2,250	53	95	0.318	0.311
1965	2,279	53	97	0.323	0.315
1966	missing				0.317
1967	2,224	53	94	0.321	0.315
1968	2,383	55	96	0.332	0.315
1969	2,426	53	97	0.333	0.316
1970	missing				0.319
1971	1,460	66	41	0.340	0.319
1972	954	66	61	0.340	0.322
1973	1,048	66	66	0.342	0.326
1974	1,504	40	80	0.331	0.333
1975	1,215	42	50	0.345	0.338
1976	1,466	42	75	0.344	0.345
1977	2,240	72	73	0.411	0.352
1978	2,635	92	70	0.417	0.363
1979	3,048	100	83	0.425	0.367
1980	3,370	100	90	0.412	0.370
1981	2,477	68	86	0.419	0.366
1982	2,316	67	84	0.417	0.365
1983	2,493	76	84	0.422	0.365

Table 5.1 (continued)

Year	Total number of			Std. dev. ln(wage) among job cells[a]	
	Job cells	Occupations	Employers	Total sample	Rolling sample (smoothed)
1984	2,748	76	86	0.425	0.368
1985	2,736	75	88	0.417	0.370
1986	2,851	76	91	0.435	0.373
1987	2,742	76	85	0.440	0.379
1988	2,668	76	84	0.447	0.383
1989	2,701	76	83	0.446	0.388
1990	2,931	75	96	0.445	0.390
1991	2,711	76	90	0.451	0.395
1992	2,512	75	89	0.456	0.400
1993	2,488	75	85	0.451	0.405
1994	2,500	83	84	0.458	0.406
1995	1,967	83	66	0.457	0.403
1996	1,694	83	57	0.441	0.397
Total	87,575				

[a] In ln(wage) points. Weight: one observation per job cell.
SOURCE: Authors' calculations from the CSS.

The situation is simplest in the years before 1980, when the CSS did not provide the entire individual-level wage distribution, but provided only mean or median wages for a job title at each employer (what we call a "job cell"). In each year, these wages can be decomposed into the sum of three differentials: an occupation effect, an effect due to working at a specific employer, and an effect due to an employer paying a specific occupation particularly poorly or well (the internal structure differential). The separation is achieved by estimating a wage equation for each city and year, which includes a complete set of indicator (dummy) variables for each employer and each occupation:

$$(5.1) \quad \text{WAGE}_{ijt} = \text{OCCUPATION}_{it} + \text{EMPLOYER}_{jt} + \text{OCCUPATION-EMPLOYER CELL}_{ijt}.$$

The WAGE$_{ijt}$ term is the logarithm of the mean or median wage of employees in occupation i with employer j (hereafter called "job cell ij") in year t. The OCCUPATION$_{it}$ term measures returns to the attributes of employees in each occupation in year t. (As a shorthand, we are combining the name of the vector of dummy variables and that of their coefficient.) Such attributes include mean human capital, any compensating differences, and perhaps features that give that occupation high bargaining power. Even fairly broad occupational categories (such as those found in the CPS) capture almost all of the variation picked up by education and age, the standard measures of human capital (Groshen 1991b). Thus, narrowly defined occupations can proxy at least as well for human capital as do standard measures. (The R^2 from occupation dummies alone is several times the R^2 from a regression with standard experience and education controls in a household survey.)

The EMPLOYER$_{jt}$ term measures the average wage differential associated with working for each employer. A positive coefficient indicates that the employer pays higher-than-average wages, conditional on its mix of occupations. As noted in Chapter 2, the evidence on low quit rates among high-wage employers suggests that a meaningful proportion of the apparently above-market wage does not only reflect high general human capital or poor working conditions.

The OCCUPATION-EMPLOYER CELL$_{ijt}$ term represents the internal wage structure effect for occupation i paid by employer j in year t. A positive OCCUPATION-EMPLOYER CELL$_{ijt}$ component indicates that employer i pays occupation j a higher differential, relative to the market, than that employer pays its average occupation. To the extent this differential is not merely measuring unobserved general skills, wage variation among occupation-employer cells indicate the extent to which internal wage structures are insulated from the external market. We measure the coefficient on an OCCUPATION-EMPLOYER CELL$_{ijt}$ (what we call the employer's "internal wage structure" for the occupation) as a residual; i.e., the cell mean wage minus its associated employer and occupation effects.

After 1980 the CSS includes individual-level wage distribution within each cell. Thus, we can estimate a more complete decomposition based on

(5.2) $\text{WAGE}_{ijkt} = \text{OCCUPATION}_{it} + \text{EMPLOYER}_{jt}$
$+ \text{OCCUPATION-EMPLOYER CELL}_{ijt}$
$+ \text{WAGE DIFFERENTIAL WITHIN AN}$
$\text{OCCUPATION-EMPLOYER CELL}_{ijkt},$

where the WAGE DIFFERENTIAL WITHIN AN OCCUPATION-EMPLOYER CELL$_{ijkt}$ measures employee k's deviation from the mean wage in job cell ij, due to such factors as individual k's skills, merit pay, and the presence of individual incentive schemes offered by the employer. The CSS does not identify individual employees, so we cannot follow a particular employee's pay over time.

Decomposing the Variance Components of Wages

This section describes the trends in the components of wage variation from 1956 through 1996.[2] We first decompose wage variation between job cells for the entire time period. We then examine within-cell variation trends separately for 1980–1996.

From Equation 5.2, we can decompose any year's between-job-cell variance of wages into four components:

(5.3) $\text{V}(\text{WAGE}) = \text{V}(\text{OCCUPATION}) + \text{V}(\text{EMPLOYER})$
$+ 2\text{Cov}(\text{OCCUPATION, EMPLOYER})$
$+ \text{V}(\text{OCCUPATION-EMPLOYER CELL}).$

When the composition of jobs is fixed over time, the change in any term in Equation 5.3 will be due to changes in either the returns to attributes or the attributes of occupations and employers over time. As Equation 5.3 expresses, the variances of the components sum to total wage variance. Below (p. 94) we discuss standard deviations because they are in natural units. For example, in a normal distribution, the standard deviation of the employer wage effects tells us roughly the percentage gap in mean wages between two employers chosen at random.

The occupation component—V(OCCUPATION)—is expected to rise over the 1980s because the returns to education increased in the CPS over the decade. Groshen (1991c) found that the trend of increase in returns to education and training are similar in the CSS and the CPS.

Previous studies suggest that wage variation by employer—V(EMPLOYER)—accounts for a large part of wage variation (Groshen 1991a,b; Haltiwanger, Lane, and Spletzer 2000; but see Abowd, Kramarz, and Margolis 1999). Although employer wage effects are correlated with employer characteristics such as industry and employer size, no single theoretical explanation for these differentials has gained a consensus.

Other studies decomposing wage variation have found mixed results on the relative importance of within- versus between-employer wage differences in explaining increased wage variation over time. Davis and Haltiwanger (1991) compared changes in total wage variability measured in the CPS with changes in between-plant wage variability in the Longitudinal Research Datafile. They concluded that total wage dispersion grew faster than between-plant wage dispersion for nonproduction manufacturing workers between 1963 and 1988. By contrast, the Hay data on managers in 1986 and 1992 found that most of the increased inequality occurred between, not within, enterprises (see Chapter 6). Results from these data sets may not generalize. For one thing, both data sets cover only manufacturing firms. In addition, Davis and Haltiwanger (1991) assumed that the estimates of wage variation from a survey of households and from a survey of plants are comparable, a problematic assumption. The Hay data set comes from a single compensation consulting firm and covers a limited number of employers. By construction, the employers in that data set use a particular compensation strategy. Thus, the results may not generalize to employers not working under that particular compensation strategy.

The internal structure component—V(OCCUPATION-EMPLOYER CELL)—measures the distinctiveness of internal pay relationships among firms (that is, OCCUPATION-EMPLOYER CELL$_{ijt}$). If this component is large, then companies frequently pay relative wages within the firm that do not match the relative wages paid in the market.

The covariance term—Cov(OCCUPATION, EMPLOYER)—enters because occupations are not equally represented within each employer. When this term is positive, high-wage firms (controlling for occupation) employ a disproportionate share of high-wage occupations. If this term grows while the distribution of jobs is held constant, it is because the firms with high and growing returns to their attributes also have more than their share of occupations with high and/or growing returns to their attributes.

Kremer and Maskin (1995) reported increased sorting between firms in several data sets. In contrast, the Hay data discussed in Chapter 6 do not show increased sorting of skills between employers during a much shorter time period (1986–1992), at least among the managers and professionals.

For the 1980s and 1990s, we can also estimate inequality within an occupation-employer cell. A large standard deviation of wages within cells suggests that skills are diverse within a job title or that employers have strong individual incentive or merit pay programs.

Because the CSS is not a random sample, it is best suited to exploring changes in the returns to attributes rather than changes in the distribution of jobs. Accordingly, we purge the data of changes in composition using a "rolling sample" technique (see Groshen 1991c). Between any two years, the change in variation is measured only for the subsamples of job cells that are present in both years. These changes are then added to the cumulative sum of previous changes plus the initial variance to estimate the effect for an unchanged job cell.

Persistence of Wage Components

The most novel contribution of this chapter is an examination of trends in the persistence of wage components over the 40 years of the CSS. Our measure of persistence is the autocorrelation of the three wage components estimated in Equation 5.2: occupation effects (corr[OCCUPATION$_{it}$, OCCUPATION$_{it-\tau}$]), employer effects (corr[EMPLOYER$_{jt}$, EMPLOYER$_{jt-\tau}$]), and internal structures (corr[OCCUPATION-EMPLOYER CELL$_{ijt}$, OCCUPATION-EMPLOYER CELL$_{ijt-\tau}$]). We perform these autocorrelations for various lag lengths τ, with a focus on lags of 1, 5, and 10 years.

Occupation autocorrelations are expected to be high because they represent the continuity in returns to training or experience and compensating differences that are held in common across firms. Despite the lack of consensus on the cause of between-employer wage differences, there is strong agreement that these differentials are persistent. Five- or six-year autocorrelations of employer differentials remain at or above 0.9 in a variety of data sets (Levine 1992; Groshen 1989; Abowd, Kramarz, and Margolis 1999; but not Leonard 1989).

The internal structure component measures the distinctiveness of internal pay relationships among firms (OCCUPATION-EMPLOYER CELL$_{ijt}$). This autocorrelation measures whether employers who pay an occupation or set of occupations well in one year continue to pay them well in subsequent years. As far as we know, this is the first study of the autocorrelation of the employer-specific internal structure, that is, corr(OCCUPATION-EMPLOYER CELL$_{ijt}$, OCCUPATION-EMPLOYER CELL$_{ijt-\tau}$).

RESULTS

We first show the pattern of increasing wage inequality and decompose its components. Then we present findings on the persistence (autocorrelations) of occupation, employer, and internal structure wage components. All references to changes being "significant" mean that a t-test of a time trend or of decade dummies supports the reported change as being statistically significant at the 5 percent level. Results of the statistical tests are available upon request.

TRENDS IN TOTAL VARIATION

The "Total sample" column of Table 5.1 shows that wage variation increased substantially over time, from a standard deviation of about 0.31 ln points in the 1950s to about 0.45 ln points in the 1990s. Since these standard deviations are taken over the medians (or means) of job cells, with a weight of 1 per cell, they control for the effect of changes in the number of workers among jobs.

The increased dispersion in the column could simply reflect the possibility that the CSS now includes more diverse occupations and employers than previously. The results in the "Rolling sample (smoothed)" column of Table 5.1 are controlled for sample changes. The column presents three-year moving averages to smooth the noise from occasional small samples and to interpolate missing years.

The results controlling for changes in the occupational mix also reflect growing inequality. Although wage inequality rose in each of the decades covered, the growth wage concentrated in the 1970s and 1980s.

Trends in Variance Components

Here we examine the separate contributions of occupation, employer, and internal structure differentials to widening inequality. We then examine the role of occupation-employer covariance and of individual wage variation within a job cell.

Inequality between occupations

Figure 5.1 shows how the three between-cell components of wage dispersion contributed to widening wage dispersion in the CSS from 1956 through 1996. The main reason for the recent widening wage inequality in these large firms is widening occupation differentials.

Figure 5.1 Standard Deviation of CSS Wage Components over Time (rolling sample, smoothed)

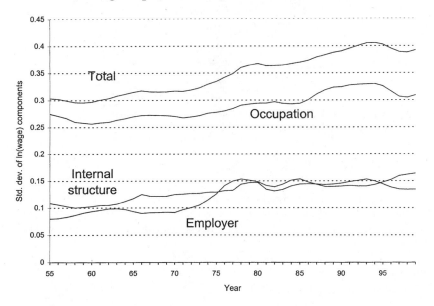

Table 5.2 Occupation Winners and Losers, 1974–1990

Occupations that gained at least 20 ln pts. rel. to 3 or more occupations	No. of occupations gained on	Occupations that lost at least 20 ln pts. rel. to 3 or more occupations	No. of occupations lost to
Cleveland[a]			
Registered nurse	10	Painter I	3
Purchasing clerk	16	Data entry operator	3
Payroll clerk II	16	Administrative secretary	3
		Stenographer	3
		Computer operator I	3
		Clerk typist	3
		Stock clerk	3
		Executive secretary	3
		Programmer II	5
		Analyst programmer I	8

Other occupations included (listed from least growth to most): telephone operators, audit analyst I, electrician, carpenter, lead computer operator.

Cincinnati[b]			
Registered nurse	8	Clerk typist	3
Audit analyst	11	Electrician	3
		Payroll clerk II	3
		Stenographer	3
		Painter I	3
		Telephone operator	3
		Stock clerk	3
		Carpenter	3
		Computer operator I	4

Other occupations included (listed from least growth to most): lead computer operator, data entry operator, payroll clerk I.

Pittsburgh[c]			
Payroll clerk II	9		
Registered nurse	12		

Other occupations included (listed from least growth to most): computer operator I, administrative secretary, telephone operator, lead computer operator, stock clerk, carpenter, data entry operator, painter I, electrician, audit analyst I, stenographer, clerk typist.

[a] Total occupations present in both 1974 and 1990: 18.
[b] Total occupations in 1974 and 1990: 14.
[c] Total occupations in 1974 and 1990: 14.

The standard deviation of occupational premiums rose from 27 percent in 1970 to 40 percent in 1996.

Which types of occupations gained relative to others during this period? One way to answer this is to identify the occupations that gained or lost most ground relative to others over a given time span. Table 5.2 presents the winning and losing occupations in each city from 1974 to 1990. Although Cleveland and Cincinnati have a number of losing occupations in common, and two occupations (registered nurses and payroll clerks II) show up as winners in all three cities, there is no clear pattern in the relative winners and losers.

A more general approach is to look for evidence of an increase in the returns to both formal education and skill in the widening occupation differentials. To do this, we merged information on job attributes from the National Crosswalk Service Center (1988) with the survey data. Although many job attributes could be examined, using just "specific vocational preparation" and an index of "general education development" generally explains 60 to 70 percent of the variation in occupational wage differentials. Specific vocational preparation measures the amount of time to learn the techniques and develop the facility needed for average performance on the job. It includes both off-site and on-site vocational training as well as the time for sufficient on-the-job learning to achieve basic proficiency. General education development is the sum of three 6-level indices indicating the level of general reasoning ability, mathematical skills, and language skills. The three indices were too collinear to disentangle changes over time in their relative importance. (Groshen [1991b] provides detailed definitions of these terms.)

For each year, we regressed the occupational wage level against the occupation's measures of specific vocational preparation and of general education development (as well as a complete set of employer dummies). Figure 5.2 shows the deviations from the mean of the two estimated coefficients over time. The estimated returns to occupation-specific and to general skills followed quite different courses. Returns to specific vocational preparation were fairly flat over the sample period, with the exception of a transitory bump up in the mid 1970s. In contrast, the coefficient on general education development rose consistently over the period except for a strong dip in the mid 1970s, followed by rapid recovery in the 1980s.

Figure 5.2 Changing Returns on Skill

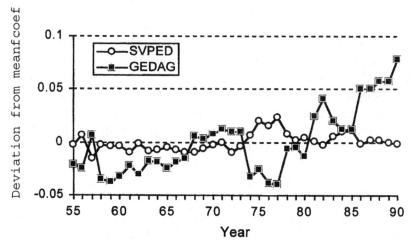

Thus, the finding in the CPS of increased returns to education is confirmed in this data set, which also shows a rising return to general skills that explains much of the increase in wage variation among occupations. Returns to specific vocational preparation, on the other hand, do not appear to have risen substantially over the last three decades.

The actual skills required by an occupation have changed over time, but our measures of skill requirements are taken from a job analysis in the mid 1980s. If the measured skill requirements were less accurate in the earlier years, one would expect a bias toward zero in the coefficients for these years. However, the explanatory power of the model should then be lower in the early years, which it is not.

Inequality among employers

The standard deviation of employer differentials is large, as in Groshen (1991b,c). Wage differentials among CSS employers widened dramatically in the late 1970s; the standard deviation of the employer effects rose from 9 percent in 1970 to 15 percent in 1980. In contrast, these differentials showed little change in the 1960s, 1980s, and 1990s. The relative stability of between-employer inequality provides no support for human capital theory's prediction of declining inequality (HumCap 2) or of the institutionalist theory's prediction of declining inequality (Inst 1).

What characterized those employers that showed large increases or decreases in their relative wages during the 1970s? Since most of the increase in the dispersion of employer differentials occurred in the second half of the 1970s, we can rank employers by the size of the change they experienced from 1974 to 1980 and then look for common traits among those with the largest changes. For 38 of the 60 employers included in the sample in both years, the estimated wage coefficients changed by less than 0.04 ln points (in either direction) or wound up closer to the mean than they started.

Among the five employers that showed declines of more than 0.04 ln wage points in their wage differentials and that increased their distance from the mean, none is even partially unionized. By industry, four are banks and one is an insurance company. In contrast, among the 17 employers with increases of more than 0.04 ln wage points that increased their difference from the mean, 14 are at least partially unionized. This is consistent with the high inflation and loose labor markets of the 1970s, and also with the fact that union wages are more likely to have cost-of-living indexing. Nine of these employers manufacture durable goods (including steel), six are utility or telephone companies, three are government agencies, and one is a nondurable-goods manufacturer.

Thus, large increases in employer wage differentials in the late 1970s were mainly due to the widening of the union wage differential and the differentials paid by durable-goods manufacturers and utilities, and perhaps to the effects of deregulation in the banking industry and unionization of federal jobs. Among the many unanswered questions about this result is why the increase in variance in the 1970s appears to be so long-lived.

Inequality due to differing internal wage structures

The standard deviation of internal wage structure differentials increased from 11 percent to 15 percent during the 1960s and the 1970s; that is, employers' internal wage structures were increasingly distinct from those paid in the external labor market. However, this form of wage variation held steady during the 1980s or 1990s. Given the rising inequality among occupations, the relative importance of firm effects and internal wage structures fell since 1980, even as their absolute importance remained steady. Again, these results provide no support for theories of widening inequality (HumCap 2) or declining inequality (Inst 1).

Occupation-employer covariance

Figure 5.3 shows the contribution of employer sorting by occupation to wage variance over time. The covariance is positive, but small. A positive value means that the premiums paid by high-wage employers tend to be received by workers in disproportionately high-wage occupations, adding to overall wage variation. However, this effect is considerably smaller than the other components of wage variation; it usually accounts for only 2 to 4 percent of the total variation. From 1978 until 1981, the covariance has a pronounced upward trend that dissipated somewhat in the 1980s and reestablished itself in the 1990s. By 1996, the covariance accounted for more than 9 percent of total variation. Thus, the CSS provides some evidence in support of

Figure 5.3 Covariance of Employer and Occupational Effects over Time (rolling sample, smoothed)

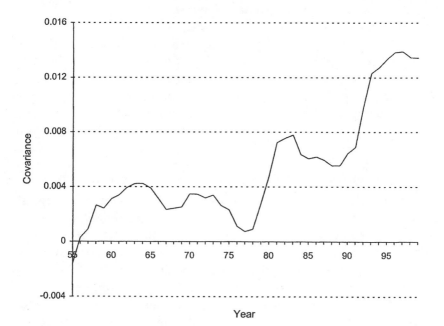

increased wage dispersion being due to increased employer sorting, although the growth starts from a low base.

Variation within employer-occupation job cells

The data allow investigation of wage variation within job cells only during the 1980s and 1990s. In 1989, a supplemental question was added to the CSS asking managers whether they had modified their pay-for-performance programs. About four-fifths of the employers in this sample reported that they implemented or strengthened their merit raise and pay-for-performance programs over the 1980s. Thus, if these schemes affect the variance of wages, we should see an increase in variation due to this component in the 1980s or 1990s.

Table 5.3 shows a decomposition of wage variation into the portions between and within job cells from 1980 to 1996. In each year, the standard deviation of wages within job cells is low, as found in BLS Industry and Area Wage Surveys (Groshen 1989, 1991b). There is only a slight upward trend in the standard deviation of cash compensation within a cell, from near 8 percent in the early 1980s to near 9 percent by the mid 1990s. The estimated trend of a 0.6 percentage point rise in within-cell inequality per decade is significant at the 5 percent level.

We replicated this analysis using data from the Hay data set (which is described further in Chapter 6). We examined job cells that had at least four incumbents at that employer. There were 4,351 such job cells in 1986 and 3,921 in 1992. The mean and median number of incumbents in each job cell were similar in both years (approximately 10 and 4).

Consistent with results in the CSS, the typical (median) job cell had a standard deviation in total cash compensation of 7.0 percent in 1986 and 7.5 percent in 1992. All job levels experienced an increase in the standard deviation of total compensation, but the increase was larger for first-line supervisors (rising from 7.3 to 8.0 percent) and smaller for professionals (6.9 to 7.0 percent). The standard deviation of wages within a job cell grew less rapidly (the 0.5 percentage point change equals about an 8 percent increase) than the standard deviation of wages in the entire sample (which rose by 11 percent).

A second dimension of within-cell inequality can be individualized bonuses. Thirty-two percent of employees in the Hay sample received

**Table 5.3 Wage Dispersion within CSS Job Cells
          during the 1980s and 1990s**

| Year | No. of observations | Standard deviation of ln(wages)[a] | | |
		Total	Between job cells	Within job cells
1980	23,475	0.353	0.342	0.086
1981	19,753	0.355	0.344	0.088
1982	18,302	0.347	0.339	0.077
1983	19,336	0.352	0.344	0.078
1984	19,379	0.355	0.345	0.082
1985	20,101	0.362	0.353	0.080
1986	20,893	0.378	0.369	0.083
1987	21,552	0.384	0.375	0.081
1988	20,293	0.397	0.388	0.088
1989	21,613	0.384	0.375	0.084
1990	22,327	0.388	0.379	0.086
1991	21,945	0.389	0.378	0.088
1992	8,769	0.368	0.352	0.099
1993	20,870	0.399	0.388	0.092
1994	18,487	0.415	0.405	0.088
1995	14,351	0.413	0.405	0.082
1996	10,932	0.418	0.408	0.093

[a] In ln(wage) points.

a bonus in 1992, up from 19.6 percent in 1986. This percentage understates the extent of bonuses, because not all who were eligible for bonuses necessarily received payment. If we instead estimate the percentage of job cells for which at least one incumbent received a bonus, the proportion rose from 27 to 47 percent over the same period. In 1986, bonus variation within job cells was, on average, a small part of total pay. The mean standard deviation of bonus/(base+bonus) within a job cell was 0.75 percent; that is, bonuses increased pay variation only modestly among people in the same job cell.

At the same time, the proportion of pay at risk in our data set as measured by the size of the bonus payments rose from 0.75 percent in 1986 to 1.03 percent in 1992. While the absolute level of these payments is low, the increase in level is particularly impressive given that 1992 was a year of low corporate profits. To the extent that bonus pools are related to corporate performance, the 1992 figures are an understatement of the true rise in the importance of bonuses.[3]

These results suggest that adoption of individual (as opposed to group-based) pay-for-performance or incentive schemes has widened wage inequality only slightly in the CSS and the Hay data sets. If such schemes are now a substantially larger source of wage variation than before, they must have largely replaced the variation from other wage-setting practices (such as seniority). Similarly, if such schemes were applied to groups rather than individuals (for example, with team-based pay or gain sharing), then they must have replaced a previous source of variation, because neither employer nor internal structure components increased variation in the 1980s.

PERSISTENCE OF WAGE COMPONENTS

We begin by comparing the overall persistence of occupational, employer, and internal structure differentials over spans of 1 to 15 years. In Figure 5.4, the vertical axis measures the correlation of estimated differentials in one year with estimates from another year. The horizontal axis indicates the number of years spanned. All possible spans in the data are combined to construct the correlations. For example, the one-year employer correlations are calculated over coefficients from every two consecutive years from each respondent firm.

Overall, estimated CSS occupational differentials have a correlation of 0.99 with the same occupation after one year, declining to 0.90 when measured 15 years apart. Although employer differentials show less stability than occupational premia (starting at 0.93 for one-year autocorrelations and declining to 0.62 over 15 years), they nevertheless suggest a high degree of permanence in employers' wage strategies—as would be expected under an internal labor market and has been found in other studies. The 15-year correlations suggest that workers can expect that, if they join a high-wage firm in the middle of their career, it will still be a fairly high-wage firm when they are nearing retirement.

The autocorrelations of internal structure differentials start at 0.76 one year apart and decline to 0.24 over 15 years. Since compositional effects (as workers are promoted into and out of the cell) can exert strong influence on cell means and medians, these differentials are expected to be less stable than employer and occupation differentials. (That is, each job cell has far fewer observations than does an entire firm or occupation, making it more sensitive to moves of a small number of individuals.) Nevertheless, they are strongly positive, indicating fairly stable divergences from market means, particularly over one- to five-year spans. That is, employers with lower relative wages for secretaries than for other employees in one year will probably have lower relative wages for secretaries for many years to come.

**Figure 5.4 Occupation, Employer and Internal Structure Wage
Differentials Autocorrelations by Length of Time
between Observations**

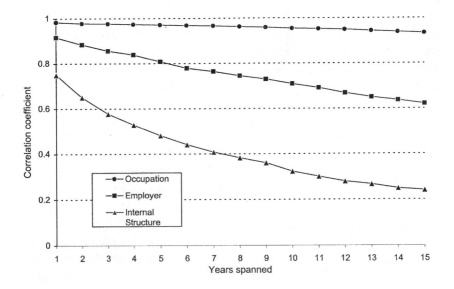

Trends in persistence

Do the autocorrelations indicate that employer wage structures have become less or more stable over the last two decades? To answer this, we graph the autocorrelations plotted in Figure 5.4 separately depending on the end year of the span. If employer and internal structure differentials have become less stable, we should see a downward drift in autocorrelations.

Figure 5.5 shows 1-, 5-, and 10-year autocorrelations for occupational wage differentials arranged by the end-year of the span. Discontinuities in the lines reflect missing data for the end year.

Autocorrelations over one- and five-year periods were very high in late 1960s (0.99), then fell in late 1970s to 0.94. We then see a slow recovery through 1982–1983 recession to 0.96–0.98 and continued growth, back to very high levels near 0.98. Ten-year autocorrelations fell from the late 1960s to a minimum near 1979 and have risen steadily since. Their quick recovery implies that some of the late 1970s drop was due to transitory changes from persistent differentials (that is, the differentials returned to the long-term patterns). If occupational wage relativities were becoming less stable (because occupational wages were now less protected from shocks, or the shocks were larger), these autocorrelations would drift down over the 1980s and 1990s. Although there is some evidence of reordering during the late 1970s (as would be expected during high inflation if wages are rigid— see Groshen and Schweitzer [1996]), there is no evidence of a similar decline in stability recently.[4] In fact, 10-year autocorrelations have been rising recently at a statistically significant pace.[5]

Figure 5.6 repeats the exercise for employer differential autocorrelations. The very early years show evidence of strengthening of the persistence of employer wage effects, as described in "golden age" descriptions of industrial relations. Again, the 1970s saw some restructuring of employer wage relativities, with recovery of stability in the 1980s and 1990s. The one-year autocorrelations are remarkably constant. They drift upward slightly ($p < 0.05$), which is certainly not what we would expect if employer wage structures were becoming less important or undergoing a major reordering. Similarly, the longer-span autocorrelations drift upward slightly (and are, again, statistically sig-

Figure 5.5 Occupation Autocorrelations over Time

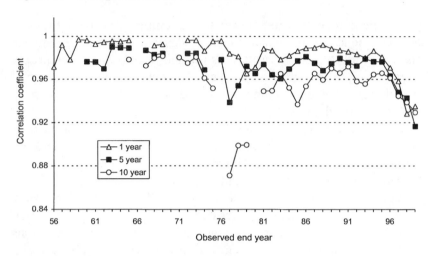

Figure 5.6 Employer Autocorrelations over Time

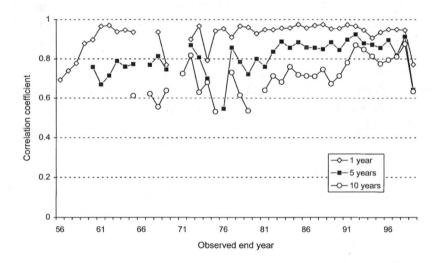

nificant), reinforcing the conclusion that employer wage differences remain as stable now (if not more so) as they were during the 1960s.

Figure 5.7 plots trends in internal structure persistence. Focusing on the one-year autocorrelations, again there is no evidence of a recent decline in the persistence of wage structures. The persistence is hump-shaped with a slow decline since the mid 1960s peak. (Fitting a quadratic in time to the series of autocorrelations is not statistically significant; thus, neither the hump nor the slow decline is statistically significant.) This peak is almost precisely when Doeringer and Piore performed the field research that led to their 1971 book on internal labor markets and again is consistent with the "golden age." Thus, it is not surprising that they stressed the stability of within-company wage structures. The mid 1970s saw a loosening of these structures. However, since 1980, the one-year autocorrelations have been constant and five-year autocorrelations have trended up ($p < 0.06$).

This pattern means that the extent to which relative wages within a company mirrored the wage ratios among occupations in the external market fell during the 1960s and 1970s, generally preceding the

Figure 5.7 Internal Structure Autocorrelations over Time

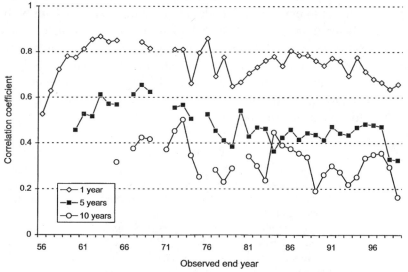

increase in wage variation among employers. Thus, this component does not appear to have grown, as might be expected if the growth of wage differentials for some employers increased their insulation from market pressures and allowed them to deviate more from external market pay ratios. Instead, growth in this component may reflect either varying lags in adjustment to external changes, an increase in uncertainty about market pay ratios, or greater insulation from the market due to a change in worker preferences. The effects of deregulation and imports are discussed in Appendix E and on page 164.

Finally, we note that the patterns over time of the variance and persistence of employer and internal structure differentials differ from each other and from that for occupation differentials. The variety of patterns calls into question any assumption that all of the differentials measure labor market returns to a single set of skill factors.

These autocorrelations can be biased down due to measurement error in the internal structure effects estimated in our data. We replicated some of the longer-term autocorrelations using three-year centered moving averages. That is, instead of correlating the 1970 and the 1980 internal wage structures, we correlated 1969–1971 average internal structures with their 1979–1981 counterparts. Autocorrelations of such moving averages are smoother over time, but otherwise are very similar in their level and evolution to those calculated without averaging. As a check to ensure outliers do not drive the results, we reran the main analyses using rank (rather than standard) autocorrelations. Again, results were very similar. There may also be measurement error because we have a sample of occupations, not all occupations in an employer's establishment. In this case, although measurement error might bias down all of the autocorrelations, there is no reason to expect this bias to have changed over time.

Notes

1. This chapter is drawn from Groshen and Levine (1998).
2. This section updates Groshen (1991c). The Community Salary Survey is described in Appendix C.
3. The mean variation within a job cell of pay attributable to bonuses was driven down because many jobs offered no bonus. For job cells with some non-zero bonuses, the mean standard deviation of percent bonus within a job cell was 2.9 percent in 1986 and 2.7 percent in 1992. This decline is misleading, however,

because (as noted in the text) the total fraction of job cells with a positive bonus rose rapidly. The small but rising importance of bonuses is better measured by the calculation in the text.

4. Alternatively, this instability may reflect a data issue. Only job cell means, not medians, are available for the 1970s. Sample means are more sensitive to outliers, so their presence may explain the apparent reduced stability for these years.

5. Statistically significant at $p < 0.05$ in a quadratic of time for the entire series, or for a linear term in time for a sample restricted to the 1980s and 1990s.

6
Job Characteristics, Skills, and Wages

All theories of wage determination that we discuss predict that job characteristics play an important role in explaining why wages differ among establishments (see Chapter 2). In this chapter,[1] we first examine the role of job characteristics in explaining employer wage effects in the Hay and Indiana/Japan data sets when treated as cross sections. We then examine the Hay data set over time.

In all the data sets, the basic technique is to run models:

(6.1) $\text{WAGE}_{ijt} = f_{1t} \text{EMPLOYER}_{jt} + \text{RESIDUAL}_{ijt}$

and

(6.2) $\text{WAGE}_{ijt} = B_t \text{ JOB CHARACTERISTICS}_{it} + f_{2t} \text{ EMPLOYER}_{jt}$
$+ \text{RESIDUAL}_{ijt},$

where i indexes occupations and j indexes employers. The occupation characteristics vary among the data sets, and f_{1t} and f_{2t} represent complete sets of employer-specific intercepts.

To be brief, human capital theory posits that employer wage effects are due to poorly measured skills. To the extent the researchers have good measures of skills, then the importance (e.g., standard deviation) of employer wage effects should decline markedly when the job characteristics are added to Equation 6.1 (that is, s.d.(f_{1t}) should be far greater than s.d.(f_{2t})).

THE DATA

We first analyze a proprietary data set collected by Hay Associates, the world's largest compensation consultant. To construct the skills measure we analyzed, the Hay system performs a detailed analysis of the skills that are needed to perform particular jobs. Hay works with the companies in developing detailed questionnaires to establish exactly what an incumbent does in a job. Separate versions are developed for each functional area such as finance, personnel, or engineering. The questionnaires cover job duties, allocation of time, responsibility, critical tasks, customer contact, and many other tasks. The questionnaires are completed for each job title, usually by a team of managers, employees holding those jobs, and Hay consultants. As described in Appendix F and in Bellak (1984), Hay goes to great lengths to create measures of skill and responsibility that are comparable across employers. Summary statistics and descriptions of the sample are found in the tables of Appendix F.

We replicate the cross-sectional Hay results with data from 1982–1983 surveys of manufacturing establishments in the Indianapolis area in the United States and from the Kanagawa prefecture (an industrial district outside of Tokyo) in Japan. (Appendix G and Lincoln and Kalleberg [1990] discuss the data in more detail; Levine 1991a presents additional results.) These surveys included information on employees and multiple measures of their job characteristics. While the Hay data use a formal job analysis, the Indiana/Japan data sets use employee self-reports of job complexity, autonomy, and other job characteristics.

RESULTS WITH THE 1986 HAY DATA

We use an ordinary least squares regression to test the model and to examine wage inequality among and within firms. We regress the logarithm of base wages against a set of firm dummies and a composite indicator of Hay points. To control for unmeasured aspects of the jobs, we include each job's occupational level in the hierarchy (five levels) and 16 indicators of the functional area within which each job is located (finance, marketing, engineering, and so forth).

We used a bootstrap technique to compute the statistical significance of the changes by running the regression models 200 times on random halves of each sample and retaining the estimated returns to

Hay points and/or the estimated standard deviation of the firm effects for each regression. To check if the differences in a coefficient over time or across specifications was statistically significant, we tested whether the distributions of the 200 coefficients in each specification differed. We performed a nonparametric Wilcoxon rank test on the two distributions of coefficients and/or standard deviations. (Using a more powerful but parametric t-test produced the same results.)

Especially because many of the wage equations involve sample sizes of over 50,000 observations, even differences that are unimportant substantively can be statistically significant. In the discussion below, we emphasize those results that are both large and statistically significant. The large sample size also implies that correcting for measurement error—when, for example, computing the standard deviation of employer wage effects—does not meaningfully affect our results (Haisken-DeNew and Schmidt 1997). As a result, we forego that extra set of computations in the results reported here.

Table 6.1 presents the main analyses. Wage inequality in this sample has increased, as indicated in the first row of the table: the standard deviation of ln(wages) has risen from 31.6 percent to 34.3 percent, that is, by about one-tenth. (For ease of exposition, we refer to 100 times logarithms as "percent.") Inequality is lower controlling for job level and function (RMSE = 24.7 percent in 1986). The rise in inequality between 1986 and 1992 is again about one-tenth. Controlling for job level and function ensures that the increase cannot be attributed to any changes in the composition of jobs across that period. (The R^2 of the regression with just the controls is almost unchanged between 1986 and 1992.)

Are Differences in Wages between Firms Primarily Due to Differences in Skill?

The first human capital hypothesis (HumCap 1) asserted that differences in average wages among employers were attributable to differences in average levels across skills. Model 1 in Table 6.1 examines base wages using only firm effects and controls for job level and function, without Hay points. The increment to the R^2 due to adding firm effects is 7.9 percent, and the standard deviation of firm effects is 12.0 percent, reinforcing the descriptive observation earlier that wages dif-

Table 6.1 Predicting Base Wages

Model	1986	1992	Change
Total wage inequality	s.d.(ln wages) = 0.316	s.d.(ln wages) = 0.343	0.027
Controls alone: job level and function	RMSE[a] = 0.247 $R^2 = 0.386$	RMSE= 0.268 $R^2 = 0.391$	0.021 0.005

Model 1: Only firm effects and controls	s.d.(firm effects) =
	    0.120
	RMSE = 0.231
	$R^2 = 0.467$
		s.d.(firm effects) =
		    0.146
		RMSE = 0.247
		$R^2 = 0.481$
			0.026***
			0.016
			0.014

Effect of adding firm effects (Model 1 minus controls alone)	ΔRMSE = –0.016 $\Delta R^2 = 0.079$	ΔRMSE = –0.021 $\Delta R^2 = 0.090$	–0.005 0.011
Model 2: Only Hay points and controls	$b = 0.203$ (s.e. = 0.0008)*** RMSE = 0.173 $R^2 = 0.700$	$b = 0.233$ (s.e. = 0.0009)*** RMSE = 0.182 $R^2 = 0.718$	0.030*** 0.009 0.018
Effect of adding Hay points (Model 2 minus controls alone)	ΔRMSE = –0.058 $\Delta R^2 = 0.314$	ΔRMSE = –0.065 $\Delta R^2 = 0.327$	–0.007 0.013

Model 3: Firm effects, Hay points, and controls	s.d.(firm effects) =
	    0.112**
	$b = 0.211$
	(s.e. = 0.0007)***
	RMSE = 0.149
	$R^2 = 0.778$
		s.d.(firm effects) =
		    0.139***
		$b = 0.239$
		(s.e. = 0.0008)***
		RMSE = 0.152
		$R^2 = 0.804$
			0.027***
			0.029
			0.003
			0.026

Effect of adding Hay points, given firm effects (Model 3 minus Model 1)	Δs.d.(firm effects) =
	    –0.008***
	ΔRMSE = –0.082
	$\Delta R^2 = 0.311$
		Δs.d.(firm effects) =
		    –0.007***
		ΔRMSE = –0.095
		$\Delta R^2 = 0.323$
			–0.001 (n.s.)
			0.013
			0.012

Effect of adding firm effects, given Hay points (Model 3 minus Model 2)	$\Delta b = 0.008$*** ΔRMSE = –0.024 $\Delta R^2 = 0.078$	$\Delta b = 0.006$*** ΔRMSE = –0.030 $\Delta R^2 = 0.086$	–0.002 (n.s.) –0.006 0.008

NOTE: The dependent variable is ln(base wage). Tests of the statistical significance of coefficient estimates (b) and changes in coefficients (Δb) are t-tests. Tests of the joint statistical significance of firm effects are F-tests. Tests of changes over time (the right-most column) are bootstrapped, as described in the text. *** = The change is significant at the 1% level; (n.s.) = not statistically significant at the 5% level.

[a] RMSE = root mean square error, a measure of within-firm inequality.

fer substantially among employers for employees with similar job titles and skills.

Model 2 shows the results of regressing ln(wages) against the composite Hay points score. This single measure of skill and responsibility is correlated 0.80 with base wages, corresponding to an R^2 of 64 percent from this single measure alone (regression not shown). By way of comparison, a standard wage equation controlling for age, education, experience, tenure, gender, race, region, and various nonlinear combinations rarely achieves an R^2 over 30 percent. A wage regression with three-digit occupational classifications—a typical proxy for job requirements and skill in other studies—and the above controls using the 1992 Current Population Survey produces an R^2 of only 31 percent. The impressive explanatory power of Hay points implies that it is a far more complete measure of skill and job requirements than those used in the past to explain wage outcomes.[2]

Model 3 includes both firm wage effects and the composite Hay points score. The standard deviation of the firm effects declines to 11.2 percent when Hay points are included, slightly less than its value of 12.0 percent when it is calculated without controlling for Hay points in Model 1. The incremental R^2 of adding Hay points and controls to firm effects is 7.8 percentage points, which is almost identical to the incremental R^2 of adding firm effects and controls alone, without Hay points (7.9 percentage points). The fact that the standard deviation of the firm effects and the incremental R^2 of adding firm effects to the equation are hardly diminished when controlling for the very detailed measures of skill represented by Hay points suggests that relatively little of between-firm inequality is due to differences in mean skill levels between firms, providing little evidence in favor of hypothesis HumCap 1. In sum, as shown in Figure 6.1 in the 1986 cross section, including Hay points in the regression reduces inequality within a firm by about one-third, but has almost no effect on inequality between firms.

These results do not imply that mean wages at an employer and mean Hay points are completely uncorrelated. When we regress the mean wage residual at each firm (that is, the firm effects from Model 1 in Table 6.1 including the controls) and the mean Hay points residual at each firm (that is, the firm effects from Model 2 in Table 6.1 including the controls), the R^2 is 0.12 in 1986 (regression not shown). This R^2 is only one-fifth as large as that obtained when we perform the regression

Figure 6.1 Decomposing Inequality

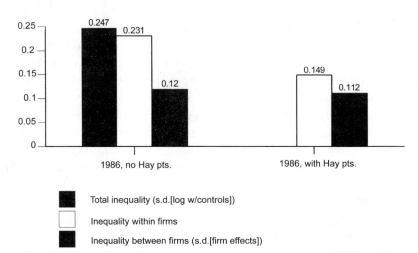

Total inequality (s.d.[log w/controls])

Inequality within firms

Inequality between firms (s.d.[firm effects])

at the individual level. Together, these results suggest that skill, as measured by Hay points, is a powerful predictor of wages within enterprises but a weak predictor of which employers pay high wages.

Robustness checks[3] found the results essentially unchanged when we

- analyzed base pay plus bonus instead of base pay alone (Table 6.2);

- omitted the detailed controls for functions and levels within the organization;

- replaced average Hay points with the know-how, accountability, and problem-solving subscores of Hay points along with their squares;

- performed the cross-section tests on a larger sample by including those employers who dropped from the sample in 1992;

- added measures for SMSA mean wages and unemployment rates;

- corrected roughly for heteroskedasticity by weighting with the term (1/Hay points);

- ran the regression separately for each job level and for the larger job functions; and

- dropped the 1 percent of the sample with the highest and lowest Hay points and wages.

Table 6.2 Predicting Base Pay Plus Bonus

Model	1986	1992	Change
Total wage inequality	s.d.(ln[base+bonus]) = 0.333	s.d.(ln[base+bonus]) = 0.363	0.033
Controls alone: job level and job function	RMSE[a]= 0.259 R^2 = 0.369	RMSE= 0.284 R^2 = 0.386	0.025 0.017
Model 1: Only firm effects and controls	s.d.(firm effects) = 0.117 RMSE = 0.243 R^2 = 0.469	s.d.(firm effects) = 0.148 RMSE = 0.265 R^2 = 0.466	0.030 0.022 −0.003
Effect of adding firm effects (Model 1 minus controls alone)	ΔRMSE = −0.016 ΔR^2 = 0.079	ΔRMSE = −0.021 ΔR^2 = 0.090	−0.005 0.011
Model 2: Only Hay points and controls	b = 0.220 (0.0008) RMSE = 0.175 R^2 = 0.724	b = 0.255 (0.0009) RMSE = 0.185 R^2 = 0.735	0.025 0.010 0.011
Effect of adding Hay points (Model 2 minus controls alone)	ΔRMSE = −0.058 ΔR^2 = 0.314	ΔRMSE = −0.065 ΔR^2 = 0.327	−0.007 0.013
Model 3: Firm effects, Hay points, and controls	s.d.(firm effects) = 0.108 b = 0.227 (s.e. = 0.0007) RMSE = 0.152 R^2 = 0.793	s.d.(firm effects) = 0.140 b = 0.261 (s.e. = 0.0008) RMSE = 0.159 R^2 = 0.808	0.022 0.034 0.007 0.015
Effect of adding Hay points, given firm effects (Model 3 minus Model 1)	Δs.d.(firm effects) = −0.008 ΔRMSE = −0.082 R^2 = 0.311	Δs.d.(firm effects) = −0.008 ΔRMSE = −0.095 R^2 = 0.323	0.013 0.0 0.012
Effect of adding firm effects, given Hay points (Model 3 minus Model 2)	Δb = 0.008 ΔRMSE = −0.024 ΔR^2 = 0.078	Δb = 0.006 ΔRMSE = −0.030 ΔR^2 = 0.086	−0.002 −0.006 0.008

NOTE: Dependent variable is ln(base pay plus bonus).
[a] RMSE = root mean square error, a measure of within-firm inequality.

Hypothesis EffWage 2 posits that the accountability factor has large incremental value in predicting wages after controlling for the know-how factor. As noted above, including the know-how, account-ability, and problem-solving subscores separately increased the explan-atory power of the model by a statistically significant amount, but the basic results were unchanged. Nevertheless, in 1986, the know-how subscore had a higher correlation with wages than our composite score; correspondingly, in a regression the accountability subscore had a small negative coefficient (results available on request). In 1992, in contrast, accountability had the largest standardized coefficient of the three subscores. Thus, these results provide inconsistent evidence on whether accountability, as a measure of importance and difficulty of monitoring above and beyond traditional human capital, has an impor-tant role in explaining wages. At the same time, due to the high multi-collinearity of the three subscores, we are not surprised by the instabil-ity of individual coefficients and we do not want to make too much of the results.

RESULTS WITH THE INDIANA/JAPAN DATA[4]

As with the Hay data, we use a baseline model with standard con-trols and employer wage dummies and then augment it with measures of job characteristics.

Baseline Results

Table 6.3 presents the basic wage equations for Indiana and Japan. The logarithm of hourly wages (in Indiana) or of annual earnings (in Japan) is regressed upon a standard list of demographic and human capital controls. As expected, wages are higher for men (especially if they are married), unmarried women in Japan, whites in the United States, and employees at large plants and plants that are branches of larger organizations. Furthermore, there are large differences in wages between industries (columns 1 and 3) and establishments (columns 2 and 4). The results in Table 6.3 accord well with past research on wages in the United States and in Japan.

**Table 6.3 The Determinants of Wages in Indiana and Japan:
Baseline Model**

Variable	Indiana	Japan
Education	0.033***	0.031***
	(0.005)	(0.008)
Age	0.011***	0.072***
	(0.003)	(0.007)
Age^2	−0.0001***	−0.0007***
	(0.00004)	(0.00009)
Age over 55	—[a]	−0.098
		(0.060)
Tenure	0.012***	0.018***
	(0.002)	(0.003)
$Tenure^2$	−0.00022***	−0.00022***
	(0.00005)	(0.00009)
Nonwhite	−0.052***	—
	(0.014)	
Male married	0.152***	0.281***
	(0.014)	(0.029)
Male unmarried	0.112***	0.194***
	(0.016)	(0.026)
Female married	−0.009	−0.207***
	(0.016)	(0.038)
Line worker	−0.350***	−0.268***
	(0.024)	(0.036)
Line supervisor	−0.217***	−0.169***
	(0.028)	(0.036)
Line manager	0.132***	−0.030
	(0.038)	(0.051)
Technical worker	−0.337***	−0.211***
	(0.025)	(0.036)
Technical supervisor	−0.202***	−0.157***
	(0.030)	(0.037)
Number of plant dummies	47	34
s.d. (coeff. on plant dummies)	0.185	0.137

(continued)

Table 6.3 (continued)

Variable	Indiana	Japan
F test	43.9***	13.7***
R^2	0.648	0.753
F test	82.2***	101.2***
N	2,740	1,715

NOTE: Four overtime dummies (Japan only) are omitted from the table. Standard errors are in parentheses. The omitted categories are "Female unmarried" and "Technical manager." Dependent variable for Indiana is ln(hourly wage); for Japan, it is ln(annual earnings) including bonus and family allowance. *** = Statistically significantly different from 0 at the 1% level.

[a] A dash (—) indicates not available in data set or not applicable.

Results with Job Characteristics

To test the hypotheses that the wage anomalies described above are due to differences in working conditions (HumCap 1, EffWage 1, CompDiff 1), 52 dummies for Indiana representing all possible responses to the 13 job characteristics measures were added to the wage equations; for Japan, 48 dummies representing 12 questions were included. The job characteristics included the complete set of dummy variables for each possible response to the three or four on-the-job training questions, three autonomy questions, three complexity questions, and three supervision questions. These results are found in Table 6.4.

Adding the job characteristics increases the R^2 of the Indiana regression from 0.65 to 0.68; the Japanese R^2 moves from 0.75 to 0.76 (Tables 6.3 and 6.4). In each data set, the rise in R^2 is statistically significant at $p < 0.01$. The "on-the-job-training" bundle is significant in both. The "complexity" and "supervision" bundles are significant for Indiana, but not for Japan; the reverse is true of the "autonomy" bundle.

The easiest way to understand the magnitude of these effects is to examine the change in wages when each characteristic increases by one point on a five-point Likert scale (approximately one standard deviation). Raising the responses to the four on-the-job training questions for Indiana increases predicted wages by 3.6 percent; for complexity, the increase is 1.8 percent. Raising each autonomy measure by

Table 6.4 The Determinants of Wages in Indiana and Japan: Model with Job

Variable	Indiana	Japan
Education	0.025***	0.024***
	(0.005)	(0.008)
Age	0.008***	0.069***
	(0.003)	(0.007)
Age^2	–0.00008**	–0.0007***
	(0.00004)	(0.00009)
Age over 55	—	–0.096
		(0.061)
Tenure	0.0099***	0.017***
	(0.0017)	(0.003)
$Tenure^2$	–0.00019***	–0.00020**
	(0.00005)	(0.00009)
Non-white	–0.036***	—
	(0.014)	
Male married	0.122***	0.265***
	(0.014)	(0.029)
Male unmarried	0.095***	0.186***
	(0.016)	(0.026)
Female married	–0.01	–0.187***
	(0.016)	(0.038)
Line worker	–0.283***	–0.225***
	(0.025)	(0.037)
Line supervisor	–0.178***	–0.146***
	(0.027)	(0.036)
Line manager	0.148***	–0.019
	(0.037)	(0.051)
Technical worker	–0.300***	–0.194***
	(0.025)	(0.036)
Technical supervisor	–0.181***	–.0148***
	(0.030)	(0.037)
On-the-job training[a]		
Time required to train=0	–0.143***	–0.16***
	(0.023)	(0.053)
Time required to train=1	–0.126***	–0.10**
	(0.021)	(0.05)
Time required to train=2	–0.103***	–0.098
	(0.02)	(0.05)

(continued)

Table 6.4 (continued)

Variable	Indiana	Japan
Time required to train=3	−0.099***	−0.09
	(0.021)	(0.05)
Time required to train=4	−0.063***	−0.08
	(0.02)	(0.05)
Time required to train=5	0.0013	−0.077
	(0.021)	(0.052)
Learning new things=1	−0.024	0.0005
	(0.02)	(0.03)
Learning new things=2	−0.009	0.015
	(0.016)	(0.023)
Learning new things=3	0.019	0.029
	(0.015)	(0.023)
Learning new things=4	0.009	0.02
	(0.012)	(0.018)
Importance of formal training=1	−0.034	0.049**
	(0.062)	(0.021)
Importance of formal training=2	−0.033	−0.10**
	(0.029)	(0.048)
Importance of formal training=3	0.00003	−0.0005
	(0.012)	(0.025)
Importance of formal training=4	0.0039	0.0009
	(0.01)	(0.018)
Importance of informal training=0	−0.008	
	(0.048)	
Importance of informal training=1	0.032	
	(0.032)	
Importance of informal training=2	0.015	
	(0.016)	
Importance of informal training=3	0.011	
	(0.01)	
Complexity[a]		
Job requires high skill=1	−0.072***	0.009
	(0.024)	(0.037)
Job requires high skill=2	−0.022	−0.018
	(0.016)	(0.026)
Job requires high skill=3	−0.02	−0.005
	(0.013)	(0.026)
Job requires high skill=4	−0.014	−0.12
	(0.011)	(0.023)

Table 6.4 (continued)

Variable	Indiana	Japan
Job is repetitive=1	−0.017	−0.016
	(0.024)	(0.029)
Job is repetitive=2	−0.006	−0.014
	(0.024)	(0.027)
Job is repetitive=3	0.007	−0.006
	(0.025)	(0.031)
Job is repetitive=4	0.038	−0.008
	(0.025)	(0.027)
Job has variety=1	0.003	−0.05
	(0.021)	(0.031)
Job has variety=2	0.005	−0.022
	(0.015)	(0.027)
Job has variety=3	0.004	−0.077
	(0.015)	(0.028)
Job has variety=4	−0.0013	−0.044
	(0.011)	(0.026)
Autonomy[a]		
Freedom how to do my work=1	−0.027	0.025
	(0.024)	(0.033)
Freedom how to do my work=2	−0.006	−0.0024
	(0.018)	(0.03)
Freedom how to do my work=3	0.002	0.006
	(0.017)	(0.031)
Freedom how to do my work=4	−0.004	0.04
	(0.014)	(0.029)
Not participate in decisions=1	0.059***	0.025
	(0.02)	(0.03)
Not participate in decisions=2	0.02	−0.028
	(0.02)	(0.024)
Not participate in decisions=3	0.019	−0.019
	(0.017)	(0.024)
Not participate in decisions=4	0.014	−0.01
	(0.016)	(0.023)
I decide work speed=1	0.012	−0.005
	(0.02)	(0.028)
I decide work speed=2	−0.014	0.029
	(0.017)	(0.023)

(continued)

Table 6.4 (continued)

Variable	Indiana	Japan
I decide work speed=3	0.002	0.0018
	(0.017)	(0.024)
I decide work speed=4	−0.002	0.029
	(0.015)	(0.021)
Supervision[a]		
Supv. has a great deal of say=1	0.018	0.036
	(0.028)	(0.042)
Supv. has a great deal of say=2	0.012	0.002
	(0.014)	(0.025)
Supv. has a great deal of say=3	0.012	0.002
	(0.013)	(0.025)
Supv. has a great deal of say=4	−0.0023	−0.004
	(0.01)	(0.02)
Supervisor lets me alone=1	0.01	0.008
	(0.025)	(0.017)
Supervisor lets me alone=2	0.017	−0.017
	(0.024)	(0.034)
Supervisor lets me alone=3	0.028	0.024
	(0.026)	(0.024)
Supervisor lets me alone=4	0.011	0.014
	(0.027)	(0.023)
Supervisor decides what I do=0	0.063***	0.024
	(0.015)	(0.023)
Supervisor decides what I do=1	0.029***	0.017
	(0.011)	(0.021)
Number of plant dummies	47	34
s.d. (coeff. on plant dummies)	0.19	0.135
F test	46.6***	12.5***
F tests on groups of characteristics		
On-the-job training	5.26***	2.37***
Complexity	2.06**	1.26
Autonomy	1.3	1.6
Supervision	2.71***	0.73
R^2	0.680	0.764
F test	49.7***	53.6***
N	2,740	1,715

Table 6.4 (continued)

NOTE: Dependent variable is ln(hourly wage) in Indiana; ln(annual earnings) incl. bonus and family allowance in Japan. Standard errors are in parentheses. Four overtime dummies (Japan only) are omitted from the table. Omitted variable for Gender × Marital Status interaction is "Female unmarried." Omitted variable for the Department × Rank interaction is "Technical manager." *** = Statistically significantly different from 0 at the 1% level; ** = statistically significantly different from 0 at the 5% level.

[a] Each variable in this section is a dummy variable equal to 1 if the response to that question was in that category, and zero otherwise. For example, the dummy "Time required to train=0" equals 1 if the response to the question equals zero ("a few hours"), and the dummy equals zero for responses equal to 1 through 6.

one point lowers wages by −0.8 percent. Lowering each supervision response by one point increases wages by 3.0 percent. In Japan, the value for on-the-job training is 4.0 percent, for complexity it is 2.1 percent. The effects of the other two sets of measures are smaller and not significant.[5]

In both countries, the effects of job characteristics on wages are similar in magnitude to the effects of education. Increasing education by one point (e.g., moving from "some high school" to "high school graduate," a little over one standard deviation) raises wages in the United States by about 4 percent and in Japan by about 3 percent. In both countries, this increase is approximately half as large as increasing each measure of on-the-job training and complexity and lowering each measure of supervision by one point each.

On average, jobs with high complexity and low supervision have slightly higher wages. These results support the hypothesis that the effects posited by the human capital, efficiency wage, and conflict theories are greater than any compensating differences from the utility of avoiding repetitive work or the disutility of being supervised. Autonomy has little effect, perhaps because the compensating difference (that is, the wage people are willing to give up to gain autonomy) approximately offsets the effects of the other theories (that is, the higher wages due to the skill and bargaining power possessed by employees working with more autonomy).

The relatively small increase in R^2 in Japan coupled with the small magnitude of the effects is consistent with past research which suggests that the characteristics of the current job are less important in Japan than in the United States because of the system of long-term employment relations (Kalleberg and Lincoln 1988).

Do Job Characteristics Reduce the Variability of Establishment Effects?

The estimated plant effects remain virtually unchanged in the presence of job characteristics (Figure 6.2). In Indiana, the standard deviation of establishment effects increases slightly from 18.5 percent in the baseline equation to 19.0 percent when job characteristics are added to the regression; the Japanese figure declines slightly from 13.7 percent to 13.5 percent. The plant effects with and without job characteristics are correlated at or above the 0.98 level in both data sets. These plant effects are very large; in both Indiana and Japan, moving from the average plant to one paying one standard deviation above average increases wages by as much as increasing education from grade school to college.

The general results reported above are robust to a variety of alternative specifications. Constraining the sample to include only men; only line workers; only workers with greater than two years experience (because of the strong nonlinearities in the returns to tenure during the first years on the job); interacting training measures with tenure; and adding education as a set of dummies (instead of as a continuous variable) did not noticeably increase the ability of the job characteristics to explain the plant wage effects.

RESULTS OVER TIME IN THE HAY DATA

The results over time are consistent with the cross-sectional results: Hay points matter greatly for changes in within-firm inequality but not for changes in between-firm inequality (Figure 6.3). Specifically, total inequality (conditional on job level and function) rose by 0.021 ln points from 1986 to 1992. This increase was slightly faster

Figure 6.2 Standard Deviation of Establishment Effects with (solid) and without (empty) Job Characteristics

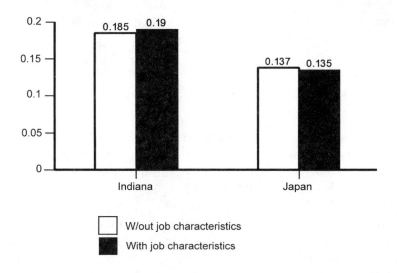

Figure 6.3 Changes in Inequity (Hay data, 1986–92)

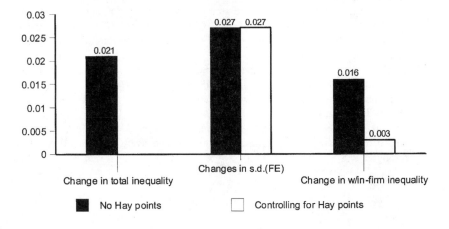

between firms (the standard deviation of firm effects rose by 0.027) than within firms (the RMSE rose by 0.016). Controlling for Hay points had no effect on the rise in the standard deviation of firm effects. In contrast, it explained nearly all of the rise in within-firm inequality, with the RMSE of ln(wages) rising a tiny 0.003.

CONCLUSION

The results from two data sets strongly suggest that measures of skills and responsibility can help predict wages. At the same time, the increased predictive ability is solely within employers. Even quite good measures of skills do little to explain which employers pay above-average wages.

Rising returns to skills help explain rising inequality in the Hay data set. At the same time, all of the increase is concentrated within the enterprise, and the rising returns to Hay points do not help us understand rising inequality among these large employers.

Notes

1. This chapter is drawn from O'Shaughnessy, Levine, and Cappelli (2001) and Levine (1991a).
2. The extremely high R^2 of this regression may also imply that employers set pay based on Hay points. Recall, however, that the employers have considerable discretion in setting pay levels and that Hay points do not translate into any unique salary recommendation.
3. Available from K.C. O'Shaughnessy at School of Business, Western Michigan University, 2333 Beltline SE, Grand Rapids, MI 49546–5936.
4. These analyses were carried out with Elizabeth Bishop on data kindly made available by Jim Lincoln.
5. The precise effect of increasing a response one point depends on the starting response. The reported responses are unweighted averages over all possible responses.

7
Changes in Attitudes toward Pay Flexibility

The literature reviewed in Chapter 3 provides mixed evidence on whether attitudes toward the employment contract have changed from the 1970s to the 1990s. A key element of the classic old employment contract was nominal and real wage rigidity; conversely, a key element of the new employment contract is increased pay flexibility. In this chapter,[1] we examine whether attitudes toward pay flexibility have, in fact, changed. We also present results on perceptions of the fair employment contract concerning layoffs.

THE DATA

We carried out our own surveys on the fairness of the employment contract, replicating questions that Kahneman, Knetsch, and Thaler asked in the mid 1980s. Thus, changes in responses test whether pay cuts are more acceptable in the late 1990s than 12 years earlier.

Kahneman, Knetsch, and Thaler performed their survey between May 1984 and July 1985 in Vancouver and Toronto. We carried out our survey in Vancouver and Toronto between March and September 1997, with a total sample of 950 respondents. We then repeated the survey in Silicon Valley between October 1997 and March 1998, with a sample of 1,059.

The protocols consist of a series of telephone surveys with questions about hypothetical situations relevant to price-setting and employment practices (Appendix H). We selected the questions relevant to labor markets from the Kahneman, Knetsch, and Thaler surveys, creating separate questionnaires for interview purposes. Each separate survey had four or five questions about standards of fairness. For each contrast we presented, comparison questions were asked of different respondents; this between-subjects design minimizes respondents' inclination and ability to answer based on guesses about the researchers' hypotheses.[2]

We collected approximately 125 replies for each question. Trained interviewers placed telephone calls to random listings in area directories, using a standard script. Eleven different people conducted the survey, so that no single individual's bias in elicitation method could greatly distort the results.

HYPOTHESES

Chapter 2 laid out the hypotheses we test. To recap: If the "new employment contract" is widely accepted, then

Attitude 1: Pay cuts are considered more fair in 1997 in Vancouver and Toronto than in the mid 1980s.

This hypothesis underlies much of the popular writing on the new employment contract, with its emphasis on employees' increasing acceptance of the market and lower reliance on and trust in employers. If custom and norms are slow to change or shocks are not as large as the media suggest, then attitudes have not changed and we have

Attitude 1': Pay cuts are not considered more fair in 1997 in Vancouver and Toronto than in the mid 1980s.

This hypothesis is more consistent with the literature on slow changes in attitudes due perhaps to rigidity of attitudes in a changing environment, or due to less change in the environment than is suggested by many proponents of the new employment contract.

We were concerned that Canadian attitudes might show no change even if such a change were evident in the United States. Given this concern, we replicated the study in the Silicon Valley, a region associated with the new employment contract. Our criterion of selecting a region specifically due to its association with the new contract led us to

Attitude 2: Pay cuts are perceived as more fair in Silicon Valley than in Canada.

Table 7.1 shows the results for 10 questions asked about decreases in compensation. Following Kahneman, Knetsch, and Thaler, we

Table 7.1 Responses to Pay Cut Questions in Canada and Silicon Valley
(% stating action is unfair)

				Difference (percentage pts.)	
Question	Canada[a] 1984/5	Canada 1997	Silicon Valley 1997/8	Canada 1997 – Canada 1984/5	Canada 1997 – Silicon Valley 1997/8
Q1: Painter goes into landscaping; lower wages. Wages reduced from $15 to $12.	37 (94)	48 (107)	37 (164)	11	11
Q2: Substantial unemployment; 12% inflation. Wages increased only 5%.	22 (129)	21 (108)	51 (175)	–1	–30***
Q3: Business has not increased as before. Wages reduced by 10%.	61 (100)	72 (109)	61 (153)	11	11
Q4: Business Ok; unemployment. Employee earning $15 quits and replacement paid $12.	27 (125)	24 (105)	33 (143)	–3	–9
Q5: Substantial unemployment and no inflation. Wages decreased by 7%.	62 (98)	76 (100)	66 (149)	14**	10
Q6: Business Ok; workers available at lower wage. Wages reduced by 5% for current workers.	77 (195)	76 (144)	63 (136)	–1	13**
Q7: Business Ok; much unemployment. Wages reduced from $15 to $12.	83 (98)	63 (119)	67 (141)	–20***	–4
Q8: Business losing money; workers available at lower wage. Wages reduced for current workers by 5%.	32 (195)	34 (122)	27 (139)	2	7

(continued)

Table 7.1 (continued)

				Difference (percentage pts.)	
Question	Canada[a] 1984/5	Canada 1997	Silicon Valley 1997	Canada 1997 – Canada 1984/5	Canada 1997 – Silicon Valley 1997/8
Q9: Business losing money, much unemployment. Wages reduced from $15 to $12.[b]	50 (153)	53 (142)	56 (128)	3	–3
Q10: Business has not increased as before. Total pay + bonus = market level. Eliminate usual 10% annual bonus.	20 (96)	44 (100)	41 (127)	24***	3

NOTE: Sample size is in parentheses. *** and ** represent statistically significant differences at the 1 and 5% levels, respectively, on the test of the equality of proportions (normal approximation to the binomial distribution, two-tailed test).

[a] Kahneman, Knetsch, and Thaler (1986) study.

[b] Question 9 asked whether the action was completely fair, acceptable, slightly unfair, or very unfair. We classify the first two categories as "fair" and the last two categories as "unfair."

report the proportion of respondents who claimed the action was unfair. The results support qualitatively the Kahneman, Knetsch, and Thaler findings of how the context of the pay cut (for example, the profitability of the employer) affected perceptions of fairness. Contradicting press reports of greatly increased acceptance of market forces, we do not find that pay cuts were substantially more acceptable in the late 1990s than in the mid 1980s. As discussed below, these results do not support Attitude 1.

Although the mean level of agreement that pay cuts are unfair has been constant, the gap between the levels of perceived fairness—i.e., of "more" and "less" fair pay cuts—has narrowed between 1984/1985 and 1997/1998. That is, respondents were a little more accepting of pay cuts when the employer had no justification, and a little less accepting when the employer had an excuse (e.g., low profits, cutting bonus not base pay).

Although we chose a region in the United States frequently associated with the new employment contract, the differences between the two nations were minor and do not tend to support Attitude 2. Unless U.S. residents were much more resistant to pay cuts than Canadians were in the past (an unlikely situation), these results suggest that employees' views of fair employer actions has been stable in the United States as well.

Changes over Time in Canada

Our results were broadly consistent with those of Kahneman, Knetsch, and Thaler. Specifically, respondents thought pay cuts solely due to the presence of unemployment were unfair: between 63 and 76 percent of respondents thought pay cuts were unfair in questions 5, 6, and 7 in the new surveys, similar to the results of Kahneman, Knetsch, and Thaler. Respondents were more willing to accept a reduction in pay when it was accomplished by a nominal increase less than inflation, when replacing a worker, when changing lines of business, or when the business was losing money. Specifically, 21 percent thought a 5 percent nominal wage increase was unfair during times of 12 percent inflation (question 2), but 76 percent thought a 7 percent nominal pay cut was unfair in times of no inflation (question 5). In addition, when a company is making a small profit and there is high unemployment and an inflation rate of 12 percent per year, 63 percent of respondents felt it was unfair to cut an incumbent worker's pay from $15 to $12 an hour (question 7). In contrast, only one-fourth of respondents thought a similar pay cut was unfair if the worker quit and a new worker received the lower pay (question 4). An intermediate proportion thought the pay cut was unfair if the painter switched to a new business and retained the incumbent worker (48 percent, question 1). If the firm is losing money instead of making a small profit (question 9 rather than question 7), 53 percent of the respondents thought the pay cut was unfair.

There is no consistent trend in responses over time, so that Attitude 1′, not Attitude 1, is supported. Two questions had large and statistically significant changes, but one change showed decreased tolerance for pay cuts and the other showed other increased tolerance. Specifically, the proportion who thought the pay cut in question 5 was unfair (cut nominal wages with no inflation) rose 14 percentage points (significant at the 5 percent level), while the proportion reporting unfair in question 7 (cut wages with high unemployment) declined 20 percentage points (significant at the 1 percent level). Other changes were small and not significant.

Comparing Canada with Silicon Valley

The results in Silicon Valley also support the presence of most of the fairness rules that Kahneman, Knetsch, and Thaler identified. Although pay cuts merely due to unemployment were not usually thought fair, pay cuts were also more acceptable when replacing a worker, when changing lines of business, or when the business is losing money. Specifically, when a company is making a small profit and there is high unemployment and an inflation rate of 12 percent a year, 67 percent of respondents felt it was unfair to cut an incumbent worker's pay from $15 to $12 an hour (question 7). In contrast, only one-third of respondents thought a similar pay cut was unfair if the worker quit and a new worker received the lower pay (question 4), and 37 percent thought the pay cut was unfair if the painter switched to a new business and retained the incumbent worker (question 1). If the firm was losing money (question 9) instead of making a small profit (as in question 7), 56 percent of respondents thought the pay cut was unfair. Respondents were also more willing to accept cuts in bonuses (41 percent "unfair" in question 10) than in base pay (61 percent "unfair" in question 3).

The largest difference between Canada and Silicon Valley was a lower acceptance of real pay cuts accomplished with a nominal pay increase of 5 percent and inflation of 12 percent. Fifty-one percent of the Silicon Valley respondents felt this situation was unfair, compared with only 21 percent of the Canadians in 1997 and 22 percent of the earlier Canadian sample (question 2). A real pay cut accomplished with a nominal pay cut but no inflation was considered unfair by even more respondents (question 5; 66 percent of Silicon Valley respondents, close to the Canadian responses), so the Kahneman, Knetsch, and Thaler finding of inflation illusion was supported (but more weakly) in the Silicon Valley sample as well.

There was little difference between Canada 1997 and Silicon Valley on the other illusion manipulation, i.e., the acceptance of pay cuts accomplished by the elimination of a customary bonus that was needed to bring compensation to the market level (question 3 vs. question 10). While there was a substantial effect for all samples, the bonus illusion was much stronger in Canada 1984/5 than in either contemporary study (question 10; 20 percent unfair vs. 44 percent or 41 percent).

The Effects of Justifications

While we qualitatively duplicate Kahneman, Knetsch, and Thaler's results, the effects of the justifications on perceived fairness were consistently weaker in the newer samples (Table 7.2). For example, Kah-

Table 7.2 Effects of Justifications in Canada and Silicon Valley

Questions	(Pct. pt. difference in % unfair)			Difference (pct. pts.)	
	Canada 1984/5[a]	Canada 1997	Silicon Valley 1997/8	Canada 1997 – Canada 1984/5[a]	Canada 1997 – Silicon Valley 1997/8
The. importance of inflation illusion (Q5 – Q2).	40***	55***	15***	15***	40***
The importance of bonus vs. wage distinction (Q3 – Q10).	41***	28***	20***	–13**	8
20% lower wage; same employee vs. new employee (Q7 – Q4).	56***	39***	34***	–17***	5
20% lower wage; same employee in new business vs. old business (Q7 – Q1).	46***	15***	30***	–31***	–15***
20% lower wage; business OK vs. losing money (Q7 – Q9).	33***	10**	11**	–23***	–1
Reduce wage by 5%. Business OK vs. losing money (Q6 – Q8).	45***	42***	36***	–3	6

NOTE: For statistical significance information, see note on Table 7.1.
[a] Kahneman, Knetsch, and Thaler (1986) study.

neman, Knetsch, and Thaler found a 41 percentage-point difference with respect to whether a pay cut was achieved by elimination of a customary bonus or by a pay reduction (question 3 vs. question 10). That gap declined to 28 percentage points in our Canadian survey and to only 20 percentage points in Silicon Valley. The effects of the justifications were larger for all six comparisons in the original study than in Canada in 1997. Kahneman, Knetsch, and Thaler found typical effect sizes of 43.5 percentage points, which shrunk by about one-third to 24–31 percentage points in our surveys. The shrinkage was due to trends toward accepting pay cuts when the company did not have the justification of low current profits, trends against accepting pay cuts when the company had low current profits, and a substantial difference for justifications not related to the firm's profitability. In short, the fairness and framing effects Kahneman, Knetsch, and Thaler identified remain prominent in the data, but became meaningfully smaller.

A summary of the comparisons is presented in Table 7.3. The main result of this chapter is that, in general, Canada showed no time trend in accepting pay cuts as unfair. In fact, the small differences indicate less acceptance of pay cuts in 1997 than in 1984/1985 (column 4, rows 1 and 2, and Figure 1).

There is a negligible difference between Canada 1997 and Silicon Valley (data column 5, row 1). At the same time, if we eliminate the questions on bonus and inflation illusion (question 2 and question 10), we see that respondents in Silicon Valley were slightly more accepting of pay cuts than were the Canadian respondents (column 5, row 2). All of this difference was due to questions where a pay cut either was not based on the firm's difficulties or where there was a shock to the employment relationship. When the company had low profits, replies in the two nations were almost identical.

These results suggesting slightly higher acceptance of the market in Silicon Valley are roughly consistent with the previous research on U.S.-Canadian attitudes referred to above. To a certain limited degree, the new employment contract, with its concomitant acceptance of market forces, may be more slightly prevalent in Silicon Valley than in Toronto and Vancouver.

In Canada, the gap in "percent responding unfair" between replies with and without a justification declined by 12 percentage points, suggesting that the justifications were somewhat less important in contem-

Table 7.3 Aggregated Results When Pay Cuts Are Fair

	% responding "unfair"			Difference (percentage pts.)		
Questions	Canada 1984/5[a]	Canada 1997	Silicon Valley 1997/8	Canada 1997– 1984/5	Canada 1997– Silicon Valley 1997/8	Silicon Valley 1997/8– Canada 1984/5
1. Mean proportion "unfair"; all 10 questions	47.1	51.1	50.2	4.0	0.9	3.1
2. Mean proportion "unfair": 8 questions excluding "illusion" questions 2 and 10	53.6	55.7	51.1	2.1	4.6**	−2.5
3. Mean proportion "unfair" when a pay cut was not based on the firm's difficulties[b]	74.0	71.7	65.3	−2.3	6.4**	−8.7**
4. Mean proportion "unfair" when the business is not doing well[c]	36.5	39.7	38.2	3.2	1.5	1.7
5. Mean change in % "unfair" between matched scenarios with vs. without a justification[d]	43.5	31.5	24.3	−12.0***	7.2**	−19.2***

[a] Kahneman, Knetsch, and Thaler (1986) study.
[b] The 3rd row includes Q5, Q6, and Q7 from Table 7.1.
[c] The 4th row includes Q1, Q4, Q8, and Q9 from Table 7.1.
[d] The 5th row is the average of (Q5–Q2) + (Q7–Q4) + (Q7–Q1) + (Q7–Q9) + (Q6–Q8) + (Q3–Q10) from Table 7.1. "Justification" includes low profits, change in employee, and the other conditions noted in Table 7.1.

porary Canada. For Silicon Valley vs. 1984/5 Canada, the effect of justifications diminishes a further 7.2 percentage points.

WHEN ARE LAYOFFS ACCEPTABLE?

In addition to studying both the reality and the attitudes toward flexibility of wages, we also studied attitudes towards layoffs. The new employment contract suggests that layoffs should typically be considered fair, especially if the employer has made clear that layoffs were expected and assists employees in finding new work. We studied how changes in the sources of the shocks to the employer, the reactions of the employer, the skills and occupations of the employees affected, and other factors affected respondents' perceptions of fairness.

The questions concerning layoffs examined variations of a model case:

A company faced lower product demand due to shifts in the market; the viability of the employer is threatened. In response, the company laid off some high-technology engineers with an average of 10 years of tenure at this employer. Before the layoff, the employer gave each employee four paid weeks to find another job elsewhere in the company. Those who could not find a new position received severance pay based on age and years of service. The company provided out-placement assistance including counseling and resume-writing workshops. Employees knew layoffs were likely in this circumstance.

Respondents were then asked if the layoff was completely fair, somewhat fair, unfair, or very unfair.

We varied this model case along a number of dimensions. We examined how respondents changed their views about the fairness of the employer if the source of lower labor demand was higher productivity due to employees' suggestions or due to new technology instead of product market shocks, and if the company had layoffs with less notice or avoided layoffs altogether instead of the relatively gentle layoffs described above. We compared results if the occupation of the employees were production workers instead of engineers. In the Silicon Valley surveys, we added the dimension of general vs. firm-specific skills. We also varied whether CEO pay either rose due to cost-cutting from layoffs or whether the CEO turned down his bonus to share the pain.

Occupation and Skills

Our scenarios covered two occupations with different gains or losses from the new employment contract. The first was an occupation that might not suffer greatly from the new contract: high-technology engineers with 10 years of tenure at this employer. Presumably, these engineers would be able to find new employment at high pay relatively easily. The second occupation was more vulnerable to the new contract: production workers who have specialized in this company's unusual technology, with an average of 10 years of tenure at the employer.

Comparison questions (for example, questions matched on all aspects except the source of the shock) were asked of different respondents. This design minimizes respondents' inclination and ability to answer based on their attempts to guess the researchers' hypotheses.

Tables later in the chapter present the mean reply to each question, coding the responses from 0 = "very unfair" to 3 = "completely fair." Because the data were ordinal, the statistical tests use the nonparametric Wilcoxon-Mann-Whitney rank-sum test (Siegel and Castellan 1988). Unlike a parametric test such as a t-test, the rank-sum test makes no assumptions about the spacing of the intervals that make up the ordinal scale. When considering the magnitude of gaps, the differences in means are easy to read and we focus on them in the text; Appendix I contains the full tabulations.

We report all differences that were statistically significant at the 5 percent level with the rank-sum test. Most of the tests involved comparisons of two groups of 250 or so respondents. With these sample sizes, differences as small as 0.10 on a 4-point scale were usually statistically significant, although the economic effects of such changes may not be important. Moreover, differences in means of less than 0.18 were usually not statistically significant using the parametric t-test.

JUSTICE THEORY HYPOTHESES

Justice theories lead to a number of hypotheses concerning how the source of shocks, company responses, and the characteristics of employees should affect perceptions of fairness.

What Shocks Justify Layoffs?

The scenarios examined four different shocks that reduce the employer's demand for labor: product demand (lower product demand due to shifts in the market; the viability of the employer is threatened); technology (higher productivity due to new technology); suggestions (higher productivity due to employees' suggestions); project (the employee's current project has ended).[3]

In general, previous research suggests that people consider it fairer to react to an exogenous shock than to take the initiative and cause harm (see the citations in Rabin 1993). Along these lines, Kahneman, Knetsch, and Thaler found that circumstances threatening the existence of the firm led many people to consider pay cuts as fair. Similarly, Brockner (1992) noted how employees perceive layoffs as less problematic when they are necessary due to external circumstances. Thus, we assume that layoffs are largely perceived as fair when the employer's health is threatened by declining product demand.

Different Shocks to Labor Demand

New technology is less exogenous to the employer than lower product demand. Thus, respondents should rate layoffs in response to the product demand shock as fairer than those due to the technology shock. Moreover, new technology that raises productivity increases the employer's ability to pay. To the extent that perceptions of fairness involve the sharing of rents and quasi-rents, layoffs due to the introduction of new technology should be perceived as less fair than layoffs due to lower product demand.

Like new technology, employees' suggestions increase employers' ability to pay. Layoffs due to employees' suggestions have yet another reason to be perceived as unfair: they violate the norm of reciprocity, which suggests that employers should respond to employee suggestions with bonuses, not with layoffs. For respondents who share this view, layoffs for this reason should seem even less fair than those due to new technology. These considerations lead to

Hypothesis 1: Layoffs are perceived as fair in cases of lower product demand, sometimes fair for the introduction of new technology, and usually unfair for employees' suggestions.

"Harsh" vs. "Gentle" Layoffs

Our scenarios considered three possible responses to a reduction in labor demand.

- "Gentle" layoffs: The company is laying off some employees. Before the layoff, the employer has given each employee four paid weeks to find another job elsewhere in the company. Those who cannot find a new position receive severance pay based on age and years of service. The company provided out-placement assistance including counseling and resume-writing workshops. Employees knew layoffs were likely in this circumstance.

- "Harsh" layoffs: The company is laying off employees with two weeks' warning. These are the first layoffs of [occupation] in the company's history.

- Hoard labor: The employer promises to avoid laying off employees, although many employees will need to be retrained in a new job and employees may need to relocate to a different city.

The gentle layoffs scenario is substantially more generous than the harsh scenario. Brockner (1992), for example, noted that layoffs are perceived as more fair when the employer provides tangible care-taking services to help soften the blow. Moreover, the gentle layoffs scenario includes advanced notice, a form of respect that Brockner et al. (1994) argued will predict high perceptions of procedural justice. This reasoning leads to

Hypothesis 2a: Gentle layoffs are perceived as significantly more fair than harsh layoffs.

More interestingly, the literature on the new employment contract predicts that gentle layoffs will generally be perceived as fair. Unlike the case of harsh layoffs, respondents will not consider these gentler layoffs as violating norms of reciprocity, even when employees have submitted productivity-enhancing ideas. For example, the severance pay may be interpreted as indicating that the employer is sharing some gains of higher productivity. This reasoning leads to

Hypothesis 2b: In contrast to hypothesis 1, the type of shock makes little difference in how fairly respondents rate gentle layoffs. (That is, harsh layoffs are considered very unfair after employee suggestions, but not too unfair after demand shocks; in contrast, gentle layoffs are considered not too unfair in any case.)

Hoarding labor is the strongest form of employment security an employer can provide. In this case, we assume hoarding labor may involve need for retraining or relocation. These were the preconditions of large Japanese and U.S. employers who provided employment security. (Recall the joke that "IBM" stood for "I've Been Moved.") If the old employment contract was perceived as fair, then we have

Hypothesis 2c: Hoarding labor, even if it means retraining and relocation, is considered fair for every type of shock.

CEO Bonuses

Theories of distributive justice often imply that lower-paid employees look to the fate of their higher-paid colleagues for fairness comparisons. In some cases, these comparisons rise to the highest ranks of the organization (Cowherd and Levine 1992). CEO pay may be particularly salient during downsizing.

For example, one high-technology company announced its CEO's record compensation the same week they announced layoffs. The employees were outraged. E-mail on the company's internal computer network contained messages such as "Morale is somewhat like it must have been just before the French Revolution; everyone wants to overthrow the royalty." (Bishop and Levine [1998] detail this case.)

Theories of procedural justice reinforce distributive concerns over relative outcomes (Bies, Tripp, and Neale 1993). People are more likely to consider a decision fair, even if it harms them, if the decision maker did not profit from it. Conversely, if a decision maker profits from a decision that harms employees, the employees have reason to doubt the objective basis of the decision (Leventhal 1976).

At the same time, some analysts have emphasized the potential benefits to shareholders that can follow from rewarding CEOs for cutting costs (Dial and Murphy 1995). This result depends heavily on whether the remaining employees perceive the CEO pay as fair or not and on employees' reaction to any perceived unfairness.

In fact, the reaction of layoff survivors appears to depend in part on the perceived fairness of the layoffs. Brockner (1992) claimed that employees perceive layoffs as more fair when cutbacks were shared at higher managerial levels. These findings lead to

Hypothesis 3a: Perceived fairness will increase when the CEO turned down his bonus that year because of the unexpected need for layoffs.

Hypothesis 3b: Perceived fairness will decrease when layoffs are accompanied by the CEO receiving a record bonus for his success in introducing the new technology or cutting costs.

Skill Specificity and Occupation

Employees' costs of layoffs are higher when the affected employees have employer-specific skills than when they have skills that are widely useful (Becker 1975). Thus, people are more likely to consider the former situation less fair. (Rousseau and Anton [1988, 1991] provide further theoretical justification for this hypothesis.)

Hypothesis 4a: Layoffs are perceived as more fair when the affected workers or engineers specialize in widely used hardware, so that their skills would be useful in another job, as compared with when they are specialists in the company's unusual technology.

Although recent data suggest that layoff rates are converging, production employees are still more likely to be laid off than are professional employees (Farber 1995). Substantial evidence indicates many people find that what is common becomes perceived as fair. Moreover, professionals typically have a higher trust relationship with the employer, providing higher commitment and working with lower monitoring. In exchange, so goes the reasoning of the traditional employment contract, the employer is supposed to provide stable employment to this type of employee. To the extent that what is common becomes perceived as fair or that professionals are working under an implicit employment contract with higher security, we have the following hypothesis

> Hypothesis 4b: Layoffs are perceived as more fair when they affect production workers rather than engineers.

Canada vs. Silicon Valley

As noted in Chapter 2, Canada has been associated with lower (and Silicon Valley with higher) acceptance of market forces than most of North America. Thus, paralleling hypothesis Inst 8a that Canadians are less accepting of pay cuts, we have

> Inst 8b: Layoffs are perceived as more fair in Silicon Valley than in Canada (specifically, Vancouver and Toronto).

These historical and cultural differences may have been heightened by recent differences in unemployment rates. In November 1997, the unemployment rate in Silicon Valley (specifically, the San Jose, California, metropolitan area) was only 2.6 percent, below the already-low U.S. average of 4.1 percent. In Canada, in contrast, average unemployment rates were substantially higher than in the United States, running about 8.9 percent; the rates in Vancouver and Toronto were slightly lower than the national rates. To the extent people find layoffs less fair when the cost of job loss is high, the U.S.-Canadian differences in notions of fairness should be increased by the much-higher Canadian unemployment rates. (Alternatively, if being in a region with many layoffs increases the perceived fairness of layoffs, then the high unemployment rates in Canada may have inured respondents to layoffs and increased how often layoffs are viewed as fair.)

In Silicon Valley, layoffs of professionals such as engineers are relatively common events.[4] Moreover, for most of the last several decades, unemployment rates for engineers in Silicon Valley have been quite low, often less than 1 percent. If a low cost of job loss leads respondents to perceive layoffs as more fair, we have the following hypothesis

Inst 8c: Compared with layoffs for production employees, layoffs of engineers are perceived as more fair in Silicon Valley than in Canada.

RESULTS

What Shocks Justify Layoffs?

The results in Tables 7.4 to 7.7 provide mixed support for hypothesis 1 that reciprocity and ability to pay mattered in determining the fairness of layoffs. As expected, Table 7.4 shows that layoffs were viewed as more fair when due to declining product demand (1.71 in Canada, 1.58 in the United States) than when due to employees' suggestions (1.37 in Canada, 1.39 in the United States). This supports the hypotheses that layoffs are not considered fair when the employers' ability to pay is high and/or when the layoffs violate norms of reciprocity.

More surprisingly, layoffs due to technological change were at least as acceptable (1.57 in Canada, 1.71 in the United States) as layoffs due to a negative product demand shock; the difference between source of shocks was not statistically significant. Thus, it appears that the violation of a reciprocity norm (not punishing employees who have given a gift of new ideas), rather than rent-sharing, is responsible for the lower perceived fairness of layoffs.

When Are Gentle Layoffs Fair?

Hypothesis 2a posited that the gentle layoffs scenario (with advance notice, attempts to find alternative placement, and so forth) would be perceived as more fair than harsh layoffs (two weeks warning, unexpected). Consistent with this hypothesis, gentle layoffs were on average rated midway between completely fair and acceptable in Canada (2.35) and acceptable in the United States (2.03; Table 7.5). Harsh layoffs were consistently rated as unfair (in both nations near 1 on the zero-to-three scale).

Table 7.4 How Does the Source of the Shock Affect the Fairness of Layoffs?

Shock characteristic	Canada	Silicon Valley	Silicon Valley – Canada	Scenarios[a]	No. obs. Can./S.V.
Source of shock					
Declining product demand	1.71	1.58	–0.13	F, M	270/253
New technology	1.57	1.71	0.14	D, E	240/256
Employees' suggestion	1.37	1.39	0.02	L, I	224/278
Project has ended	1.75	1.56	–0.18**	J, S	216/272
Differences among shocks					
Technology – product demand	–0.14	0.13	0.27**		
Product demand – suggestions	0.34***	0.19	–0.15		
Technology – suggestions	0.20**	0.32***	0.12		
Combined other shocks – suggestions	0.31***	0.22**	0.09		

NOTE: Mean perceived fairness: 3 = completely fair, 0 = very unfair. *** and ** represent statistically significant differences at the 1 and 5% levels on a Wilcoxon-Mann-Whitney rank-sum test (two-tailed) for one-way comparisons and on a two-tailed t-test for differences in differences. Results may not sum due to rounding.

[a] Appendix H contains full text of the questions referenced in the "Scenarios" column.

Importantly, the literature on new employment contract suggests that layoffs, even following employees' suggestions, are seen as more consonant with norms of reciprocity when employers try to cushion the blow. Thus, hypothesis 2b posited that the type of shock makes little difference in how fairly respondents rate gentle layoffs. The hypothesized interaction was that gentleness of layoffs would be more important for layoffs created by employee suggestions than for layoffs motivated by downturns in demand.

For both Canada and Silicon Valley, the gaps in perceived fairness between harsh and gentle layoffs is slightly smaller for layoffs following suggestions (1.36 and 0.86 points, not shown) than the gap for lay-

Table 7.5 How Do Employer Reactions Affect the Fairness of Layoffs?

Employer reaction	Canada	Silicon Valley	Silicon Valley– Canada	Scenarios[a]	No. obs. Can./S.V.
Focal scenario: demand shock, professionals, and special skills					
Hoard labor	2.67	2.01	–0.66***	P	24/138
Gentle layoffs	2.55	2.12	–0.43***	E	131/133
Harsh layoffs	0.92	0.98	0.05	M	139/120
Hoard – gentle difference	0.12	-0.11	–0.23**		
Gentle – harsh difference	1.63***	1.15***	–0.48***		
Pooling sources of shocks and characteristics of employees for matched scenarios					
Gentle	2.35	2.03	-0.31***	E, I, J, M	468/544
Harsh	0.88	1.05	0.17***	D, F, L, S	482/515
Gentle – harsh difference	1.46***	1.00***	–0.48***		

NOTE: Mean perceived fairness: 3 = completely fair, 0 = very unfair. *** and ** represent statistically significant differences at the 1 and 5% levels on a Wilcoxon-Mann-Whitney rank-sum test (two-tailed) for one-way comparisons and on a two-tailed t-test for differences in differences. Results may not sum due to rounding.
[a]Appendix H contains full text of the questions referenced in the "Scenarios" column.

offs following demand shifts (1.63 and 1.15 points, Table 7.5). These results do not support the hypothesis that gentleness matters more when suggestions lead to layoffs.

Hypothesis 2c posited that hoarding labor, even if it means retraining and relocation, would always be viewed as fair. In fact, hoarding was rated between acceptable and completely fair, not substantively different from the rating on gentle layoffs.

Do CEO Bonuses Matter?

Theories of upward equity comparisons and theories of procedural justice lead to the prediction that layoffs are perceived as more fair when the CEO shares in the pain of downsizing than when the CEO receives a bonus for successful downsizing. Supporting hypothesis 3a, respondents felt layoffs were substantially more fair when the CEO refused a bonus than when CEO pay was not mentioned (1.48 vs. 1.00, $p < 0.01$; Table 7.6). We also find some support for hypothesis 3b: paying the CEO a bonus reduced perceptions of fairness relative to not mentioning a bonus, although the difference in means was only 0.10 on the four-point scale (0.90 vs. 1.00, $p < 0.05$).

Does Skill Specificity and Occupation Matter?

As expected, layoffs of employees with generally useful skills (hypothesis 4a) were perceived as slightly more fair than layoffs when the employees are specialists in the company's unusual technology, with an average of 10 years tenure with the employer (gap of 0.18 in the United States, $p < 0.05$; Table 7.7).

The results for occupation (hypothesis 4b) were mixed. As hypothesized, laying off production workers was perceived as slightly more fair than laying off professionals in Canada (0.95 vs. 1.12, $p < 0.05$). The gap was smaller and not significant in the United States (1.11 vs. 1.18).

Do Canada and Silicon Valley Differ?

Averaging over all matched scenarios, respondents in Silicon Valley rated layoffs as fair as did respondents in Canada (a difference of 0.004 points). This provides no support for hypothesis 5a, that Silicon Valley respondents would be more accepting of layoffs than Canadians.

While the mean fairness rating did not differ between the nations, the gap between the perceived fairness of harsh and gentle layoffs was substantially larger in Canada, 1.63 points vs. 1.15 (see Table 7.5). Silicon Valley respondents thought hoarding labor and gentle layoffs were less fair than Canadians by about 0.5 point on a 3-point scale ($p < 0.01$). Given the number of comparisons we tested, sampling variation

Table 7.6 How Does CEO Compensation Affect the Fairness of Layoffs?

Compensation	Canada	Silicon Valley	Silicon Valley – Canada	Scenarios[a]	No. obs. Can./S.V.
CEO bonus record high[b]		0.90		H, Q	0.272
CEO bonus not mentioned	0.92	1.00	0.08	D, F	238/262
CEO bonus refused[b]		1.48		C, N	247
Differences					
Bonus high, not mentioned		–0.10**			
Bonus refused, not mentioned		0.48***			

NOTE: Mean perceived fairness: 3 = completely fair, 0 = very unfair. *** and ** represent statistically significant differences at the 1 and 5% levels on a Wilcoxon-Mann-Whitney rank-sum test (two-tailed) for one-way comparisons and on a two-tailed t-test for differences in differences. Results may not sum due to rounding.
[a] Appendix H contains full text of the questions referenced in the "Scenarios" column.
[b] Question was asked only in the United States.

Table 7.7 Do Employee Characteristics Affect the Fairness of Layoffs?

Compensation	Canada	Silicon Valley	Silicon Valley – Canada	Scenarios[a]	No. obs. Can./S.V.
Type of skills					
Employer-specific		1.15		F, G, K, S	0/517
Generally useful		1.33		A, B, O, R	0/540
Specific–general skills		0.18***			
Type of employee					
Professional	0.95	1.11	0.16	F, S	246/257
Production	1.12	1.18	0.06	G, K	228/260
Professional – production	–0.17**	–0.07	0.10		

NOTE: Mean perceived fairness: 3 = completely fair, 0 = very unfair. *** and ** represent statistically significant differences at the 1 and 5% levels on a Wilcoxon-Mann-Whitney rank-sum test (two-tailed) for one-way comparisons and on a two-tailed t-test for differences in differences. Results may not sum due to rounding.
[a] Appendix H contains full text of the questions referenced in the "Scenarios" column.

suggests that not much should be made of these differences on specific questions. Overall, Canadians were a bit more likely to respond with the extreme answers of "completely fair" or "very unfair" (43.2 percent to 39.6 percent; both the test of equality of proportions and the χ^2 test give $p = 0.06$, two-tailed). Other differences between the two nations were both small and not statistically significant.

Hypothesis 5b posited an interaction wherein layoffs of professionals would be relatively more acceptable in Silicon Valley than in Canada. The divergences are in the hypothesized direction, but the results were small and not statistically significant.

CONCLUSION

In summary, the results support previous findings about the perceived fairness of pay cuts rising when the employer had an excuse for the pay cut. At the same time, there is little evidence that Anglophone Canadians were more accepting of pay cuts in 1997 than in 1985; nor was there evidence that residents of Silicon Valley were more accepting of pay cuts than were Canadian respondents. Thus, unless U.S. respondents were more accepting in the 1980s, it appears that there has not been a trend to increasing acceptance of pay cuts.

The results concerning the perceived fairness of layoffs also supported most of the hypotheses. Layoffs were perceived as more fair if the company was in financial distress, if it gave advance notice and severance pay to employees, if the CEO shared the pain, and if the employee had general skills. At the same time, consistent with the results on pay cuts, Anglophone Canadians were not more accepting of layoffs than were residents of Silicon Valley.

Notes

1. Parts of this chapter are drawn from Charness and Levine (2000, forthcoming).
2. Gorman and Kehr (1992) mailed Kahneman, Knetsch, and Thaler questions to U.S. executives, but used a within-subject design. Frey and Pommerehne (1993) asked the Kahneman, Knetsch, and Thaler questions relating to fairness in pricing decisions in Switzerland, obtaining results similar to those of the original study. Neither study was able to examine changes over time.

3. Follow-up interviews led us to believe that respondents did not interpret this condition as we had intended. That is, the scenario we had in mind was of a company with employees who moved from project to project. In the "old" employment contract, the employer found new positions for employees as each project ended (e.g., a new version of a project shipped). In the "new" contract, employees must seek new employment within the enterprise or outside of it as each project ends. Apparently, some respondents had in mind a different scenario where the employee was hired for a single project, the employer had no ongoing or start-up projects, and then the single project ended. This ambiguity led us to drop a separate analysis of this condition, although we did retain these respondents for other conditions.

4. To get a feel for the frequency of publicly visible announcements, we searched the Computer Database produced by Information Access Company for articles concerning layoffs at computer companies. In the relatively prosperous year of May 4, 1997, to May 4, 1998 (chosen to be the most recent at the time of the search), 46 articles appeared with the word "layoff" in the title. The list included former bastions of the "old" contract such as IBM and DEC, innovators in creating the new contract such as Apple, and new software companies that have always grown up with an atmosphere of exciting prospects coupled with low job security such as Netscape, Sybase, and Informix. The results of this quick search are merely suggestive. On the one hand, many of the layoffs were not specifically in Silicon Valley. On the other hand, many smaller employers that closed down or laid off employees would not have merited articles in this database.

8
Conclusions

In this chapter, we summarize our results by topic and then discuss how these results compare with the predictions of the various theories. We discuss a number of interpretations for our findings in terms of general human capital and other deductive theories. We conclude with a discussion of implications for managers, policymakers, and researchers.

PREDICTIONS AND STUDY RESULTS

In the classic old employment contract, wages were not strongly responsive to the labor market. Instead, each company had a distinctive company wage level and pattern. In most settings, the presence of an internal labor market depended on the organization reaching sufficient size. Thus, the theory of internal labor markets also predicted that large employers would have distinct levels and structures of wages from nearby small employers. These descriptive models yield the following predictions:

1) Large employers pay higher wages (assuming size correlates with more difficulty monitoring and higher ability to pay);

2) Large and small employers reward employee characteristics such as age and education differently;

3) Wage levels of large and small employers within a region are only weakly related;

4) Wage levels among large employers within a region have large and persistent deviations from one another;

5) Internal wage structures within large employers have large and persistent deviations from the market;

6) Large employers have higher-skill employees and those from demographic groups managers prefer; and

7) Employees hold strong norms against pay cuts in most cases.

As others have also found, all of these predictions are supported in our analyses of Chapters 4–7.

Did Large Firms Pay Higher Wages?

Large employers (more than 1000 employees) paid wages 21 percent higher than small employers (fewer than 100 employees); from CPS 1979 data; see Chapter 4.

Did Large Firms Pay Distinct Returns for Characteristics?

The pattern of returns for employee characteristics at large and small employers often differed; for example, large employers paid substantially higher returns for education (CPS).

Did Large Firms Largely Ignore Local Labor Markets?

Large employers did not appear to set wages with great attention to the local labor market. Controlling for many observable characteristics, metropolitan areas or states whose small employers paid wages 20 percent above (or below) the small-firm national average had large employers that paid wages only about 10 percent above (or below) the large-firm national average (CPS). More dramatically, the average wage rates in the surrounding metropolitan area were not useful in predicting the wage levels of first-line supervisors and professionals working at the large companies that participated in the Hay survey.

Did Large Firms Pay Distinctive Average Wages?

As noted above, controlling for detailed occupation (CSS) or the Hay measure of skills and responsibility (Hay) wage levels among large employers still resulted in large and persistent deviations. The standard deviation of employer wage effects was over 11 percent in both data sets. In addition, the persistence (autocorrelation) of employer wage effects was high in the early period (1950s to 1970s in the CSS).

Did Large Firms Maintain Distinctive Internal Wage Structures?

In addition to distinctive wage levels, large employers also paid distinctive wage structures; that is, the wage relativities between occupations at one employer differed from those paid in the market (Hay, CSS). Moreover, although less persistent than the wage levels, these distinctive internal differentials also persisted many years.

Was Sorting of Skills and Demographics Prevalent?

Theories of general human capital stress that high-wage employers will hire employees high on both observable and unobservable skills. Theories of internal labor markets disagree that wages clear the market, as high-wage primary-sector employers with strong internal labor markets pay above-market wages. Nevertheless, the institutionalist theory predicts the employers with internal labor markets will have their pick of employees, so they will hire stable, well-educated employees, particularly from preferred demographic groups (adult white males for primary-sector jobs, females for clerical jobs, etc.).

Consistent with both sets of theories, large employers (in the CPS) hired workers with above-average levels of observable skills. Inconsistent with the institutionalist theory predictions of internal labor markets in the classic period (but as others have found, e.g., Holzer 1998), large employers hired a disproportionate share of black employees at least as far back as 1979. Moreover, high-wage employers in the CSS, Hay, and Indiana/Japan data sets hired workers disproportionately from higher-wage occupations (CSS) and workers with slightly higher observable skills (as measured by Hay points in the Hay data set or by survey responses in the Indiana/Japan data sets).

Were Nominal Pay Cuts Viewed as Unfair?

North Americans' views of fair wage determination were largely consistent with the observed wage rigidities. When Kahneman, Knetsch, and Thaler (1986) asked Canadians in 1984/1985 whether pay cuts were fair in the presence of unemployment, the vast majority replied the cuts were unfair.

HAVE INSTITUTIONS AND WAGE STRUCTURES WEAKENED?

The standard reading of recent business history suggests that the wage structures associated with internal labor markets (as described by Doeringer and Piore 1971) weakened between 1980 and 1996 (e.g., Cappelli 1995; Kanter 1987; Manicatide and Pennell 1992; and Stiles et al. 1997). Such a view has a number of implications for the wage differentials discussed above.

Have Wage Levels at Large and Small Firms Converged?

If internal labor markets have declined, we should see wage levels at large and small employers becoming more similar (Inst 2). The data support this hypothesis. Mean wages in 1979 at employers with over 1,000 employees were 36 percent higher than at employers with fewer than 100 employees. This ratio declined to 26 percent in 1993. Controlling for standard demographic, human capital, and occupational controls reduced the 1979 gap to 18 percent, and the 1993 gap to 14 percent (Figure 8.1).

Have Returns at Large and Small Firms Converged?

In addition to differences in mean wages, theories of labor market dualism emphasize that primary-sector (typically large) employers paid higher wages for education and tenure. If internal labor markets have declined, then the returns to education and tenure in large and small employers have converged (Inst 3a). More generally, we should see returns at small and large firms converging (Inst 3b).

In contrast to Hypothesis Inst 3a, the CPS results show no convergence in returns to education between large and small employers. More generally, the results do not support hypothesis Inst 3b that returns at large and small employers are converging. Intuitively, in Figure 8.1, the size-wage gap is about three-tenths smaller whether one

Figure 8.1 The Size-Wage Gap

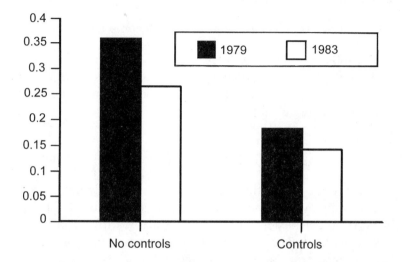

does or does not control for observable employee characteristics; this result implies sorting is not changing that much.

Are Local Labor Markets Increasingly Important for Large Employers?

In a classic multisite internal labor market, wages are set largely with reference to internal wage norms, not to the external market. Thus, local wages usually have a muted effect on internal wage relativities. If internal labor markets have declined, we should see the correlation between average wages in a local labor market (state or large metropolitan area) and large-company wages rising from 1979 to 1993 (Inst 4). In fact, in neither the CPS (1979 to 1993) nor the Hay data set (1986 to 1992) has the correlation between average wages in a local labor market and large-company wages risen by a statistically significant amount.

Even if the average returns to employer size remained steady, the patterns of returns (for example, the coefficients on education) at large and at nearby small employers might have converged (Inst 5). In fact, the region-specific coefficients estimated on employees from large

firms have not become systematically closer to the coefficients estimated on employees from small firms.

Did the Distinctive Average Wage Levels Become Less Important?

The 1960s saw increased dispersion and persistence of employer
wage levels. The standard deviation of employer wage effects
remained near 11 percent in both the CSS and Hay data sets. In addition, the persistence (autocorrelation) of employer wage effects
remained similar in the 1990s to those in the early 1980s (CSS).

Did Large Firms Maintain Distinctive Internal Wage Structures?

As with wage levels, the 1960s saw increased dispersion and persistence of employer internal wage structure differentials. During the
early 1970s, the persistence of internal structure differentials peaked;
then, they gradually became more flexible. At the same time, the variability and persistence of distinctive internal wage structures remained
constant from the early 1980s to the 1990s (CSS).

In sum, capitalizing on the perspective provided by our long time
period, the changes we detect in employer structures since 1980 are
minor. This historical perspective is missing from many analyses of
recent labor market changes, because many important data sets (such
as those based on the Displaced Worker Survey) have been around for
only about half as long as the CSS.

Did Sorting of Skills Decline?

The evidence on changes in sorting over time is mixed. In the Hay
data set, sorting of the very good measure of observable skills was similar in 1986 and 1992. In the Current Population Survey, the mean
characteristics of employees at large and small employers either
remained constant or converged substantially between 1979 and 1993,
with the exception of race. In the Cleveland survey, the correlation
between an employer's average wage (conditional on its occupation
mix) and the mean wage of the occupations it hired rose by an economically meaningful amount.

Do Attitudes Increasingly Accept the Market?

In the popular version of the "new employment contract," employers both can and must adjust wages or employment to match the market, and the old rigidities are no longer expected or demanded by employees. In fact, we did not find that market forces have become more legitimate justifications for wage reductions. To study this hypothesis, we used the Kahneman, Knetsch, and Thaler (1986) questions on pay cuts and fairness. Their initial survey was May 1984 to July 1985 in Vancouver and Toronto. We replicated the survey in those two Canadian cities from March to September 1997. Because the Canadian experience might be different from that in the United States, we also replicated it in Silicon Valley in October 1997 to March 1998.

As Kahneman, Knetsch, and Thaler found, respondents were more likely to report a pay cut as fair if the company was losing (not making) money; if there was a real pay cut accomplished by a nominal wage increase less than inflation (not a nominal pay cut in times of low inflation); if it was for a new (not the same) employee; if it was for a company changing lines of business (not remaining in the same business); and if it was a cut to a recurring bonus (not to base pay). The bottom line result is that, on average, respondents' views of whether pay cuts were fair (averaging over all questions) were almost identical in Canada in 1997 to what they had been in 1984/1985 (rejecting Inst 7). It was also identical in Silicon Valley in 1997/1998. These results provide no evidence of a shift in norms that are more accepting of pay flexibility.

The new employment contract, the popular press recounts, emphasizes that employees "own" their own careers and ensure their own employability by constantly increasing their skills. As such, we expected layoffs to be widely considered fair. The old employment contract, in contrast, emphasized retaining employees unless business conditions required a layoff. In both Silicon Valley and in Canada, attitudes toward layoffs in 1996/1997 were largely consistent with those of the traditional employment contract. Although none of the following effects were large, layoffs were perceived as more fair, as we expected, if

- they were due to lower product demand, not caused by employee suggestions;
- they were with advance notice, job-hunting assistance, and sever-ance pay, not unexpected and with no notice;
- the CEO shared the pain, not if the CEO received a record bonus for success in cutting costs;
- they involved production employees or employees with general skills, not professionals or employees with firm-specific skills.

Contrary to expectations, layoffs and pay cuts were not more accepted in Silicon Valley. Given that we selected Silicon Valley spe-cifically with the intent of finding regional differences, these results suggest that the U.S.-Canadian gap in attitudes towards the market may not be that large. Lipset (1990) surveyed the larger literature on U.S.-Canadian gaps in attitudes; he found many cases of differences and many cases of similarity; our results fall in the latter category, at least for English-speaking Canada.

Summary of Evidence Concerning Institutional Decline

To identify an "internal" labor market, one must identify a rigidity that keeps wages distinct from those in the external labor market. The strategy in this study has been to identify a number of rigidities (size-wage effect, between-firm inequality, employee attitudes concerning pay cuts, etc.) and look for a decline in each.

To some extent the patterns differ as we look across the many dif-ferent dimensions of pay rigidity. Nevertheless, the basic result of this volume is clear: there is no pattern of declining importance of pay rigidities, or of institutional forces more generally, in determining com-pensation. The fairly consistent attitudes opposing most pay cuts may have constrained the spread of any new contract and may also indicate that the new contract is not widely accepted as fair.

STUDY RESULTS IN TERMS OF THEORY

General Human Capital Theory

The theory of general human capital has been widely used to explain the recent rise in inequality: changes in technology and in global trade have increased the demand for skill. With a constant degree of sorting by skill, general human capital theory suggests that inequality among employers and the variability of wage structures within an employer should have increased proportionately with inequality among occupations. For example, Davis and Haltiwanger (1991) interpreted widening inequality among manufacturing plants, particularly between large and small plants, as evidence of rising returns to unobserved skills. Juhn, Murphy, and Pierce (1993) made the same argument concerning the rising earnings gap between whites and blacks.

By a number of measures of skills, returns to skills rose in U.S. labor markets from the mid 1970s to the mid 1990s. Consistent with the results in other data sets, returns to skills rose in the three data sets studied here. Specifically, we see rising returns to Hay points and to education in the CPS. In the CSS, inequality among occupations increased. We attached to each CSS occupation an estimate (from the Department of Labor's *Dictionary of Occupational Titles*) of the typical educational requirements for that occupation and of the typical specific vocational training for that occupation. The returns to the typical educational level of an occupation rose at the same pace as did returns to education in the CPS. In contrast, returns to typical specific vocational training remained constant.

If companies pay different wages due to differences in skill, variation in pay for apparently identical employees (that is, the standard deviation of the coefficients on the firm effects) should be substantially smaller when controlling for skills than when not controlling for skills (HumCap 1). In fact, the standard deviation of the firm effects was almost unaffected when controlling for skills in all of the Hay, Indiana, and Japan data sets. This result is particularly surprising, because the Hay data sets measure of skills correlated 0.80 with wages in the early period.

If inequality between firms largely proxies for unobserved skills and returns on those skills have risen, we have hypothesis HumCap 2: wage inequality between firms should increase at the same pace as returns to skills increase. Consistent with this hypothesis, inequality among employers rose in the Hay data set; inconsistent with this hypothesis, inequality among employers was stable in the CSS data set even as inequality rose within firms. Similar logic leads to HumCap 3: the returns to size have risen. As noted above, returns to size declined in the CPS, providing no support for this hypothesis.

Moreover, the increase in the standard deviation of the coefficients on the firm effects was essentially unaffected whether controlling for skill or not controlling for skill. This result contradicts HumCap 4. Extending this argument, Kremer and Maskin (1995) showed that if a model of human capital is sufficiently rich to generate sorting of skills among employers, then rising returns to skill will increase the sorting of employees by skill among employers; that is, high-wage employers will increase their concentration of high-skill occupations. This increased sorting suggests that the variability of employer wage effects will rise more rapidly than the variability of occupation wage effects. Our results are inconsistent with the prediction that employer and internal structure differentials rose in tandem with occupational differentials during the 1980s and 1990s (contradicting HumCap 4).

The observed variation in the pace and size of changes casts doubt on the simple hypothesis that all increased wage variation is due to enhanced returns to human capital. Thus, if these differentials represent returns to unmeasured ability, those returns did not keep pace with returns to measured ability during the 1980s and 1990s. Alternatively, these differentials may reflect other factors in addition to unmeasured human capital.

There is, however, some support for the hypothesis that sorting by ability has increased. In the CSS, the correlation between the average wage of the occupations employed at a firm and the firm's average pay rose meaningfully, but from a very low base. This increase supports certain theories of human capital (e.g., Kremer and Maskin 1995).

Theory of Compensating Differences

The theory of compensating differences posits that observed wage gaps are due to differences in working conditions (undesirable vs. desirable). Thus, controlling for relevant working conditions should remove most of the unexplained wage variation between employers (CompDiff 1). In fact, the failure of the measures of working conditions in the Hay and the Indiana/Japan data sets to reduce observed wage gaps between employers by meaningful amounts casts doubt on compensating difference explanations for the wage gaps.

The theory of compensating differences also posits that observed wage gaps should offset differences in benefits. Thus, total pay (that is, base pay plus bonus) should be more equal among firms than is base pay (CompDiff 2). As with the first hypothesis, there is no support for this one either. As is usually true, unobserved differences in skill or in the difficulty of monitoring can account for the failure of compensating differences to appear in the data if people with high skills, efficiency wages, or bargaining power receive both high wages and high average bonuses.

Rent-Sharing and Bargaining Theories

Rent-sharing, insider-outsider, and bargaining theories of wage structures assume that some employers have high rents and purchase their workers' cooperation with high wages. Such employers have incentives to maintain rigid wage structures to reduce employee bargaining and influencing activities with their supervisors (Milgrom and Roberts 1990; Williamson 1975). In addition, high-wage employers should find it easier to maintain a rigid internal wage structure (Reynolds 1951) that can insure employees against downturns (Bertrand 1999) and provide incentives based on long-term contracts (Valletta 2000).

Most studies find that increased ability to pay (as measured by past high profits per employee, product-market innovations, or declining costs of inputs) predict higher wages (e.g., Blanchflower, Oswald, and Sanfrey 1996; Carruth and Oswald 1989). Consistent with Groshen (1990), there was no consistent relationship between lagged profits and current wages in either the Hay or Cleveland data sets. These results may be due to our small sample of firms and to problems measuring ability to pay.

Substantial evidence also suggests that increased product-market competition from increased international trade, deregulation, and other forces have eroded many employers' long-standing product-market rents, which should reduce between-firm wage inequality due to rents. If product-market rents have declined, then companies are less able to make and keep commitments to employees. Thus, we should see smaller and less persistent employer and internal structure differentials (Bargaining 1). In fact, the variability and persistence of both types of differential have been stable in the CSS, giving no support for this hypothesis. (While many writers have claimed that competition has increased due to globalization and deregulation, the evidence for this proposition is weak. The very high stock market valuations of the late 1990s were consistent with profit rates that were higher than in previous decades.)

Moreover, we expect to see these declines in structure variability and rigidity, particularly in industries subject to deregulation or that have rising foreign competition. We tested whether employer wage structures measured in the CSS declined most rapidly in industries that underwent deregulation or faced rising import penetration. The regressions have small sample sizes and several problems of measurement.

With these cautions in mind, the results are easy to summarize: industries undergoing deregulation or experiencing above-average increases in import penetration did not experience notable declines in the variation or persistence of deviations from the market wage level and structure. Companies with falling profits did not have below-average wage growth. Thus, our results do not indicate that the shocks to ability to pay that we measured either increased wage flexibility or lowered employee rents.

Most innovative workplace practices (such as employee involvement and total quality management) are most common at large employers. Some analysts suggest that, on average, these innovations reduce employees' bargaining power. If so, the size-wage effect should have decreased (hypothesis Bargaining 3). In contrast, Lindbeck and Snower (1996) posited that pervasive organizational changes have increased employees' bargaining power. Thus, their theory suggests the size-wage effect should have increased (Bargaining 3'). As discussed above, the size-wage effect has decreased, providing indirect support for the hypothesis that the innovations found in large firms reduce employees' bargaining power (or that computers and organizational change have disseminated to smaller firms and increased employees' skills or bargaining power there).

Finally, if larger firms were forced to pay high wages due to employee bargaining power, then the employers would hire employees with high levels of both observed and unobserved skills. In this setting, a reduction in the relative bargaining power of employees at large firms should both reduce the size-wage effect and reduce the sorting of employees by firm size (Bargaining 4). As noted above, in the CPS the size-wage effect has declined and the sorting of employees on most characteristics has also declined, supporting this hypothesis.

Efficiency Wage Theories

Efficiency wage theories posit that some jobs are difficult to monitor, have outputs that are highly responsive to employee effort, or have high turnover costs. In such models, employers sometimes pay high wages to motivate and retain employees. If we measure the job characteristics that indicate monitoring difficulty and the other factors that drive the efficiency wage payments, then the otherwise-mysterious high wages should be less important. In terms of employer wage effects, efficiency wage theories imply that the standard deviation of the estimated employer wage effects should be lower in equations with extensive controls for relevant working conditions than in equations with no such controls (EffWage 1). As noted in discussing the identical predictions of the human capital and compensating differences theories, the standard deviation of the employer wage effects was almost unaffected by extensive measures of job characteristics in both the Hay and Indiana/Japan data sets.

In some fairness versions of efficiency wage theories, large wage differentials lead to a large psychic cost for low-wage employees (Levine 1991b; Akerlof and Yellen 1990). Thus, when wage differentials widen, high-wage employers have an incentive to outsource low-wage occupations such as janitors or security guards. Conversely, low-wage employers have an incentive to outsource high-wage occupations such as accountants and lawyers. Such outsourcing will lead to an increased sorting of high-wage occupations into high-wage employers, as found in the Cleveland Survey. At the same time, our direct test in the Current Population Survey did not find that high-wage industries were disproportionately shedding low-wage business services.

Incentive Theories

Classic internal labor markets provided career incentives based on the possibility of promotion; at the same time, individual-level incentives within a job title were muted. Correspondingly, if internal labor markets have broken down then we might expect stronger incentives within jobs using merit pay or bonuses.

Pay variation among employees with the same job title at a single employer has increased (Incentives 1). In the 1980s and 1990s, the CSS has data on inequality for employees sharing a job title at an employer. The standard deviation of wages within a job cell is low, as found in BLS Industry and Area Wage Surveys (Groshen 1989, 1991b). There is only a slight upward trend in the standard deviation of cash compensation within a cell—from near 8 percent in the early 1980s to near 9 percent by the mid 1990s. The Hay data set on managers and professionals has similar results: the typical (median) standard deviation in total cash compensation within a job cell had a standard deviation of total pay of 7.0 percent in 1986 and 7.5 percent in 1992.

One element of individualized pay has increased in importance: the bonus. Thirty-two percent of employees in the Hay sample received a positive bonus in 1992, up from 19.6 percent in 1986. At the same time, for those job titles with multiple incumbents, wage variation within a job title due to the bonus was a trivial portion of pay, typically less than 1 percent. An increase in the incidence of bonuses also shows up in other samples collected by consulting firms, e.g., Hansen (1998). (These other consultants' samples, like the Hay sample, are not representative. The Hay sample has the advantage that we analyze a panel of employers, not just a repeated cross section.) These bonuses contributed relatively little to pay variance, as relatively little pay was at risk.

The popular literature on changing compensation emphasizes that incentive pay has also increased at the group and company levels. However, we do not observe higher short-lived variance between jobs, as team-level or division-level gain sharing would induce. To the extent compensation is now tied to company-specific performance more than to market pay levels, we have the hypothesis that pay variation among employers has increased (Incentives 2). In contrast, the CSS exhibits no increase in the variance of employer wage effects, as theories of increased company-wide incentives would suggest.

If the company-specific pay is largely paid in bonuses, not base pay, then between-company inequality should be higher with total pay than with base pay (Incentives 3, but not CompDiff 2). In fact, inequality among employers is almost identical for base pay and for base pay + bonus. That is, in the Hay data analyzed in Chapter 6, the standard deviation of employer effects in models with similar controls (either just the baseline controls in model 1, or also with Hay points in model 3) were almost identical whether looking at wages (Table 6.1) or base pay + bonus (Table 6.2).

IMPLICATIONS OF THIS RESEARCH

The rhetoric of the new employment contract suggests that product markets are increasingly turbulent and competitive (but see Levine and O'Shaughnessy 1999). This higher turbulence, in turn, implies that employers can no longer promise security of employment or of pay. Instead, employers have to reduce pay and shed employees whenever higher productivity permits downsizing or lower output demand requires it. Moreover, proponents of the new employment contract emphasize how flexible employees have become, moving from job to job in search of higher wages and more opportunities for learning.

The results contained here do not support this chain of logic. Our survey results do not show that employees' norms toward pay cuts and layoffs are different than in a traditional employment contract. Moreover, companies' pay policies—presumably in part reflecting this stability in norms—do not appear vastly more flexible and market-oriented.

At the same time, the rhetoric of the old employment contract was inflated as well. For all of U.S. history, most people who worked as employees worked for small and medium-sized employers. Even at the height of the old contracts' acceptance by the business press, a vast proportion of U.S. employees lacked job security, company-provided health insurance and pensions, and stable earnings.

Here we discuss the implications of these findings for managers, union leaders, and public policymakers. In each section, we first present the implications of stability of the perceived fair contract and the lack of increase in the rate of employment mobility of American workers. We then present implications of the always-high level of mobility.

Implications for Managers

For managers, the results in this volume suggest that traditional internal labor market policies (such as minimizing layoffs) may still be useful in promoting high levels of skill and effort. Moreover, when layoffs are necessary, it appears that providing a justification from an exogenous source, having top executives share the pain, and providing notice and assistance all can improve perceptions of fairness. These results echo prescriptions found elsewhere in the literature (e.g., Brockner 1992).

Importantly, respondents did not feel that layoffs following higher productivity due to employees' suggestions were as fair as layoffs due to other causes. This result highlights the tension between efforts to reduce costs via employee involvement and via downsizing. Managers should be aware that reassuring employees their suggestions will not lead to downsizing may increase employees' willingness to contribute ideas.

The results also suggest that traditional internal labor market policies such as avoidance of nominal pay cuts are still useful in promoting high levels of effort. Neither the costs nor the benefits of the classic promises of attempting to buffer employees from shocks appear to have diminished.

In fact, many new organizational forms depend on a higher degree of trust in the employment relationship than did older Taylorist models (Levine 1995), and many grant employees additional discretion (Snower 1998). Given that employees appear to retain norms of reciprocity, in such cases employers should consider increasing—not decreasing—the assurances they give employees. In a dynamic world, few of these assurances will involve no-layoff guarantees. At the same time, employees appear to consider it more fair if layoffs do not result from the employees' suggestions, if the employer attempts to find the employee another position, and if the top executives forgo bonuses at times of downsizing.

The United States never had many employers with credible promises of long-term employment. At the same time, even employers without a promise probably often acted to mitigate shocks and to maintain employment of at least professional and managerial employees, while some large unionized employers coupled high layoff rates with recall rights determined by seniority. It is plausible that this commitment declined during the era of downsizing and delayering. At the same time, there is no evidence that employees find this shift to be particularly fair.

Our results also suggest that new organizational forms (particularly those invoking a degree of trust in the employment relationship) will find it efficient to preserve some buffering from shocks in short-run labor demand. While the implicit labor contract may eventually need to change, public acceptance has not yet arrived. The panoply of studies on the costs of violating the employment contract should caution managers against implementing policies that employees perceive as unduly harsh. In short, employers that commit to avoiding layoffs except when external events (e.g., downturns in the product market) lower ability to pay will probably still reap the benefits of higher loyalty and discretionary effort that existed in previous decades.

A further managerial implication of our findings concerns the relative cost of locating in the United States vs. Canada. Canadians' reputation for norms that are less responsive to the market than those held by U.S. residents may have dissuaded some managers from choosing to site new workplaces in Canada. For managers, our results suggest that U.S. respondents in one of the most market-oriented portions of the nation had norms regarding layoffs similar to those of Anglophone Canadians. Thus, these results suggest that concerns about a U.S.-Canadian attitude gap may not be warranted.

Implications for Union Leaders

The business press has long commented that union policies are inconsistent with the demands of the market. The new employment contract, with short-term jobs and high degrees of wage and skill flexibility, is even less consistent with union policies than was the old contract.

On the one hand, unions have never had an easy time organizing or representing temporary workers, independent contractors, employees at small employers, highly skilled employees, and other large sectors of the U.S. workforce. Some of these limitations were due to U.S. labor law, which was designed with large and stable employers in mind. Thus, regardless of changes in the employment contract, unions have always needed to look for models for the large sector of the American workforce ill-suited to industrial unionism.

Craft unionism in construction and movie-making, for example, provides powerful models of high-skill workforces in which the unions create stable institutions that enhance both members' lives and industry productivity. Employees can keep their union-organized benefits such as pensions and health care regardless of their current employer. Importantly, union-organized and certified training programs such as apprenticeships can add value for both employers and employees. Thus, unions already have models that can apply for other sectors with short-term employment such as temporary workers.

At the same time, the death of the old contract has been greatly exaggerated. Just as managers should not assume that all employees endorse the "new employment contract" and its promise (for them) of low-cost layoffs, unions may want to take advantage of those employers who prematurely use the "new" rules of the game before the employees perceive them as fair.

Absolute job security has always been difficult and often highly unprofitable for employers to sustain. At the same time, these results hold promise that unions that can ensure fairness when layoffs are necessary, can perhaps enhance legitimacy of the layoffs and, thus, increase employees' loyalty to the employer enough to reduce the costs of layoffs. These results also suggest the kind of layoffs that union members may resent the most: specifically, those that break norms of reciprocity, especially when executives do not share the pain.

Finally, these results suggest several policies that members value when layoffs occur: advance notice, assistance in new job placement, and severance pay. Many unions have fought for these policies, and the findings support the importance of these policies to employees.

Implications for Public Policy[1]

Many aspects of Americans' lives have been influenced by the normative role the old employment contract has played in legitimizing the design of many important institutions. For example, unlike in other industrialized nations, pensions and health care in the United States are largely provided through employers. Training decisions after college are largely decentralized to the employer, with no visible means of certifying to future employers what was learned on the job.

Affirmative action policies have emphasized increasing employment of underrepresented groups by large employers. This focus makes sense only to the extent that jobs at large employers are above-average jobs in quality, as was typically true in the old model. Local economic development efforts largely focus on attracting large manufacturing plants (most famously, auto assembly plants), usually with a combination of public spending on infrastructure and with tax breaks. These policies are motivated by the sense that auto plants create high-wage and stable manufacturing jobs.

Unemployment compensation is only available after a fairly lengthy period of work and is unavailable for temporary workers and independent contractors. More generally, labor laws often do not apply to workers with short-term or nonstandard relations with their employer. In the extreme case, the law recognizes no employment relation at all for many workers who are formally independent contractors but largely work for one employer.

The new contract has important implications for each of these policies, indicating how poorly suited the policies are for a mobile workforce with complex employment relations. On the one hand, the research presented in this volume suggests that mobility has not shown a marked increase. This result might make some confident that the old policies made sense in the past and continue to make sense today. For example, affirmative action may still want to target large employers, as they continue to provide jobs with above-average wages. On the other hand, North American labor markets have always had high mobility. Thus, public policies based exclusively on the old model never fit the careers and lives of many Americans.

For example, health insurance or pensions should never have been based on an employment model of lifetime employment. Instead, public policies should encourage portability of pensions and health insurance. Government connection to learning should never have stopped after college; instead, the government should oversee a system of industry-designed certifications for general skills. These recommendations make sense due to the high level of mobility in the United States, regardless of any recent increases in that mobility.

At the same time, the results in this volume do not imply that labor market policy should abandon a focus on creating stable jobs. Product market and organizational forces—or simply management ideology—may keep the supply of such jobs below demand, but employees apparently have rather traditional ideas about what is fair treatment. Similarly, the evidence does not suggest that large employers are blithely ignoring employees' desires for stability. On the one hand, many large employers have reduced their commitments to long-term relationships and of pay predictability for some of their managerial and professional employees. On the other hand, most large employers often make efforts to reduce the need for layoffs and, when layoffs occur, follow the procedures that signal respect and regret to the existing employees.

Implications for Researchers

Table 8.1 summarizes the theories of internal labor markets we have discussed and our results. Our results are surprisingly unsupportive of any single theory about changes in wage structures at large U.S. employers.

Consistent with the theory of human capital, measures of skill—ranging from education and tenure (CPS) to occupation (CSS) to Hay points—predict wages. Consistent with the hypothesis of a general increase in the returns to skill, returns to all of these measures of skill rose from the early to the later period.

Our results are inconsistent with mainstream interpretations that use human capital theory as a unifying framework for understanding wage differences among employers or rising inequality (Juhn, Murphy,

Table 8.1 Summary of Hypotheses

Observable	Hypotheses
The standard deviation of the coefficients on the firm effects	Was substantially smaller when controlling for skills and working conditions than when not controlling for skills: HumCap 1, EffWage 1, CompDiff 1
Wage inequality between firms over time	Increased: HumCap 2, Inst 1′, Bargaining 1, Incentives 2 Declined: Inst 1, Bargaining 1 Higher (lower) when looking at base pay + bonus: Incentive 3, (CompDiff 2)
Change in wage inequality between firms over time controlling for job characteristics	Risen: HumCap 2 Much smaller rise with controls: HumCap 4 Risen: Incentives 2
Persistence of employer wage effects	Declined: Inst, 1, Bargaining 1 Increased: Bargaining 1′
Size and persistence of employer wage effects in sectors with declining ability to pay	Declined: Bargaining 2
Compensation levels at large and small employers	Converged: **Inst 2, Bargaining 3** Diverged: HumCap 3, Bargaining 3′
Returns paid for employee characteristics at large and small employers	The returns of education and tenure in large and small employers have converged: Inst 3a Converged overall: **Inst 3b**
Employee characteristics at large and small firms	Converged due to breakdown of ILM: Inst 6b Converged due to lower employee rents at large firms: Bargaining 4 High-wage (low-wage) industries have reduced their relative employment intensity of low-wage (high-wage) business services: Inst 6a. Diverged due to rising skill demands: HumCap 5
Returns to characteristics common at large firms	Risen: HumCap 6
Wage levels at large and nearby small employers	Converged: Inst 4
Returns paid for employee characteristics at large and nearby small employers	Converged: Inst 5

(continued)

Table 8.1 (continued)

Observable	Hypotheses
Attitudes toward pay cuts and layoffs	More accepting in 1990s than 1980s (data only for pay cuts): Inst 7
	More accepting in Silicon Valley than Canada: Inst 8a, b.

NOTE: Hypotheses in **bold** type are largely supported. Unless otherwise noted, "Inst" hypotheses refer to institutionalist predictions when labor market rigidities decline, "HumCap" hypotheses refer to human capital theory predictions when returns to general skill increase (in ways uncorrelated with firm size).

and Pierce 1993; Davis and Haltiwanger 1991). In the early period, controlling for skills did not systematically reduce the estimated wage gap between high- and low-wage employers (Hay, CSS, Indiana/Japan). Moreover, controlling for measures of skills did little more (CSS) or nothing more (Hay) to undo the rising inequality among employers. If economists use human capital theory to explain increases in wage differentials for race and plant size that occur when returns on measured skill rise, they should also confront wage differentials that remain constant or barely rise (as we find) or that decline (e.g., the gender differential; see Blau and Kahn 1997).

The hypothesis of declining rigidities receives mixed support. At the same time, the institutionalist theory of rigidities never fully specified the mechanism (efficiency wages, bounded rationality, organizational inertia, or rent-sharing) that led to the deviations from the competitive market wage.

The failure of the job characteristics measured in the Hay and the Indiana/Japan data sets to predict the employer wage effects presents a serious challenge to all theories of wage determination. Employers pay very different levels of compensation, and so far economic theories yield little insight as to why.

Regardless of the data, numerous combinations of these and other theories can (*ex post*) explain the patterns we observe. A complete test of the changing size-wage gap and the changing variance of wages among employers will require more detailed data that permits us to open up the black box of the employer wage-setting decision.

Our survey results bear on current models where a person's happiness is affected by nonpecuniary considerations such as equity and reciprocity (e.g., Rabin 1993; Bolton and Ockenfels 2000; Fehr and Schmidt 1999; Charness and Rabin 1999). One of the major debates in this area is whether the apparent concern for fairness observed in many experiments is driven more by a desire to equalize payoffs (sharing of rents) or by a desire to reciprocate for kind or harsh actions. Our results—that respondents judged layoffs after suggestions as much less fair than layoffs after the introduction of new technology—suggest that, in these contexts, norms of reciprocity are more important than are norms of rent-sharing. That is, it is likely that the ability to pay and quasi-rents rise after new technology is introduced, but respondents did not find technology improvements illegitimate reasons to lay off redundant employees.

An important question motivating this volume is the relationship between changes in internal labor markets and rising inequality. Although we do not have longitudinal data on individuals, our findings are broadly consistent with the longitudinal data from the National Longitudinal Survey of Youth (NLSY), Panel Study of Income Dynamics (PSID), and CPS. Rising pay inequality is due in large part to increased pay variability when people change jobs (Gottschalk and Moffitt 1994; Cameron and Tracy 1998). Consistent with the past research, we have not uncovered increasing variability within an employer's wage structure over time.

The bottom line result of maintained rigidities poses a puzzle for institutional theories of these rigidities. Most of the rigidities (employer wage effects, size-wage effect, etc.) have historically been linked to large employers with high ability to pay. This high ability to pay, in turn, was linked to product-market rigidities or imperfections such as oligopolies, unions, product-market regulation, and limited international competition. The last quarter of the twentieth century witnessed a decline in all of these product-market rigidities, but without a corresponding decline in rigidities in compensation outcomes examined here. (For a survey of the ways that deregulation and other institutional changes have mattered, see Fortin and Lemieux 1997.) At a theoretical level, these findings suggest that fairness considerations (and other micro-level determinants of bargaining power and the payoff to efficiency wages) may play a relatively larger role in determining wage patterns and rigidities than many researchers previously thought.

At the same time, all of the justifications that Kahneman, Knetsch, and Thaler described had weaker effects in 1997–1998 in both Canada and Silicon Valley than in their earlier study. Kahneman, Knetsch, and Thaler wrote a timeless and placeless paper: a model of human cognitive and emotional processing. They treated fairness as cognitive psychologists have often treated heuristics such as framing (Tversky and Kahneman 1986), that is, as hard-wired in. In fact, fairness is a perception that is shaped by culture (e.g., Roth et al. 1991). Our results show that the specific features that determine respondents' perceptions of fairness depend on both time and place.

LIMITATIONS AND FUTURE RESEARCH

To some extent, this research has shown largely negative results. We see only limited changes in organizational pay practices, and we find only limited support for human capital theory as an explanation for the wage structures and changes that we do observe. Both sets of results call for more research.

The results finding limited changes are suspect because we omit several important forms of compensation and several potentially important sets of organizations. The compensation measures we examine do not include deferred compensation. Thus, they omit some elements of compensation that are probably still small on average, yet are growing in importance. ESOPs and profit sharing cover a large share of employees, although the ratios are not exploding. As noted in Chapter 3, stock options appear to be increasing both in terms of grants for highly paid executives (Rock 1998) and in terms of the proportion of employees who receive any (Gilles 1999). Future studies should examine all forms of compensation, not just the cash compensation that we could examine in these data sets.

As noted above, the large and persistent employer wage effects remain a challenge for all theories of wage determination. Future research should include detailed job analyses on larger sets of organizations. In addition to the sensible forms of job analysis in the Hay and Indiana/Japan data sets, additional forms may be helpful. Only a large data set with information on both employees and employers can permit us to disentangle the various theories. Preferably the data set should be longitudinal and linked to financial performance data. The 1998 Workplace Employee Relations Survey in the United Kingdom is coming close to this standard (Marginson and Wood 2000).

The samples of organizations we studied omitted some sets of organizations. For example, the CSS and Hay data sets do not include small and newly founded organizations. Our tests showed these samples were representative of other large organizations in their industry, but some industries were underrepresented. Even within the sample of large organizations, the structure of the survey implied that organizations or subunits using very different bases for pay such as straight commissions or broadbanding are often not included in the survey population. Future research should use administrative data from tax, unemployment insurance, or social security records to examine the population of employees and organizations (e.g., Hellerstein, Neumark, and Troske 1999).

The attitude surveys have their own limitations. Many people perceive what is common as fair. Should the new employment contract become widespread, it will probably become more acceptable. At the same time, the persistence we find of traditional norms may slow the diffusion of new contracts.

In addition, the 13-year span of the two fairness surveys was not long, even in a rapidly changing economy. It is worth examining changes in the perceived fair contract over greater spans of time.

For social scientists, these results emphasize the need for understanding the foundations of fairness judgments. Consider the many reasons why the wage-bonus distinction might matter more in one region than in another. People in one region might view the bonus as more of an entitlement, where the creation of entitlement is socially constructed. (That is, traditional bonuses may become normative more rapidly in some nations than others.) Alternatively, respondents in one region could put more value on all entitlements, a difference in underlying social values. Thirdly, a cognitive difference might drive the results if respondents in the second region were less influenced by a change in framing. For example, citizens who have experienced inflation probably understand the real vs. nominal distinction better.

Furthermore, salience may differ, as people who have experienced a cut in pay or bonus may reply differently than others. In addition, individual differences ranging from gender to religion to political beliefs can affect perceptions of the fairness of pay cuts and of other elements of the employment contract. For example, top-level managers endorse pay cuts more readily than others (Gorman and Kehr 1992; Rousseau 1995, p. 213).

Future research should look at wider differences in space (e.g., more countries), analyze more of the individual differences underlying responses (e.g., responses of managers vs. low-level employees), and investigate more of the rationales and justifications underlying the responses.

In general, the results do not come down strongly in favor of any of the theories we examine. Proponents of each theory can easily add additional features of employees or employers that were omitted from our many data sets, and claim that better measurement of these factors would have provided more support for their hypothesis. The challenge for all social scientists is to go out and measure those many candidate factors and see if, in fact, they help explain wage patterns within and between organizations.

Note

1.   The arguments in this section are developed more fully in Levine (1998).

Appendix A

An Illustrative Model of Human Capital Theory

This section outlines a simple human capital model of wage determination. Although we do not expect any such simple model to be literally true, it provides a useful benchmark when we move to the data. We have designated several propositions as testable assumptions and several as testable implications from the model. While we recognize that even the testable assumptions are implications of underlying assumptions, they are sufficiently close to each other to treat them as equivalent.

Assume the true model is completely neoclassical, where ln(wages) of an individual i (w_i) are purely a reward for general skills (S_i) with a rate of return B; then $w_i = BS_i$. Assume further that some employers have higher average returns to skills than do other employers. Thus, employers will sort employees, leading employers to differ in their average skill levels. If we regress individual-level wages against a vector of firm-specific dummies, then the estimated coefficients on the dummies will capture the amount of sorting by skill. We refer to the coefficients on the dummies as the *firm wage effects* (or as the *between-firm variation in wages*). Combined with the assumption that wages measure skills, we have the testable assumption that mean wages differ by firm. This assumption holds in the data sets studied here (Indiana/Japan, Hay, CSS).

Because mean wages at a firm are captured by firm-specific intercepts (hereafter, "firm effects"), this assumption implies that in a regression of wages on firm-specific intercepts,

$$(\text{A.1}) \quad w_i = f_1 \times (\text{firm effects}_i) + e_{i1},$$

the coefficients on the vector of firm wage effects (f_1) will differ from each other. The standard deviation of the coefficients on the firm wage effects, s.d.(f_1), indicates how much employers differ in their average skill levels. The standard deviation of the estimated residual e_{i1} measures the extent of skill (and therefore wage) variation within each firm.

Assume we now have an imperfect but fairly accurate measure of skills, $s_i = S_i + u_i$, where u_i is a well-behaved error term uncorrelated with skill or firm. In this case, we can decompose the variance of the skill measure into a component due to the variance of skills and a component due to the error: $V(s) = V(S) + V(u)$. We can now correlate our measure of skills with wages, yielding a testable assumption that the measure of skills is correlated with wages. This assumption also holds in the data sets studied here (Indiana/Japan, Hay, CSS).

We then add our measure of skills to the regression in Equation A.1, yielding:

(A.2) $w_i = b_2 \times (s_i + f_2(\text{firm effects}_i) + e_{i2}$.

Now the standard deviation of the firm wage effects, s.d.(f_2), indicates how much employers differ in their average skill levels for those skills not measured by the imperfect skill measure s_i. That is, the imperfect measures of skills, s_i, picks up some of the sorting of skills that was captured by the firm effects in Equation A.1. This yields:

HumCap1:   The standard deviation of the coefficients on the firm effects, s.d.(f_2), is smaller when controlling for skills in Equation A.2 than in Equation A.1 with no such controls, s.d.(f_1).

To the extent that the measure of skills s_i is highly correlated with wages, the measurement error on skills (u_i) is low. We will now make two further testable assumptions.

Consider the case with data from two time periods, early and late. Assume similar amounts of sorting of both measured (s_i) and unmeasured (u_i) skills between employers both early and late. We can test for similar sorting of measured skills by measuring how the average level of observable skills varies between employers. Specifically, if we regress firm effects against observable skills, $s_i = f_3(\text{firm effects}) + e_i$, we can examine the variance of the firm effects. Under this simple model of human capital, the variance of the firm effects should be similar early and late, as is roughly true in the Hay data set.

Assume further that the returns to skill (B) has increased over time. Together these assumptions imply that the variance of firm wage effects with no controls for skills (as in Equation A.1) has increased proportional to the variance of ln(wages).

HumCap 2:   The standard deviation of the coefficients on the firm effects in Equation A.1 are proportionally larger in the later periods, and the R^2 should remain constant.

With constant measurement error of true skills, u_i, we have the testable assumption that the returns on skill (the estimated coefficient b from the equation

(A.3) $w_i = bs_i + e_{i3}$

rose over time. This assumption holds in the data sets examined here (CSS, Hay). The error term in this regression, e_{i3}, measures the returns on unmeasured skills times the amount of unmeasured skills, u.

Assume further that the measurement error in our imperfect measure of skills is constant; that is, the ratio of true variance $V(S_i)$ to measured variance $V(s_i)$ is constant. (Alternatively, assume that the returns to both the measured and unmeasured components of skill both increase equally.) This yields a further testable implication that the higher estimated returns to skill explain most of the rise in the variance of ln(wages). Specifically, the estimated R^2 of Equation A.3 should not have increased over time. The standard error of the equation should have increased proportionately with the square root of the increase in the estimated returns to skill, b.[1]

Finally, to the extent that differences in mean wages between employers (firm wage effects) are due to differences in mean human capital, controlling for observable skill (s_i) should eliminate most of the increase in the standard deviation of the estimated firm.

HumCap 4: The variance of firm effects in an equation which controls for skill has risen much less over time than the variance of firm effects in an equation with no such controls.

Note

1. To see this result, recall that R^2 of Equation A.3 is $V(Bu) / [(V(Bu) + V(Bs)]$. Thus, the R^2 does not change when the coefficient on skills, B, rises. The variance of the error, $V(e_3)$ also rises linearly with B, that is, $V(e) = BV(u)$. The standard error of the equation is the square root of $V(e_3)$, so it should increase with the square root of b.

Appendix B

The Current Population Survey

We analyze the Pension and Benefits supplements to the May 1979 and April 1993 Current Population Surveys (CPS). A requirement for this analysis is that the data include information on the size of the respondents' employer, as measured by employment of the firm. The benefits supplements are the largest microdata sample of the United States labor force with such information.[1] In addition, the benefits supplements collect data on wages, pensions, health benefits, and service with the current employer, which are useful to this investigation.

We analyze the workforce from ages 16 to 75, excluding the self-employed, those employed in business services, and those reporting wages of under $1.00 per hour or more than $100.00 per hour, and records which contain missing data. The 1979 wage data has been converted into real dollars using the CPI-U-X1.

The most important decision for this analysis is the definition of large and small employers. There is no universally accepted definition; indeed, there is disagreement over whether size should be measured by employment or by capital stock (Belman and Groshen 1998). We have chosen to treat employers with 1,000 or more employees as "large" and those with less than 100 employees as "small." Our upper limit certainly includes most firms which have historically provided internal labor markets, but it may be diluted by firms that are large and do not provide internal labor markets. Nevertheless, as formal employment structures such as internal labor markets are relatively rare in employers with less than 100 employees, this approach should reveal changes in wages and other characteristics of employees in the large firms that do provide internal labor markets. Our approach is then to use cut points of 100 and 1,000, leaving medium-sized employers (100–999) as the omitted group.

Our typical regression specification incorporates controls for age, its square, and education, as well as indicator variables for marital status, union membership, race, gender, residence in a metropolitan area, and major occupation. The education variable reported in the CPS was changed in 1992 from a measure of years of education completed to a measure of degree attainment. (We converted the measure of degree attainment back into a measure of continuous education using computer code kindly provided by Jared Bernstein.) The public sector is excluded from our analysis because their labor markets and career systems operate differently than those in the private sector. Agriculture is omitted due largely to concerns about measurement error. We also omit business service industries because one hypothesis for declining internal labor markets is the outsourcing of business services (e.g., janitorial, security, accounting) to business-service employers.

This study uses both descriptive statistics and regression to analyze changes in internal labor markets between 1979 and 1993. The use of sample weights is needed to obtain representative descriptive statistics from the CPS. In contrast, economists typically do not use sample weights in running regressions. Because the regression equations are used to form both in- and out-of-sample predictions of wages and other factors and because weighted data is used in making these predictions, we have estimated our regressions using the supplement weights in the CPS. This assures that the predictions and decompositions add up correctly. The weighted regressions are unbiased, and the treatment of means are consistent. Moreover, as we include the factors that are presumed to be used in stratifying the CPS and creating the weights (race, age, etc.) in our regressions, the weighted regressions are essentially identical to the unweighted regressions. The standard errors of the regression estimates are obtained using the Huber-White correction for heteroskedasticity.

1. The coding of the employer size variable was altered in 1988 by a change in the top-coding of establishment size from 1,000 to 250. In both years, individuals are first asked the employment at the establishment in which they work, then whether they work for a multi-establishment firm and then, if they do, the employment of the firm. All questions were reported as discrete categories. In 1970, establishment size was top-coded at 1,000 employees, but it was top-coded at 250 in 1993. As a result, there are a small number of individuals who worked in large, single-establishment firms in 1993 who are classified as being in firms of 100–499 employees rather than being properly recorded as working in firms of 500–999 or 1,000 or more.

Table B.1 Coefficients and Gap in Large- and Small-Firm Coefficients, 1979–1993

| Variable | 1979 Coefficients | | | | 1993 Coefficients | | | | Change in the gap 1979–93 | |
| | Large firm | | Small firm | | Large firm | | Small firm | | | |
	Coefficient	t	Coefficient	t	Coefficient	t	Difference	t	Difference	t
Constant	2.3392	73.3	2.1203	62.8	1.9902	60.6	1.9720	50.1	-0.201	-2.9
Education	0.0403	16.6	0.0295	11.3	0.0544	16.6	0.0580	19.0	-0.014	-2.5
Education^2	0.0014	3.0	-0.0002	-0.4	0.0044	6.4	0.0027	4.0	0.000	0.2
Age	0.0053	8.9	0.0056	10.2	0.0065	9.9	0.0074	10.8	-0.001	-0.4
Age^2	-0.0003	-9.9	-0.0004	-15.0	-0.0004	-11.3	-0.0003	-9.5	-0.000	-2.2
Tenure	0.0135	9.5	0.0100	5.7	0.0197	13.6	0.0128	6.5	0.003	1.0
Tenure^2	-0.0003	-4.7	-0.0001	-1.0	-0.0004	-6.3	-0.0002	-2.3	0.000	0.1
Tenure < 1 yr.	-0.0406	-2.4	-0.0399	-2.3	-0.0654	-3.4	-0.0729	-3.5	0.008	0.2
Tenure 1–2 yr.	-0.0043	-0.2	-0.0510	-2.5	-0.0250	-1.0	-0.0377	-1.5	-0.034	-0.8
Married	0.0476	4.2	0.0544	4.2	0.0562	4.8	0.0493	3.5	0.014	0.5
Union	0.0554	4.5	0.2391	11.9	0.1063	7.1	0.2352	7.6	0.055	1.3
Black	-0.0463	-2.7	-0.0825	-3.9	-0.0671	-4.0	-0.0853	-3.3	-0.018	-0.4
Female	-0.2463	-20.3	-0.2618	-18.2	-0.1331	-11.1	-0.2113	-13.7	0.063	2.3
Metropolitan	0.0760	6.5	0.0831	6.6	0.1248	9.0	0.1391	9.3	-0.007	-0.3
Northeast	-0.0673	-4.5	-0.0374	-2.2	-0.0063	-0.4	-0.0690	-3.6	0.093	2.7
North Central	-0.0535	-3.6	-0.0365	-2.1	-0.0668	-4.4	-0.1341	-7.4	0.084	2.6
South	-0.1095	-7.0	-0.0885	-5.2	-0.0795	-5.3	-0.1461	-8.2	0.088	2.7
Manager	0.2712	9.7	0.3271	10.5	0.3255	10.6	0.3334	8.8	0.048	0.8
Professional	0.2243	7.6	0.2055	5.6	0.3039	9.4	0.1845	4.5	0.101	1.4

(continued)

186

Table B.1 (continued)

Variable	1979 Coefficients				1993 Coefficients				Change in the gap 1979–93	
	Large firm		Small firm		Large firm		Small firm			
	Coefficient	t	Coefficient	t	Coefficient	t	Difference	t	Difference	t
Technical	0.1025	2.9	0.3072	4.9	0.2263	6.4	0.2665	5.3	0.164	1.7
Sales	0.1068	3.5	0.2124	6.7	0.1547	5.4	0.2054	5.6	0.055	0.9
Clerical	0.0145	0.6	0.1165	3.9	0.0573	2.0	0.1361	3.7	0.023	0.4
Protective	0.0140	0.2	-0.2549	-1.5	0.1080	1.3	-0.0547	-0.4	-0.106	-0.4
Service occ.	-0.1050	-3.4	-0.0558	-1.9	-0.0627	-2.1	-0.0576	-1.6	0.044	0.7
Craft	0.0961	3.8	0.1942	7.0	0.1564	5.2	0.1436	4.0	0.111	1.9
Operative	0.0240	1.0	0.0557	1.8	-0.0182	-0.6	-0.0579	-1.3	0.071	1.1
Transport. operative	-0.0011	-0.0	0.0854	2.4	0.0259	0.7	0.0178	0.4	0.095	1.3
Mining	0.3971	11.2	0.3481	4.0	0.4779	8.3	0.4049	4.5	0.024	0.2
Construction	0.4906	12.3	0.3273	14.7	0.3459	7.3	0.2917	10.5	-0.109	-1.5
Nondurable mfg.	0.2007	10.6	0.1746	6.9	0.2928	13.7	0.1691	5.3	0.098	2.0
Durable mfg.	0.2685	15.6	0.2161	9.1	0.3376	16.5	0.2907	9.7	-0.005	-0.1
Transport. ind.	0.3813	15.2	0.1250	3.7	0.4127	16.2	0.1733	4.7	-0.017	-0.3
Communications	0.2673	9.6	0.2891	4.0	0.2939	9.1	0.1606	1.8	0.155	1.3
Utilities	0.2590	7.9	0.2368	2.5	0.3977	10.4	0.3843	4.1	-0.009	-0.1
Wholesale	0.2978	10.4	0.2289	9.4	0.3271	10.8	0.2335	8.3	0.025	0.4
FIRE	0.2046	9.6	0.2484	10.4	0.2918	13.7	0.2809	9.6	0.055	1.1
Service ind.	0.0123	0.3	0.0945	3.8	-0.0016	-0.1	0.0763	2.7	0.004	0.1
Prof. serv.	0.1425	6.5	0.1751	9.1	0.1801	8.8	0.2312	10.8	-0.018	-0.4

Table B.2 The Gap in Means of Characteristics, 1979–1993

Variable	1979 Means				1993 Means				Change in the gap 1979–93	
	Large firm		Small firm		Large firm		Small firm			
	Mean	t	Mean	t	Mean	t	Mean	t	Difference	t
Education	12.6875	357.5	11.8937	297.8	13.4165	386.7	12.7129	1207.8	-0.0902	-0.1
Education²	167.0189	1031.8	149.1125	682.9	185.1459	1292.0	167.6523	640.6	-0.4128	-0.4
Age	36.5471	199.2	35.3541	163.2	37.3103	205.3	36.8517	5372.3	-0.7344	-0.7
Age²	1497.2000	592.7	1469.9030	395.7	1530.0820	485.7	1523.5250	15531.1	-20.7400	-4.5
Tenure	8.8727	65.3	4.4947	45.3	8.5505	95.1	4.9192	90.6	-0.7467	-0.7
Tenure²	167.2564	65.4	66.0728	36.2	148.8618	97.1	64.7474	51.5	-17.0693	-5.2
Tenure < 1 yr.	0.1635	30.6	0.3174	47.2	0.1425	23.3	0.2489	156.4	0.0475	0.0
Tenure 1–2 yr.	0.0787	20.2	0.1171	25.2	0.0605	14.6	0.0949	184.0	0.0039	0.0
Married	0.6639	97.4	0.5773	81.0	0.6005	85.9	0.5705	1271.5	-0.0566	-0.1
Union	0.3391	49.6	0.0952	22.5	0.1919	63.3	0.0484	22.5	-0.1004	-0.1
Black	0.0823	20.7	0.0790	20.3	0.1195	33.4	0.0687	90.5	0.0476	0.0
Female	0.3449	50.3	0.4649	64.6	0.4608	65.3	0.4894	1144.5	0.0914	0.1
Metropolitan	0.7720	127.5	0.7116	108.8	0.8040	130.5	0.7443	833.0	-0.0007	-0.0
Northeast	0.2741	42.6	0.2399	38.9	0.1990	35.5	0.1953	3535.9	-0.0305	-0.0
North Central	0.3111	46.6	0.2759	42.8	0.2725	43.9	0.2610	1526.5	-0.0237	-0.0
South	0.2606	41.1	0.3134	46.8	0.3181	48.8	0.3081	2063.0	0.0628	0.1
Manager	0.1203	25.6	0.1026	23.4	0.1256	27.5	0.1186	1135.9	-0.0107	-0.0

(continued)

Table B.2 (continued)

Variable	1979 Means				1993 Means				Change in the gap 1979–93	
	Large firm		Small firm		Large firm		Small firm			
	Mean	t	Mean	t	Mean	t	Mean	t	Difference	t
Professional	0.1109	24.5	0.0693	18.9	0.1162	27.9	0.0959	317.2	−0.0214	−0.0
Technical	0.0297	12.1	0.0096	6.8	0.0481	20.4	0.0287	98.7	−0.0006	−0.0
Sales	0.0601	17.5	0.0896	21.7	0.1502	30.9	0.1369	686.4	0.0428	0.0
Clerical	0.2010	34.7	0.1766	32.1	0.1844	35.7	0.1588	415.6	0.0012	0.0
Protective	0.0050	4.9	0.0010	2.2	0.0043	6.2	0.0024	85.9	−0.0021	−0.0
Service occ.	0.0630	18.0	0.1923	33.8	0.0929	17.1	0.1813	137.1	0.0409	0.0
Craft	0.1609	30.3	0.1604	30.3	0.1035	22.2	0.1244	397.7	−0.0215	−0.0
Operative	0.1745	31.8	0.0978	22.8	0.0882	26.4	0.0595	138.6	−0.0480	−0.0
Transport. operative	0.0324	12.7	0.0467	15.3	0.0409	13.5	0.0486	421.6	0.0066	0.0
Mining	0.0212	10.2	0.0039	4.4	0.0085	8.5	0.0051	97.5	−0.0138	−0.0
Construction	0.0161	8.9	0.1122	24.6	0.0133	3.0	0.1077	76.2	0.0017	0.0
Nondurable mfg.	0.1543	29.6	0.0678	18.7	0.1181	34.2	0.0640	79.1	−0.0325	−0.0
Durable mfg.	0.3236	47.9	0.0854	21.2	0.1815	49.1	0.0741	46.1	−0.1309	−0.1
Transport. ind.	0.0568	17.0	0.0358	13.3	0.0664	23.8	0.0405	104.9	0.0048	0.0
Communications	0.0398	14.1	0.0057	5.2	0.0329	32.0	0.0053	12.9	−0.0066	−0.0
Utilities	0.0256	11.2	0.0033	4.0	0.0223	23.0	0.0047	18.0	−0.0048	−0.0

Wholesale	0.0338	13.0	0.0666	18.5	0.0351	9.9	0.0673	139.7	0.0006	0.0
FIRE	0.0796	20.4	0.0691	18.9	0.1060	29.9	0.0677	118.2	0.0277	0.0
Service ind.	0.0162	8.9	0.0590	17.4	0.0347	10.1	0.0627	149.6	0.0148	0.0
Prof. serv.	0.0804	20.5	0.1746	31.9	0.1539	25.9	0.2309	200.4	0.0172	0.0

Table B.3 Are Returns at Large and Small Firms Converging?

Variable	Calculation using 1979 characteristics			Calculation using 1993 characteristics		
	X^S_{79}	Excess B^a	Product	X^S_{93}	Excess B^a	Product
Constant	1.0000	-0.2007	-0.2007	1.0000	-0.2007	-0.2007
Education	-0.1092	-0.0144	0.0016	0.7129	-0.0144	-0.0103
Education^2	7.6696	0.0002	0.0018	6.5427	0.0002	0.0016
Age	-0.5075	-0.0005	0.0003	0.8517	-0.0005	-0.0004
Age^2	225.477	-0.0002	-0.0339	166.1998	-0.0002	-0.0250
Tenure	-2.4589	0.0034	-0.0084	-2.0808	0.0034	-0.0071
Tenure^2	53.2425	0.0000	0.0004	44.8787	0.0000	0.0004
Tenure < 1 yr.	0.3174	0.0082	0.0026	0.2489	0.0082	0.0020
Tenure 1–2 yr.	0.1171	-0.0340	-0.0040	0.0949	-0.0340	-0.0032
Married	0.5773	0.0137	0.0079	0.5705	0.0137	0.0078
Union	0.0952	0.0548	0.0052	0.0484	0.0548	0.0027
Black	0.0790	-0.0181	-0.0014	0.0687	-0.0181	-0.0012
Female	0.4649	0.0626	0.0291	0.4894	0.0626	0.0307
Metropolitan	0.7116	-0.0071	-0.0051	0.7443	-0.0071	-0.0053
Northeast	0.2399	0.0926	0.0222	0.1953	0.0926	0.0181
North Central	0.2759	0.0843	0.0233	0.2610	0.0843	0.0220
South	0.3134	0.0876	0.0275	0.3081	0.0876	0.0270
Manager	0.1026	0.0481	0.0049	0.1186	0.0481	0.0057
Professional	0.0693	0.1006	0.0070	0.0959	0.1006	0.0097

Technical	0.0096	0.1645	0.0016	0.0287	0.1645	0.0047
Sales	0.0896	0.0549	0.0049	0.1369	0.0549	0.0075
Clerical	0.1766	0.0232	0.0041	0.1588	0.0232	0.0037
Protective	0.0010	-0.1062	-0.0001	0.0024	-0.1062	-0.0003
Service occ.	0.1923	0.0441	0.0085	0.1813	0.0441	0.0080
Craft	0.1604	0.1109	0.0178	0.1244	0.1109	0.0138
Operative	0.0978	0.0714	0.0070	0.0595	0.0714	0.0042
Transport. operative	0.0467	0.0945	0.0044	0.0486	0.0945	0.0046
Mining	0.0039	0.0240	0.0001	0.0051	0.0240	0.0001
Construction	0.1122	-0.1091	-0.0122	0.1077	-0.1091	-0.0118
Nondurable mfg.	0.0678	0.0976	0.0066	0.0640	0.0976	0.0062
Durable mfg.	0.0854	-0.0055	-0.0005	0.0741	-0.0055	-0.0004
Transport. ind.	0.0358	-0.0170	-0.0006	0.0405	-0.0170	-0.0007
Communications	0.0057	0.1551	0.0009	0.0053	0.1551	0.0008
Utilities	0.0033	-0.0088	-0.0000	0.0047	-0.0088	-0.0000
Wholesale	0.0666	0.0246	0.0016	0.0673	0.0246	0.0017
FIRE	0.0691	0.0547	0.0038	0.0677	0.0547	0.0037
Service ind.	0.0590	0.0042	0.0002	0.0627	0.0042	0.0003
Prof. serv.	0.1746	-0.0184	-0.0032	0.2309	-0.0184	-0.0043

NOTE: Education, age, and tenure are centered to have mean = 0 in the entire sample. Omitted occupation is laborer, region is West, and industry is retail trade.

[a] "Excess B" = coefficient estimated on sample from large firms – coefficient from small firms.

Table B.4 Are Employee Characteristics at Large and Small Firms Converging?

Variable	Calculation using 1979 coefficients			Using 1993 coefficients		
	Excess X^S	b^S_{79}	Product	Excess X^S	b^S_{93}	Product
Constant	0.0000	2.1203	0.0000	0.0000	1.9720	0.0000
Education	-0.0931	0.0295	-0.0027	-0.0931	0.0580	-0.0054
Education^2	1.7586	-0.0002	-0.0003	1.7586	0.0027	0.0047
Age	-0.5961	0.0056	-0.0033	-0.5961	0.0074	-0.0044
Age^2	37.2089	-0.0004	-0.0156	37.2089	-0.0003	-0.0129
Tenure	-0.7003	0.0100	-0.0070	-0.7003	0.0128	-0.0089
Tenure^2	-5.5199	-0.0001	0.0004	-5.5199	-0.0002	0.0012
Tenure < 1 yr.	0.0475	-0.0399	-0.0019	0.0475	-0.0729	-0.0035
Tenure 1–2 yr.	0.0039	-0.0510	-0.0002	0.0039	-0.0377	-0.0001
Married	-0.0566	0.0544	-0.0031	-0.0566	0.0493	-0.0028
Union	-0.1004	0.2391	-0.0240	-0.1004	0.2352	-0.0236
Black	0.0476	-0.0825	-0.0039	0.0476	-0.0853	-0.0041
Female	0.0914	-0.2618	-0.0239	0.0914	-0.2113	-0.0193
Metropolitan	-0.0007	0.0831	-0.0001	-0.0007	0.1391	-0.0001
Northeast	-0.0305	-0.0374	0.0011	-0.0305	-0.0690	0.0021
North Central	-0.0237	-0.0365	0.0009	-0.0237	-0.1341	0.0032
South	0.0628	-0.0885	-0.0056	0.0628	-0.1461	-0.0092
Manager	-0.0107	0.3271	-0.0035	-0.0107	0.3334	-0.0036

Professional	-0.0214	0.2055	-0.0044	-0.0214	0.1845	-0.0040
Technical	-0.0006	0.3072	-0.0002	-0.0006	0.2665	-0.0002
Sales	0.0428	0.2124	0.0091	0.0428	0.2054	0.0088
Clerical	0.0012	0.1165	0.0001	0.0012	0.1361	0.0002
Protective	-0.0021	-0.2549	0.0005	-0.0021	-0.0547	0.0001
Service occ.	0.0409	-0.0558	-0.0023	0.0409	-0.0576	-0.0024
Craft	-0.0215	0.1942	-0.0042	-0.0215	0.1436	-0.0031
Operative	-0.0480	0.0557	-0.0027	-0.0480	-0.0579	0.0028
Transport. op.	0.0066	0.0854	0.0006	0.0066	0.0178	0.0001
Mining	-0.0138	0.3481	-0.0048	-0.0138	0.4049	-0.0056
Construction	0.0017	0.3273	0.0006	0.0017	0.2917	0.0005
Nondurable mfg.	-0.0325	0.1746	-0.0057	-0.0325	0.1691	-0.0055
Durable mfg.	-0.1309	0.2161	-0.0283	-0.1309	0.2907	-0.0380
Transport. ind.	0.0048	0.1250	0.0006	0.0048	0.1733	0.0008
Communications	-0.0066	0.2891	-0.0019	-0.0066	0.1606	-0.0011
Utilities	-0.0048	0.2368	-0.0011	-0.0048	0.3843	-0.0018
Wholesale	0.0006	0.2289	0.0001	0.0006	0.2335	0.0001
FIRE	0.0277	0.2484	0.0069	0.0277	0.2809	0.0078
Service ind.	0.0148	0.0945	0.0014	0.0148	0.0763	0.0011
Prof. serv.	0.0172	0.1751	0.0030	0.0172	0.2312	0.0040

NOTE: "Excess X^S" = mean from large-firm sample minus mean from small-firm sample.

Table B.5 Are Returns Rising for Characteristics Common at Large Firms?

Varible	1979 Base			1993 Base		
	$(X^L_{79} - X^S_{79})$	$(b^L_{93} - b^L_{79})$	Product	$(X^L_{93} - X^S_{93})$	$(b^L_{93} - b^L_{79})$	Product
Constant	0.0000	-0.3490	0.0000	0.0000	-0.3490	0.0000
Education	0.7967	0.0141	0.0113	0.7036	0.0141	0.0100
Education^2	-1.1505	0.0031	-0.0036	0.6082	0.0031	0.0019
Age	1.0546	0.0012	0.0013	0.4585	0.0012	0.0006
Age^2	-63.6661	-0.0001	0.0050	-26.4572	-0.0001	0.0021
Tenure	4.3316	0.0062	0.0269	3.6313	0.0062	0.0226
Tenure^2	38.7962	-0.0001	-0.0055	33.2763	-0.0001	-0.0047
Tenure < 1 yr.	-0.1539	-0.0248	0.0038	-0.1064	-0.0248	0.0026
Tenure 1–2 yr.	-0.0384	-0.0207	0.0008	-0.0345	-0.0207	0.0007
Married	0.0866	0.0086	0.0007	0.0300	0.0086	0.0003
Union	0.2439	0.0509	0.0124	0.1435	0.0509	0.0073
Black	0.0032	-0.0208	-0.0001	0.0508	-0.0208	-0.0011
Female	-0.1200	0.1132	-0.0136	-0.0286	0.1132	-0.0032
Metropolitan	0.0604	0.0488	0.0029	0.0597	0.0488	0.0029
Northeast	0.0342	0.0610	0.0021	0.0037	0.0610	0.0002
North Central	0.0351	-0.0133	-0.0005	0.0114	-0.0133	-0.0002
South	-0.0528	0.0300	-0.0016	0.0100	0.0300	0.0003
Manager	0.0177	0.0543	0.0010	0.0070	0.0543	0.0004

Professional	0.0417	0.0796	0.0033	0.0202	0.0796	0.0016
Technical	0.0201	0.1238	0.0025	0.0194	0.1238	0.0024
Sales	-0.0295	0.0479	-0.0014	0.0133	0.0479	0.0006
Clerical	0.0244	0.0428	0.0010	0.0255	0.0428	0.0011
Protective	0.0040	0.0940	0.0004	0.0019	0.0940	0.0002
Service occ.	-0.1293	0.0423	-0.0055	-0.0884	0.0423	-0.0037
Craft	0.0005	0.0603	0.0000	-0.0209	0.0603	-0.0013
Operative	0.0767	-0.0423	-0.0032	0.0287	-0.0423	-0.0012
Transport. operative	-0.0143	0.0269	-0.0004	-0.0077	0.0269	-0.0002
Mining	0.0172	0.0808	0.0014	0.0035	0.0808	0.0003
Construction	-0.0961	-0.1447	0.0139	-0.0944	-0.1447	0.0137
Nondurable mfg.	0.0866	0.0921	0.0080	0.0541	0.0921	0.0050
Durable mfg.	0.2383	0.0692	0.0165	0.1074	0.0692	0.0074
Transport. ind.	0.0211	0.0314	0.0007	0.0258	0.0314	0.0008
Communications	0.0341	0.0266	0.0009	0.0275	0.0266	0.0007
Utilities	0.0223	0.1387	0.0031	0.0175	0.1387	0.0024
Wholesale	-0.0328	0.0293	-0.0010	-0.0322	0.0293	-0.0009
FIRE	0.0105	0.0871	0.0009	0.0383	0.0871	0.0033
Service ind.	-0.0428	-0.0139	0.0006	-0.0280	-0.0139	0.0004
Prof. serv.	-0.0942	0.0376	-0.0035	-0.0770	0.0376	-0.0029

Table B.6 Do Employees at Large Firms Increasingly Have Characteristics Large Firms Reward Well?

Variable	1979 Calculation			1993 Calculation		
	$(b^L_{79} - b^S_{79})$	$(X^L_{93} - X^L_{79})$	Product	$(b^L_{93} - b^S_{93})$	$(X^L_{93} - X^L_{79})$	Product
Constant	0.2189	0.0000	0.0000	0.0182	0.0000	0.0000
Education	0.0108	0.7290	0.0079	-0.0036	0.7290	-0.0026
Education^2	0.0015	0.6317	0.0010	0.0018	0.6317	0.0011
Age	-0.0003	0.7632	-0.0002	-0.0008	0.7632	-0.0006
Age^2	0.0001	-22.0692	-0.0016	-0.0001	-22.0692	0.0017
Tenure	0.0035	-0.3222	-0.0011	0.0069	-0.3222	-0.0022
Tenure^2	-0.0002	-13.8837	0.0029	-0.0002	-13.8837	0.0028
Tenure < 1 yr.	-0.0007	-0.0209	0.0000	0.0075	-0.0209	-0.0002
Tenure 1–2yr.	0.0467	-0.0182	-0.0009	0.0127	-0.0182	-0.0002
Married	-0.0068	-0.0635	0.0004	0.0069	-0.0635	-0.0004
Union	-0.1837	-0.1472	0.0270	-0.1289	-0.1472	0.0190
Black	0.0363	0.0373	0.0014	0.0182	0.0373	0.0007
Female	0.0155	0.1159	0.0018	0.0781	0.1159	0.0091
Metropolitan	-0.0072	0.0321	-0.0002	-0.0143	0.0321	-0.0005
Northeast	-0.0299	-0.0751	0.0022	0.0627	-0.0751	-0.0047
North Central	-0.0170	-0.0386	0.0007	0.0673	-0.0386	-0.0026
South	-0.0211	0.0575	-0.0012	0.0665	0.0575	0.0038
Manager	-0.0559	0.0053	-0.0003	-0.0078	0.0053	-0.0000

Professional	0.0188	0.0052	0.0001	0.1195	0.0052	0.0006
Technical	-0.2047	0.0185	-0.0038	-0.0402	0.0185	-0.0007
Sales	-0.1056	0.0902	-0.0095	-0.0507	0.0902	-0.0046
Clerical	-0.1019	-0.0166	0.0017	-0.0788	-0.0166	0.0013
Protective	0.2689	-0.0006	-0.0002	0.1627	-0.0006	-0.0001
Service occ.	-0.0492	0.0299	-0.0015	-0.0051	0.0299	-0.0002
Craft	-0.0981	-0.0574	0.0056	0.0128	-0.0574	-0.0007
Operative	-0.0316	-0.0862	0.0027	0.0397	-0.0862	-0.0034
Transport. operative	-0.0865	0.0085	-0.0007	0.0081	0.0085	0.0001
Mining	0.0490	-0.0126	-0.0006	0.0730	-0.0126	-0.0009
Construction	0.1633	-0.0028	-0.0005	0.0542	-0.0028	-0.0002
Nondurable mfg.	0.0261	-0.0362	-0.0009	0.1237	-0.0362	-0.0045
Durable mfg.	0.0524	-0.1422	-0.0074	0.0469	-0.1422	-0.0067
Transport. ind.	0.2563	0.0095	0.0024	0.2393	0.0095	0.0023
Communications	-0.0218	-0.0070	0.0002	0.1333	-0.0070	-0.0009
Utilities	0.0221	-0.0033	-0.0001	0.0133	-0.0033	-0.0000
Wholesale	0.0689	0.0013	0.0001	0.0936	0.0013	0.0001
FIRE	-0.0438	0.0264	-0.0012	0.0109	0.0264	0.0003
Service ind.	-0.0822	0.0185	-0.0015	-0.0780	0.0185	-0.0014
Prof. serv.	-0.0327	0.0735	-0.0024	-0.0511	0.0735	-0.0038

Appendix C

The Cleveland Community Salary Survey

We used data from 1956 through 1996 that was gathered in the annual Community Salary Survey (CSS) conducted by the Federal Reserve Bank of Cleveland personnel department. The department uses the survey, which covers employers in Cleveland, Cincinnati, and Pittsburgh, to formulate its yearly salary budget proposal. In return for their participation, surveyed companies receive the results for their own use. Salary surveys such as the CSS currently offer the only longitudinal microdata on wages that include both detailed occupation and employer identity information.

Our analysis was subject to several limitations. First, we measure employer wage levels relative to the market means measured within CSS sample. To the extent that all CSS employers are large and pay above-market wages, our measure of employer wage levels will understate the true employer wage effect.[1] Moreover, this approach will misstate trends in average employer wage effects relative to the entire market if the CSS sample has diverged from similar companies.

We have no reason to believe that the bias from this omission has changed over time. Some indirect evidence suggests that the bias will be small. As noted above, government and large employers' share of jobs is large and has remained relatively constant. In addition, essentially all large employers participate in wage surveys such as the one we analyze (Lichty 1991; Belcher, Ferris, and O'Neill 1985). Finally, Appendix D presents evidence CSS participants are representative of similar large employers in terms of sales growth, and other measures, and their employees are similar to employees in the CPS.

Second, our measures of relative wages move when companies' workforce compositions change (for example, due to hires and promotions of particularly skilled or unskilled employees). Such compositional changes within an occupation add noise to our measures. More seriously, our measure will overstate the effect of structures if companies keep rigid differentials between a junior and senior occupation within a job ladder but have increased the variance in the time spend in the junior occupation. Similar problems occur if employers overcome rigidities by granting workers inflated occupational titles.

Third, our data do not contain information on noncash compensation. There is some evidence that noncash benefits such as employee stock ownership and stock options are increasingly distributed to non-executives (Lawler, Mohrman, and Ledford 1995). Such a trend would bias some of our estimated changes over time. At the same time, most plans distribute relatively little stock to the vast majority of employees (Blasi and Kruse 1991); thus, the bias to our results should be small. Furthermore, Atrostic (1983) and Pierce (1998) found that as individuals' wages rise, more of their total compensation is in nonwage benefits. Thus, the differentials estimated here (particularly inter-firm ones) probably understate total effects.

Note

1. We thank Rob Valletta for pointing this out.

Table C.1 Occupations in the Cleveland Community Salary Survey (1955–96)

Account executive	Clerk typist C	IBM unit head	Press operator I
Accounting clerk I	Clerk typist II	Information processor II	Press operator II
Accounting clerk II	Comp. & benefits admin.	Information security analyst II	Programmer I
Accounting manager	Comp. & benefits manager	Internal audit manager	Programmer II
Accounting supervisor	Comp. analyst	Inventory control clerk	Programmer/analyst III
Accounts payable clerk	Computer operations manager	Job analyst	Proof clerk
Addressograph operator	Computer operations supervisor	Junior auditor	Proof machine checker
Administrative asst. I	Computer operator I	Junior computer operator	Proof machine operator
Administrative asst. II	Computer operator II	Junior economist	Protection manager
Administrative asst. III	Console operator	Junior stenographer	Public relations specialist
Administrative secretary	Contracts administrator	Lead carpenter	Purchasing agent
Analyst programmer I	Correspondence clerk	Lead check processor	Purchasing clerk
Analyst programmer II	Custodian	Lead computer operator	Receptionist
Asst. analyst programmer	Custodian II	Lead mail clerk	Receptionist clerk
Asst. console operator	Data entry operator	Lead painter	Records/files clerk
Asst. dept. manager	Data processing manager	Lead programmer	Registered nurse
Attorney	Data processing supervisor	Lead stock clerk	Research statistician
Attorney II	Dayporter	Librarian	Secretary to adm. officer
Audit analyst I	Department PC specialist	Mail clerk	Secretary to CEO
Audit analyst II		Mail clerk I	Securities proc. clerk

(continued)

Table C.1 (continued)

Audit analyst III	Dept. manager	Mail supervisor	Security guard
Audit clerk	Dept. manager	Maintenance mechanic I	Senior proof machine operator
Audit manager	Dept. manager II	Maintenance mechanic II	Senior attorney
Audit team manager	Dept. secretary	Mechanic I	Sergeant of the guard
Bookkeeping machine operator	Dept. secretary II	Mechanic II	Senior audit clerk
Budget analyst	Division head	Messenger	Senior budget clerk
Budget manager	Duplicating operator	Methods analyst I	Senior functional expense clerk
Building engineer I	Economic advisor	Methods analyst II	Senior keypunch operator
Building engineer II	Economist	Multilith operator	Senior stenographer
Building equipment mechanic	Economist II	Night cleaner–male	Senior supervisor
Building manager	Editor	Office equipment mechanic I	Senior systems analyst
Camera operator	Editor–house publications	Office equipment mechanic II	Statistical clerk
Captain of the porters	EDP audit analyst I	Offset pressman	Statistical clerk I
Carpenter	EDP audit analyst II	Operating engineer	Stenographer
Charwoman	Electrician	Operating engineer	Stock clerk
Charwoman–night	Employee benefits counselor	Operations research analyst I	Supervisor
Check adjustment clerk	Employee benefits specialist	Operations research analyst II	Systems analyst
Check adjustment clerk II	Employment interviewer	Org. development specialist	Systems consulting analyst
Check processing clerk I	Employment supervisor	Painter	Systems project manger
Check processing clerk II	Executive secretary	Paymaster	Tabulating operator
Check processing clerk III	File clerk	Payroll clerk I	Tape librarian

Check processing supervisor	File clerk A	Payroll clerk II	Telephone operator
Chief building engineer	Forms designer	Payroll supervisor	Trainee keypunch operator
Chief electrician	General clerk C	Personal interviewer	Training coordinator
Chief maintenance mechanic	General ledger bookkeeper	Personnel clerk	Unit head
Chief mechanic	Graphics illustrator	Personnel interviewer	Washroom maid
Clerk typist	Guard supervisor	Personnel manager	Word processor
	Head telephone operator	Personnel receptionist	

NOTE: Not all occupations were present in all years.

Appendix D

How Representative is the Community Salary Survey?

This appendix examines whether the Community Salary Survey wage patterns are similar to those of the CPS, whether CSS employers are similar to matched employers in Compustat, and whether joining or leaving the CSS sample is correlated with unusual movements in wages. (See Groshen [1996] for more detail on salary surveys in general and the CSS in particular.)

In general, Cleveland, Cincinnati, and Pittsburgh are more urban, have more cyclically sensitive employment, and have undergone more industrial restructuring than the nation as a whole. Prior to the 1980s, wages in these three cities were higher than the national average. Now, they are approximately average for the country.

COMPARISONS WITH OTHER DATA ON EMPLOYEES

The CSS is not a random sample either of occupations or employers; thus, it is important to place our results in context of the U.S. economy. In particular, the CSS covers common nonproduction occupations at large employers in three Midwestern cities. Table D.1 compares some features of the CSS to the 1995 Current Population Survey (CPS) Outgoing Rotation File. (The CPS is the broadest and most-studied household survey.) The top panel compares weekly wage statistics in the CSS with those of the CPS and three subsets. The first subset selects the 44 two-digit CPS occupations into which the (more narrow) CSS occupations would fall. The second subset is the states of the East North Central census region (which includes Ohio). The final subset is the most exclusive: CSS occupations in the East North Central region.

As expected, weekly earnings in the CSS sample exceed those of the average U.S. worker. The contrast between overall CPS wage levels and those in CSS occupations suggests that much of this difference is due to the occupations surveyed in the CSS. Restricting the CPS sample to Midwestern states does not noticeably narrow the gap. Remaining differences in wage levels probably reflect the fact that CSS respondents are urban and large; these characteristics correlate with high wages (Brown and Medoff 1989).

Wage variation is considerably lower in the CSS. In this case, restricting the CPS samples to CSS occupations does not improve the correspondence. This result is consistent with the CSS pulling less than the full range of narrow occupations within each two-digit CPS occupational code. In addition, the concentration of large employers in the CSS would also have this effect, because wage variation between large and small firms is omitted.

**Table D.1 Comparison of Weekly Earnings in the 1995 CSS with the
1995 CPS Outgoing Rotation File**

		Current population survey			
Statistic	CSS	Whole sample	CSS occupations only[a]	East north central region	CSS occs. in ENC region
Weekly earnings					
Mean ($)	646	500	614	511	616
Median ($)	577	403	504	423	520
ln(Median)	6.36	6.00	6.22	6.05	6.25
Std. dev. ($)	280	365	415	369	412
Std. dev. of ln(median)	0.413	0.817	0.773	0.839	0.793
No. of observations	14,351	169,781	40,230	27,544	6,316

	CPS (all U.S.A.)			CPS (East north central)	
Correlation	Pearson correlation	Spearman (rank order)		Pearson correlation	Spearman (rank order)
CSS–CPS correlations[b]					
Mean	0.790	0.798		0.785	0.796
Median	0.757	0.783		0.750	0.765
ln(Median)	0.787	0.783		0.766	0.765
Std. dev.	0.776	0.779		0.708	0.772

[a] "CSS occupations only" denotes observations in the 44 two-digit CPS occupational codes corresponding to occupations in the CSS.

[b] In the CSS data, the 83 occupations were aggregated into 44 occupational groups corresponding to the two-digit CPS codes. All correlations are statistically significant at above the 0.1 percent level.

SOURCE: Authors' calculations from the Federal Reserve Bank of Cleveland Community Salary Survey and the Current Population Survey Outgoing Rotation File, 1995.

Nevertheless, the lower panel shows that the occupational relative wage structure of the CSS closely follows that of the CPS. Standard and rank-order correlation coefficients are shown for the whole United States and for the East North Central region. The first three rows show that occupations' mean and median wages across the two samples have correlation coefficients of almost 0.8. The bottom row shows that this correspondence also holds for within-occupation wage dispersion.

Similar comparisons between the CSS and published occupational means in Bureau of Labor Statistics Area Wage Surveys (AWS) for Cleveland, Cincinnati, and Pittsburgh for the late 1970s and early 1980s yielded correlations in the range of 0.9 and above. The AWS also oversampled large employers. The movements of mean wages for similar occupations were highly correlated across the two surveys, and levels were usually within 5 percent of each other. CSS respondents appear representative of the broader AWS samples in the three cities. These comparisons increase our confidence that the findings in the CSS sample are indicative of national conditions for nonproduction employees of large U.S. firms.

COMPARISONS WITH OTHER DATA ON EMPLOYERS

Table D.2 reports several tests of whether CSS members are representative of similar-sized firms in their industries. In the first year that an employer appears in both the CSS and Compustat, we matched it to the Compustat company in the same two-digit SIC code that is closest in ln(sales). We then compared the CSS and matched firms on a variety of accounting measures. We followed the two firms until the end of the sample (1996) or until one of the firms dropped out of Compustat, typically due to a merger or acquisition. Our sample for these analyses was reduced to only 52 companies because many employers—such as those that are privately held or in the nonprofit and public sectors—could not be matched to Compustat.

Based on a simple *t*-test, none of the differences between the two samples was statistically significant. For example, the difference in median return on assets in the first year of each match is small: 17.3 percent for CSS versus 16.3 percent for Compustat. Similarly, the two samples both have median debt-to-equity ratios of about 22 percent in the first year of the match. Growth rates of sales and the above ratios are also very similar between the samples.

Survival in the Compustat database mainly measures avoidance of bankruptcy, merger, or acquisition. We cannot measure the mix of reasons that companies dropped out of either database. However, a merger or acquisition need not lead to attrition from the CSS if participation continued under the new ownership. This may explain why employers in the CSS sample exit slightly

Table D.2 Comparisons of CSS and Matched Compustat Employer

Variable	Sample medians		Test for hypothesis that median difference = 0	
	CSS employers	Compustat matches	Statistic	Value
Sales (millions of 1966 dollars)	649	632	Not applicable[a]	—
Change in ln(sales)	+4.6	+3.0	t-statistic	1.56
Return on assets (%)	17.3	16.3	t-statistic	0.64
Change in return on assets (pct. pt.)	–0.14	-0.07	t-statistic	–0.51
Debt/equity (%)	21.7	22.4	t-statistic	–1.26
Change in debt/equity (pct. pt.)	+0.4	+0.2	t-statistic	1.36
Share of sample that survived until sample end in 1996 (%)	62	53	Z-statistic[b] p-value	–1.2 0.23

NOTE: Levels were measured from the first year the focal firm was in the CSS and in Compustat, which was also the year the matched firms were chosen. Changes were measured to the last year that both firms were in Compustat.

[a] Samples were matched on ln(sales).

[b] Z-statistic and associated p-value of the Gehan generalization of the Wilcoxon-Mann-Whitney test for differences in survival times in the Compustat database between CSS and matched firms (Stata 1995). This test adjusts for censoring of the data by the end of the sample in 1996.

less often than the matched sample (37 percent versus 48 percent, respectively), although the difference is not statistically significant. Median lifetimes in the sample (33 years for CSS, 31 for matches) were similar. A variety of tests for differences in survival times (Wilxocon-Gehan, Mantel-Haenszel, and log-rank) could not reject equal probabilities. (These tests all adjust for censoring of still-existing companies [Stata 1995, p. 202].) Thus, the CSS sample looks reasonably representative of Compustat firms of the same industry and size.

TESTS FOR CSS EFFECTS ON WAGE STRUCTURES

It is possible that information from the CSS could be a key component in employers' maintenance of rigid internal labor markets. If so, respondents who do not maintain internal labor markets will not join the CSS, while those who decide to weaken their internal labor markets will drop out of the CSS. In either case, employers outside the CSS would have very different wage structures than those inside the survey. Our investigations reveal little evidence of such differences.

First, evidence was presented above (pp. 205–207) that the occupational wage structure (in means and standard deviations) in the CSS matches U.S. patterns (as measured by the CPS and AWS) reasonably well. In addition, comparisons with matched Compustat firms are similarly reassuring. Moreover, in a supplement added to the CSS in 1989, few participants reported that they used the CSS as their main source of wage-setting information.

To further explore this possibility, we took advantage of the entry and exit of firms from the sample. We isolated the behavior of firms in the years immediately after they joined the CSS and before they left it. If participants in the CSS were markedly different from the rest of the market, new entrants would have had differing wage structures that then converged to the rest of the CSS as participation continued. In addition, respondents that were about to drop out would have shown signs of divergence or reordering in the years preceding their departure from the sample.

One-year employer autocorrelations for entrants in their first year participating in the CSS are negligibly lower than for the whole CSS population sample (0.92, compared with 0.93), while those about to exit show no difference at all (data not shown). In wage level, new entrants pay an average of 4 percent below the sample mean in their first year. Those about to exit pay about 2 percent above the CSS mean in the last year before they leave the sample. Both of these wage-level differences dissipate in the years further from entry or exit.

Internal structure wage differentials are again slightly less persistent for newcomers' first years (0.72) relative to the rest of the sample (0.76). This result is consistent with some reordering but not a major realignment, since the difference is small and occurs only in the first year. Companies that are about to exit the sample do not have noticeably different autocorrelations from stayers in the years just prior to exit (data not shown).

These probes suggest that it is unlikely that CSS respondents are extremely different from the rest of the market. Nevertheless, some of the results are consistent with a mild conforming influence of participation in the CSS, and some changes could take place in the years before entry or after exit. However, the 2 percent wage premium associated with imminent exit is inconsistent with a characterization of leavers as those who are reverting to a low-wage, spot-market employment strategy.

Appendix E

Did Deregulation or Growing Imports
Weaken Wage Structures?

In this appendix, we examine how two shocks to product-market rents—deregulation and increases in foreign trade—affected the level, structure, and rigidity of wages. Coupled with the hypothesis that high ability to pay predicts high wage levels, this hypothesis implies that employers with product-market rents were more easily able to pay high wage levels, maintain wage structures that differ from the market, and keep rigid relative wages over time.

We tested these hypotheses by performing a difference-in-difference quasi-experiment. Specifically, we tested whether companies weakened their internal labor markets when their industries underwent deregulation or faced rising import penetration. To control for secular trends that affected all employers, these comparisons were made in reference to companies that were never regulated, or that were always regulated, or that faced constant levels of international competition. (In this sample, the always-regulated category includes completely public-sector employers.) Our time-series cross-section results also correct for first-order serial correlation for each employer.

EFFECTS OF DEREGULATION

We measured the effects of deregulation on four wage aspects of internal labor markets: the level and persistence of employer wage effects and the standard deviation and autocorrelation of internal wage structures. Our measures of deregulation derived from the list of industries in Fortin and Lemieux (1997, p. 82). The measurement of the effects of industry deregulation on wage levels has no advantage over similar regressions performed on the industry level (e.g., Fortin and Lemieux 1997, and the citations therein). Thus, the main contribution of this section is the results on the employer wage structures and the persistence of employer wage effects.

Wage level impacts (for the 18 employers we can track) are most simply estimated by comparing mean estimated employer effects for the three to five years prior to deregulation with those after deregulation. In some industries, the process of deregulation involved several regulatory or legislative changes. In such cases, we compared from three to five years prior to the first deregulatory change in the law to three to five years after the final deregulatory change listed by Fortin and Lemieux (1997). This comparison is a difference-in-difference estimate because employer effects are estimated relative to the rest of the sample. Three to five years before deregulation, companies in industries that would be deregulated were low-wage employers, paying 3.9 percent less than the mean. Three to five years after deregulation, the mean of companies that underwent deregulation increased to +2.3 percent, for a statistically significant rise of 6.1 percentage points. Moreover, outliers do not drive the change in the mean; 16 of 18 employer wage effects rose relative to the CSS mean.

Our results contrast with a body of research on the wage effects of regulation that largely finds that product-market regulations raise wages. Possible reasons for the divergence are 1) that our sample of employers undergoing deregulation includes many financial firms, whose nonunion employees may have extracted few rents under regulation; or 2) sampling error due to the small number of employers in the industries that underwent deregulation, worsened by the fact we had only five industry-level deregulation events.

We also detected little impact of deregulation on other measures of internal labor markets (see the right three columns of Table E.1). Employers had slightly higher standard deviations of internal wage structures after deregulation. Moreover, deregulated employers had the same standard deviation as always-regulated employers (although both were lower than never-regulated

Table E.1 The Effect of Deregulation on Measures of Industrial Labor Markets

Deregulation status	Dependent variable Employer wage effect	Standard deviation of internal wage structure	One-year change in employer wage effect	One-year autocorrelation of internal wage structure
Pre-deregulation	−0.053 (0.016)[a]	−0.004 (0.003)	0.0003 (0.002)	0.017 (0.020)
Near-deregulation	−0.0424 (0.017)	0.017 (0.005)	0.001 (0.003)	−0.011 (0.032)
Post-deregulation	−0.027 (0.016)	0.025 (0.004)	0.002 (0.002)	0.008 (0.022)
Always-regulated	Note b	0.006 (0.004)	−0.001 (0.002)	0.039 (0.020)
Never-regulated	0.006 (0.013)	0.131 (0.002)	0.033 (0.001)	0.747 (0.008)
No. of observations	1,405	3,100	2,709	2,580

[a] Standard errors are in parentheses.

[b] Regression did not include always-regulated dummy.

employers). Thus, there is no evidence that regulation, per se, permits internal wage structures to deviate from the market. Finally, there was no statistically significant effect of regulation or deregulation on the persistence of employer or internal wage structures.

EFFECTS OF RISING IMPORT PENETRATION

Similar to the results for deregulation, we find no evidence of the expected effects of trade penetration on wage levels, structures, or their persistence (Table E.2). Our measure of import penetration is drawn from the NBER trade database (Feenstra 1996). We use the industry imports/shipments ratio to measure trade penetration. Because changes in trade may take a long time to affect wage levels and structures, we analyzed non-overlapping 10-year changes in three-year averages of wage structure components and of trade penetration. That is, we examine how the level of trade penetration in 1968–1970 minus 1958–1960 predicts wage levels, persistence, internal wage structure magnitude, and persistence during that decade. We repeat the test for 1978–1980 minus 1968–1970, for 1988–1990 minus 1987–1980, and for 1994–1996 minus 1984–1986.[1] In the analyses other than those on employer wage effects, we included industries with no trade data; in those cases, we code import penetration as zero in all years. In each case, the trade penetration measures have no economically or statistically significant effect on our measures of internal labor market strength and persistence.

Table E.2 The Effect of Foreign Competition on Measures of Internal Labor Markets

Regression variable (Dependent variable)	Intradecade change[a] in			
	Employer wage effect	Standard deviation of internal wage structure	One-year change in employer wage effect	One-year autocorrelation of internal wage structure
Decadal change in industry import penetration ratio[b]	0.702 (0.586)	0.050 (0.086)	–0.027 (0.095)	0.644 (0.547)
No. of observations	93	253	240	222

NOTE: Standard errors are in parentheses.
[a] For dependent variables, changes are calculated as the difference between three-year averages at the beginning and end of the decade.
[b] Industry imports/sales.

Two aspects of this exercise may bias the results against finding a trade effect. First, as with the previous test, the effect of imports can be estimated for only a subset of CSS employers. In most decades, only about 32 firms in 16 industries had positive import penetration. Second, if employers with consistently rigid pay structures paid wages far from the market level, industries with such employers will have high costs and will be more likely to attract imports (Bertrand 1999). Thus, our results may understate the correlation between rising imports and declining internal labor markets. Nevertheless, conditional on the small samples, the deregulation and trade regressions do not suggest that product-market shocks lead firms to reduce idiosyncratic employer or internal wage effects and start paying wages more similar to the market.

Note

1. As a robustness check, we reran the analyses with the data centered on 1955, 1975, 1985, and 1995. The results were similar.

Appendix F

The Hay Data

The measure of skill created by Hay includes three groups of capabilities. "Know-how" measures the capabilities, knowledge, and techniques needed to do the job. The skills captured by this measure include the kind of formal knowledge usually associated with years of education. "Problem solving" measures how well-defined and predictable job tasks are (less-defined and predictable tasks make greater demands on employees). Finally, "accountability" measures how much autonomy or individual discretion employees have in decision making. The three dimensions are then combined into a single index known as "Hay points" that is designed to measure the extent of job requirements that workers must perform.[1] Hay's intention is to make these scores comparable across occupations, companies, and over time.

Hay maintains a database on what its client companies in different industries pay for occupations having a given number of Hay points. Individual clients choose a comparison set of employers (e.g., by size, industry, and location) and decide how they would like their overall wage structure to be positioned relative to those paid by the comparison set, e.g., at the median or at the 75th percentile. Clients also exercise discretion in deciding how to position the pay of individual jobs in their organization compared with that reference set. They may decide to pay some jobs more or less than the levels prevailing in the data set, for example, to establish wage structures that facilitate internally consistent promotion pathways or job ladders consistent with the unique set of jobs in their company.

ARE THE HAY MEASURES VALID?

Data from Hay compensation surveys have been analyzed by a number of researchers (e.g., Smith and Ehrenberg 1981; Cappelli 1993; and Gibbs and Hendricks 1995). Nevertheless, the data set is not standard, and it is important to understand its merits and drawbacks.

An important goal of the Hay systems is that the measure of skill created by its job analysis be consistent both within and among organizations because one of the services they are effectively selling is salary comparisons based on skill across firms. Hay asserts that "compensation lines are *directly* comparable from one organization to another" (their emphasis [Hay Group, no date, p. 8]). The comparability of the measures across jobs and firms is especially important for our purposes.

At each employer, a team of the company's managers that is trained and led by a Hay consultant defines the requirements of jobs and attaches Hay points to each job. The team begins the process by analyzing a set of benchmark jobs, such as nurses, secretaries, or accountants, that represent common occupations easily identifiable in the labor market. The skill requirements for these benchmark jobs are reasonably constant among employers and are largely general (as opposed to firm-specific). After the team has completed its analyses of the skill requirements of the benchmark jobs, the Hay consultant does another, independent evaluation of these jobs. These results are compared with the scores produced by the team in order to check for any biases. After attempting to correct biases in the team's judgments and then revising the scores, the consultant does yet another comparison, this time with the average scores generated across client companies for the same benchmark jobs. A correction factor is generated from that comparison and is applied to all of the job analyses generated by the team, for benchmark and nonbenchmark jobs. If, for example, the scores produced by the team for its benchmark jobs are 5 percent higher than the average across other companies, then the consultant calculates a correlation factor that will reduce the scores produced by the team for all of the jobs in the company by 5 percent.

As a final check on the consistency of these skill measures, the company maintains an internal Job Measurement Quality Assurance Group to check on the comparability of the scores produced among client companies. The consultants in this group are senior practitioners known as "correlators," who are certified by Hay for their ability to apply the Hay system consistently among client companies. After a consultant and the client team complete their analysis of jobs and pay, including any corrections, the correlators come out to the client company and assess the results for consistency with Hay practice elsewhere. Every three years after a compensation system has been introduced, a Hay consultant returns to the client to evaluate the system and ensure its consistency.[2]

In addition to these internal checks, external pressures also help ensure the reliability of the Hay procedures. First, the fact that Hay Associates has been using essentially the same job evaluation process for more than 50 years provides opportunities to identify and eliminate obvious sources of error. Hay Associates' success in the market over many decades implies that many employers find their job evaluation and weighting scheme to be useful. The tens of thousands of dollars that employers spend and the hundreds of hours that their managers spend working on job analyses suggests that employers consider the services Hay provides as highly valuable. Second, the fact that Hay Associates relies on repeat business from large corporations provides important incentives to maintain reliable systems: a client would immediately recognize and find it disturbing if the Hay job evaluation system generated different skill point values in subsequent years for jobs that the employer knew had not changed.

Further, the Hay measures have widespread influence on how jobs are structured and evaluated in the economy as a whole and, in that sense, they have good external validity. During the 1980s, for example, over 2 million employees were in jobs evaluated by Hay, and its system was used by 40 percent of the Fortune 1000 (Labich 1992, pp. 116–117). Moreover, comparisons by non-Hay firms with these establishments extend the influence of the Hay system even further.

In addition to the issue of consistency or reliability, it is also important to consider explicitly whether the Hay measures are valid; specifically, whether they do a better job at measuring the dimensions of skill than alternative measures that are available. The Hay measure of skills and responsibility—as with any such measure—is subject to several constraints. The process of determining which tasks and responsibilities should be included in job descriptions is somewhat arbitrary, and matching actual job duties with Hay Associates' compensable factors also introduces errors. How to weight different factors in determining an overall measure of skill is also somewhat arbitrary. In fact, almost every large organization in the United States carries out the same basic processes of job analysis, creating metrics of job requirements, attaching wage rates to them, and adjusting wages to create a coherent pay structure as in the Hay system. Thus, criticism of the ad hoc aspects of this process is muted by the fact that they cannot be avoided just by avoiding the Hay system of job analysis and market comparison. Moreover, the fact that the Hay system is the most widely used job evaluation system suggests it has relatively high validity.

Finally, it is helpful to contrast the Hay measures and the various procedures they use to guard against biases with alternative measures of skills that are typically used in research. Job titles and education levels are the most common alternative measures. Both education and job-title data are typically self-reported and come with all the associated biases, everything from ego-enhancing reporting to simple memory problems. Education is typically measured in years attended, with few efforts to adjust for the quality or type of education received (except in some cases where the type of degree completed is included). Job titles often differ among organizations for similar positions, especially for managerial jobs. Efforts to generate consistent job titles, such as those used by the Census Bureau, confront the same type of matching analysis performed by Hay, but with far fewer quality checks than Hay has.

THE SAMPLE

Our data set examines over 50,000 managerial positions per year in 39 companies in 1986 and 1992, with the number of managers employed per company ranging between 129 and 5,813. The data captures the population of managerial-level jobs in each company and includes the characteristics of the jobs rather than of the incumbents. For each job, we can identify its level in the organization chart or hierarchy and the firm to which it belongs: CEO or division president; other senior executives with company or division-wide responsibilities; middle management (that is, managing other managers or supervisors); supervisors; and exempt nonsupervisors. (This last category is largely professional jobs such as accountants.) We also know the functional area of each job, such as marketing or finance, location (zip codes), base salary, total salary, midpoint on the salary scale for each job class, and skill points (both total and broken out into the three subscores for know-how, problem solving, and accountability skills).

The 39 companies are headquartered throughout the United States, and the employees in each company are often dispersed throughout the country. About 200 of the locations have at least 10 managerial employees. We analyze pay data for two years for each company, 1986 and 1992. In 1989, the midpoint in that period, the companies ranged in size from 584 to over 60,000 employees, with a mean of 16,604 and a median of roughly 9,500.

We first analyze the logarithm of annual base wages, because base wages are the component of compensation that should be most closely linked to the Hay points measures of skills and responsibility. We then present the analyses on total pay, defined as base pay plus annual bonuses. We merge into our data set information on total company employment taken from Compustat.

The data set does not have information on stock options and other forms of long-term incentive pay. Moreover, it lacks information on stock ownership, a form of implicit incentive that can be very important for many top executives (Hall and Liebman 1998). Thus, our results for the very highest levels of executives may not be representative, given that stock ownership is an important part of their total compensation. We replicated all results on a sample without top executives to focus on employees for whom base and bonus payments constitute the bulk of their compensation.

CHECKS FOR REPRESENTATIVENESS

An important issue in data sets such as this one is the question of sample self-selection. To test whether the firms in this sample were distinctive from employers of similar size in their industry, we used Compustat data to match each firm in the Hay data set to the firm closest in 1986 sales within its two-digit SIC industry. We then performed a Wilcoxon signed rank test to compare the Hay firms with the matched firms.

We found no statistically significant difference between the firms in the Hay data set and the matched firms in the level of sales, employment, or debt-to-equity ratios in 1992, or in rate of change in sales, employment, or debt-to-equity ratios from 1986 to 1992. We also found no statistically significant difference in profitability (return on assets) in 1986 or 1992. Using the acquisitions line on Compustat, we found no significant difference between the mean size of acquisitions over this time period and no difference in the number of acquisitions per year. In short, there is no evidence that these employers are in any way nonrepresentative of the population of large industrial firms. (This population, of course, is not representative of all employers.)

Notes

1. For ease of presentation, we divide the Hay point total by 100; this normalization has no effect on the results. We replicated all analyses described below with the three subscores entered separately and with various interactions. Alternative formulations did not affect the results.
2. This description of the quality control process at Hay was provided by Ken Welde, Director of Information Services, at the Hay Group's Philadelphia headquarters office (private communication, December 22, 1997).

Table F.1 Summary Statistics of Hay Data

	1986		1992	
Variable	Mean	s.d.	Mean	s.d.
Base pay ($)	41,607	17,649	43,361	19,593
Total compensation ($)	42,837	21,760	45,277	25,230
Hay points	206.6	119.9	201.4	112.4
Sample size	54,080			55,298

Table F.2 Hay Skill Points

							Difference of means
Management	1986	1992	1986		1992		
level[a]	n	n	Mean	s.d.	Mean	s.d.	t-statistic
M = 0	39	39	1,352	838	1,340	950	1.12
M = 1	496	479	661	307	580	450	4.36**
M = 2	4,762	4,102	363	127	356	116	2.36**
M = 3	22,695	19,297	198	71	204	72	7.07***
M = 4	26,088	31,308	171	56	168	51	7.17***
All	54,080	55,225[b]	206.6	119.9	201.4	112.4	7.3***

NOTE: *** = statistically significantly different from 0 at the 1% level; ** = statistically significantly different from 0 at the 5% level.
[a] M = 0 is CEO or division president, 1 is other senior executives with company or division-wide responsibilities, 2 is division managers (managing other managers or supervisors), 3 is supervisor, and 4 is exempt, nonsupervisory positions, generally professional jobs.
[b] Sample sizes sometimes vary due to missing values on some variables.

Table F.3 Base Pay

					Difference of means
Management	1986 ($)		1992 ($)		
level	Mean	s.d.	Mean	s.d.	t-statistic
M = 0	220,000	141,982	231,150	158,205	2.09**
M = 1	119,682	58,175	11,636	55,062	0.89
M = 2	62,722	18,026	67,884	22,493	11.49***
M = 3	41,610	10,422	44,531	13,183	24.23***
M = 4	35,970	9,379	38,039	11,105	23.34***
All	41,607	17,649	43,361	19,593	15.5***

NOTE: All figures expressed in 1986 dollars. *** = statistically significantly different from 0 at the 1% level; ** = statistically significantly different from 0 at the 5% level.

Table F.4 Total Compensation (Base Pay + Bonus)

Management level	1996 ($) Mean	s.d.	1992 ($) Mean	s.d.	Difference of means t-statistic
M = 0	268,235	194,394	310,526	256,258	2.17**
M = 1	141,669	81,657	141,498	85,027	0.03
M = 2	67,242	23,450	74,557	29,925	12.3***
M = 3	42,315	11,424	46,107	14,875	28.2***
M = 4	36,552	9,720	38,969	11,418	26.72***
All	42,837	21,760	45,277	25,230	17.1***

NOTE: All figures expressed in 1986 dollars. *** = statistically significantly different from 0 at the 1% level; ** = statistically significantly different from 0 at the 5% level.

Table F.5 Industry Breakdown of Respondents

SIC	Description	N
20	Food and kindred products	4
26	Paper and allied products	3
27	Printing, publishing, and allied inds.	1
28	Chemicals and allied inds.	2
29	Petroleum refining and related inds.	3
30	Rubber and misc. plastics	1
32	Stone, clay, glass, etc.	2
33	Primary metals	2
34	Fabricated metal products	1
35	Industrial and commercial machinery and computer equipment	4
36	Electronic and other electric	3
37	Transportation equipment	1
38	Measuring, analysis, and controlling inst.	1
40	Railroad transport	2
49	Electric, gas, and sanitary services	6
50	Durable goods trade	2
51	Nondurable goods trade	1

Table F.6 Functional Breakdown of Respondents

Job function	Number of incumbents		Mean skill points		Mean base salary	
	1986	1992	1986	1992	1986	1992
General mgmt./multifield	630	415	690.638	661.665	105,370.5	112,063.2
Strategic/corporate planning	128	104	339.945	313.75	61,921.54	65,260.56
Finance/acctg.	3,768	3,954	211.476	207.482	41,023.2	44,167.9
Info sys./ data proc.	3,259	4,995	190.122	185.256	38,803.74	39,827.39
Human resources	2,185	2,331	208.05	203.616	41,523.28	44,421.57
Legal	504	426	305.821	303.857	55,680.49	60,438.94
Marketing	8,604	9,638	214.176	204.039	39,585.22	39,808.25
Public relations	286	327	234.804	222.419	47,261.31	48,819.96
Facility services	1,409	1,554	177.51	155.693	38,711.61	37,431.81
Research and development	1,756	1,878	236.203	231.952	44,202.21	50,116.17
Engineering	7,691	8,125	203.966	195.092	42,156.84	45,317.06
Materials mgmt.	1,979	2,175	177.155	175.845	36,024.76	38,458.5
Purchasing/contracting	906	938	207.422	192.788	41,049.23	42,737.76
Plant engr.	2,015	1,814	198.984	196.135	42,775.41	46,094.92
Mfg. or prod. engr.	1,314	1,445	200.524	198.531	39,373.31	44,038.31
Quality assurance	964	1,000	194.01	191.762	39,269.54	42,441.18
Prod./mfg. operations	6,222	4,644	184.834	191.496	38,986.15	42,989.94
Rail transport operations	2,942	2,197	181.673	181.675	44,526.31	39,645.18
Power generation	854	525	193.987	195.796	45,438.89	47,716.31
Power transmission	630	555	179.438	180.975	42,661.45	43,458.86

Gas transmission	200	152	172.25	172.316	45,670.52	47,869.42
Utility customer service	503	495	159.823	153.556	36,356.89	36,533.89
All others	5,331	5,538	203.934	224.96	40,479.98	42,957.59
Total	54,080	55,225[a]				

[a] Sample sizes sometimes vary due to missing values on some variables.

Appendix G

The Indiana/Japan Data

These data are from 1982–1983 surveys of manufacturing establishments in the Indianapolis area in the United States and from the Kanagawa prefecture (an industrial district outside of Tokyo) in Japan. The population was sampled from lists of employers provided by the Chambers of Commerce and government agencies. Within this population, organizations were stratified by employment size and by industry and were randomly selected. Forty-seven out of the 140 Indiana establishments (34 percent) and 34 out of the 90 Japanese establishments (38 percent) that were contacted provided usable data.

The establishments were spread among seven manufacturing industries: printing, electronics, chemicals, metals, food, machinery, and transportation. Within each establishment, a structured interview was conducted with top management personnel and arrangements were made to administer a questionnaire to a sample of full-time, nontemporary employees.

WAGES

Only full time workers were included in the sample. For Indiana, the wage measure is the logarithm of hourly earnings. (All Indiana results were replicated using the logarithm of annual earnings.) For Japan, the wage measure is the logarithm of annual earnings, including the annual bonus and various family-based bonuses. In all Japanese wage equations, a set of four dummy variables are included that control for the average number of overtime hours worked per month.

JOB CHARACTERISTICS

Four broad categories of job characteristics are used in this study: on-the-job training, autonomy, complexity, and supervision. All job characteristics were derived from questionnaires filled out by the workers themselves. Most questions were five-point Likert scales, with 1 implying agreement with a statement and 5 implying disagreement. In all regressions, the five possible scores were converted into a set of five dummy variables. This procedure avoids the assumption of cardinality in using the ordinal Likert scales.

On-the-job training measures include the time required to train someone for the job (0 = "a few hours," 6 = "five years or more"); the level of agreement that "My job makes me keep learning new things," (1 = "strongly disagree," 5 = "strongly agree"); the importance of formal on-the-job training in this company as a source of skills (0 = "never had," 4 = "very important"); and (in Indiana only) the importance of informal on-the-job training in this company as a source of skills (0 = "never had," 4 = "very important").

The data sets include several measures of autonomy, all using the same set of response codes; for example, "My job gives me freedom as to how I do my work" (1= "strongly disagree," 5 = "strongly agree"). There were three measures of complexity; for example, "There is a lot of variety in the kinds of things that I do." Finally, three questions measure supervision; for example, "My supervisor has a great deal of say over what I do."

LIMITATIONS OF THE DATA SET

While the data set has the advantage of covering two nations, it has the disadvantage of covering only specific regions within each nation. Furthermore, the sample is limited to manufacturing.

An important limitation of the data set is its reliance on questionnaires filled out by the workers themselves. While there is no way to avoid all subjectivity in measuring job characteristics, more accurate descriptions could be achieved if the questionnaires were supplemented with interviews of supervisors, observations of the work being performed, and so forth. (Past studies of wage differentials have also relied heavily on worker self-reports of job characteristics; e.g., Krueger and Summers [1988]; Brown and Medoff [1989]; and Kruse [1992].)

The use of multiple measures for each of the principal constructs of interest (i.e., on-the-job training, autonomy, complexity, and supervision) should increase reliability. Most past studies of wages and job characteristics have used smaller data sets and have not usually had so many measures of each construct.

The data set includes subsets of several standard instruments widely used in behavioral science research. Hackman and Oldham's Job Description Inventory (JDI), for example, has been used in numerous previous studies of workplaces (Hackman and Oldham 1980). Responses are reasonably highly correlated to behaviors such as voluntary turnover and absenteeism, increasing our confidence in the validity of the measures.

Appendix H

The Survey Questions Concerning Layoffs

This study analyzes 19 questions about layoffs in Silicon Valley and 11 questions in Canada. Each respondent answered three or four layoff questions and two pay cut questions. No respondent was asked closely comparable questions. The full text of the pay cut questions were taken verbatim from Kahneman, Knetsch, and Thaler.

The questions concerning layoffs involved scenarios where a shock to the employer led to the decision to hoard or lay off employees. The layoff could be gentle, harsh, or labor hoarding. The employees could be either high-technology engineers or production workers. Workers developed either employer-specific or generally useful skills. In Silicon Valley, some questions included mention of a CEO either receiving a record bonus or refusing a bonus.

The first sentence in every survey question describes why the layoff is occurring:

a1) "A company faced lower product demand due to shifts in the market; the viability of the employer was threatened."

a2) "A company has higher productivity due to the introduction of some new technology."

a3) "A company has higher productivity due to the employees' suggestions."

a4) "The current project for a group of high-technology engineers [a4′: production workers] has ended. The company has decided to lay them off."

The second sentence (except in the case of a4 or a4′ above) describes the type of worker being laid off:

b1) "Thus, the company is laying off some high-technology engineers."

b2) "Thus, the company is laying off some production workers."

The third sentence mentions the type of skills developed by the affected workers:

c1) "These workers are specialists in this company's unusual technology, with an average of ten years' tenure at this employer."

c2) "The affected engineers [production workers] have an average of ten years' tenure at this employer and specialize in widely used hardware, so that their skills would be useful in another job."

The next sentence states the employer's response to the shock:

d1) "The company is laying off the employees with two weeks' warning. These are the first layoffs in the company's history."

d2) "Before the layoff, the employer gave each employee four paid weeks to find another job elsewhere in the company. Those who could not find a new position received severance pay based on age and years of service. The company provided out-placement service including counseling and resume-writing workshops. Employees knew layoffs were likely in this circumstance."

d3) "Although the company has a surplus of workers, it has decided to keep a set of high-technology engineers [production workers] on the payroll until work can be found for them. The company may shift the workers to a new line of work, and may require them to relocate."

Finally, a CEO bonus might be mentioned:

e1) No mention.

e2) "The CEO received a record bonus for his success in cutting costs [introducing the new technology]."

e3) "The CEO turned down his bonus this year because of the unexpected need for layoffs."

The 19 questions consist of concatenations of these sentences, in the following combinations:

A. a1, b1, c2, d1, e1
B. a4, b2, c2, d1, e1
C. a1, b1, c1, d1, e3
D. a2, b1, c1, d1, e1
E. a2, b1, c1, d2, e1
F. a1, b1, c1, d1, e1
G. a4, b2, c1, d1, e1
H a1, b1, c1, d1, e2
I. a3, b1, c1, d2, e1
J. a4, c1, d2, e1
K. a1, b2, c1, d1, e1
L. a3, b1, c1, d1, e1
M. a1, b1, c1, d2, e1
N. a2, b1, c1, d1, e3
O. a4, b1, c2, d1, e1
P. a1, b1, c1, d3, e1
Q. a2, b1, c1, d1, e2

R. a1, b2, c2, d1, e1
S. a4, b1, c1, d1, e1

For example, question I combines elements a3, b1, c1, d2, and e1:

A company has higher productivity due to the employees' suggestions. Thus, the company is laying off some high-technology engineers. These workers are specialists in this company's unusual technology, with an average of ten years' tenure at this employer. Before the layoff, the employer gave each employee four paid weeks to find another job elsewhere in the company. Those who could not find a new position received severance pay based on age and years of service. The company provided out-placement service including counseling and resume-writing workshops. Employees knew layoffs were likely in this circumstance.

Questions A, B, C, H, N, O, Q, and R were asked only in Silicon Valley.

Appendix I

Complete Results of Layoff Questions

The number of respondents who gave each response for perceived fairness of the scenario. C = completely fair (i.e., a value of 3 in calculations presented in the text); A = acceptable (2); U = slightly unfair (1); and V = very unfair (0).

	Canada					Silicon Valley				
	C	A	U	V	mean	C	A	U	V	mean
A. Demand shock, professionals, general skills, harsh layoffs						8	34	64	31	1.14
B. Project end, production, general skills, harsh layoffs						15	49	50	19	1.45
C. Demand shock, professionals, special skills, harsh layoffs, CEO refused bonus						11	49	40	21	1.41
D. New technology, professionals, special skills harsh layoffs	2	26	56	39	0.93	8	21	55	34	1.03
E. New technology, professionals, special skills, gentle layoffs	50	49	15	3	2.25	67	53	10	8	2.30
F. Demand shock, professionals, special skills, harsh layoffs	5	27	59	48	0.92	5	22	58	35	0.98
G. Project end, production, special skills harsh layoffs	8	32	42	27	1.19	9	33	55	26	1.20
H. Demand shock, professionals, special skills, harsh layoffs CEO record bonus						9	25	43	57	0.90
I. Employees' suggestions, professionals, special skills, gentle layoffs	45	35	23	8	2.05	32	69	17	20	1.82
J. Project end, professionals, special skills, gentle layoffs	61	44	3	1	2.51	36	64	19	16	1.89
K. Demand shock, production, special skills, harsh layoffs	4	30	55	30	1.07	7	32	73	25	1.15
L. Employees' suggestions, professionals, special skills, harsh layoffs	1	11	53	48	0.69	14	20	53	53	0.96

(continued)

	Canada					Silicon Valley				
	C	A	U	V	mean	C	A	U	V	mean
M. Demand shock, professionals, special skills, gentle layoffs	77	50	3	1	2.55	62	40	16	15	2.12
N. New technology, professionals, special skills, harsh layoffs, CEO refused bonus						25	34	51	16	1.54
O. Project end, professionals, general skills, harsh layoffs						17	60	39	19	1.56
P. Demand shock, professionals, special skills, hoard labor	16	8	0	0	2.67	40	65	27	6	2.01
Q. New technology, professionals, special skills, harsh layoffs, CEO record bonus						19	19	31	69	0.91
R. Demand shock, production, general skills, harsh layoffs						22	30	33	50	1.18
S. Project end, professionals, special skills, harsh layoffs	6	25	37	39	0.98	21	29	49	38	1.24

Reference List

Aaronson, Daniel, and Daniel Sullivan. 1998. "Recent Trends in Job Displacement." *Chicago Fed Letter* 136: 1–4.

Abowd, John A., and Thomas Lemieux. 1993. "The Effects of Product Market Competition on Collective Bargaining Agreements: The Case of Foreign Competition in Canada." *Quarterly Journal of Economics* 108: 983–1014.

Abowd, John M., Francis Kramarz, and David N. Margolis. 1999. "High Wage Workers and High Wage Firms." *Econometrica* 67(2): 251–333.

Academy of Management Executive. "Careers in the 21st Century." Special issue: November 1996.

Akerlof, George. 1982. "Labor Contracts as Partial Gift-Exchange." *Quarterly Journal of Economics* 97: 543–569.

_____. 1984. "Gift Exchange and Efficiency Wage Theory." *American Economic Review* 74(2): 79–83.

Akerlof, George, and Janet Yellen. 1990. "The Fair Wage-Effort Hypothesis and Unemployment." *Quarterly Journal of Economics* 105: 255–283.

Akerlof, George A., Andrew K. Rose, and Janet L. Yellen. 1988. "Job Switching and Job Satisfaction in the U.S. Labor Market." *Brookings Papers on Economic Activity* 2: 495–594.

Allen, Steven, Robert Clark, and Sylvester Schieber. 2000. "Has Job Security Vanished in Large Corporations?" In *On the Job: Is Long-Term Employment a Thing of the Past?* David Neumark, ed. New York: Russell Sage Foundation, pp. 196–226.

Allen, Timothy, Deena Freeman, Richard Reizenstein, and Joseph Rentz. 1995. "Just Another Transition? Examining Survivors' Attitudes over Time." *Academy of Management Journal: Best Papers Proceedings*, pp. 78–82.

Annable, James. 1997. Quoted in *The Wall St. Journal*, "Insecure Executives Make the Economy Grow." April 28.

Aoki, Masahiko. 1988. *Information, Incentives, and Bargaining in the Japanese Economy*. Cambridge, New York, and Melbourne: Cambridge University Press.

Atrostic, B.K. 1983. "Alternative Pay Measures and Labor Market Differentials." Working paper no. 127, U.S. Department of Labor Office of Research and Evaluation, Bureau of Labor Statistics, March.

Baily, Martin Neil. 1974. "Wages and Employment under Uncertain Demand." *Review of Economic Studies* 41: 37–50.

Baker, George, and Bengt Holmstrom. 1995. "Too Many Theories, Too Few Facts." *American Economic Review* 85: 255–259.

Baker, George, Michael Gibbs, and Bengt Holmstrom. 1994. "The Wage Policy of a Firm." *Quarterly Journal of Economics* 109(4): 921–955.

Barnard, Chester Irving. 1962. *The Functions of the Executive.* Cambridge, Massachusetts: Harvard University Press (originally published 1938).

Batt, Rosemary. 1996. "From Bureaucracy to Enterprise? The Changing Jobs and Careers of Managers in Telecommunications Services." In *Broken Ladders: Managerial Careers in Transition*, Paul Osterman, ed. New York: Oxford University Press.

Beaudry, Paul, and John DiNardo. 1991. "The Effect of Implicit Contracts on the Movement of Wages over the Business Cycle: Evidence from Micro Data." *Journal of Political Economy* 99(4): 665–688.

Becker, Gary. 1975. *Human Capital.* 2nd ed. Chicago: University of Chicago Press.

Becker, Gary, and George Stigler. 1974. "Law Enforcement, Malfeasance, and the Compensation of Enforcers." *Journal of Legal Studies* 3(1): 1–13.

Belcher, D.W., N. Bruce Ferris, and John O'Neill. 1985. "How Wage Surveys Are Being Used." *Compensation and Benefits Review* 17(Sept./Oct.): 34–51.

Bellak, Alvin O. 1984. "Specific Job Evaluation Systems: The Hay Guide Chart-Profile Method." In *The Handbook of Wage and Salary Administration*, Milton Rock, ed. New York: McGraw-Hill.

Belman, Dale, and Erica L. Groshen. 1998. "Is Small Beautiful for Workers?" In *Small Consolation: The Dubious Benefits of Small Business for Job Growth and Wages*, Dale Belman, Erica L. Groshen, Julia Lane, and David Stevens, eds. Washington, D.C.: Economic Policy Institute, pp. 5–57.

Belman, Dale, and David I. Levine. 2001. "Have Internal Labor Market Wage Structures Declined in Large Employers?" Photocopy, University of California, Berkeley.

Belous, Richard S. 1989. "How Human Resource Systems Adjust to the Shift toward Contingent Workers." *Monthly Labor Review* 112: 7–12.

Belzer, Michael H. 1995. "Collective Bargaining after Deregulation: Do the Teamsters Still Count?" *Industrial and Labor Relations Review* 48: 636–655.

Bertrand, Marianne. 1999. "From the Invisible Handshake to the Invisible Hand? How Product Market Competition Changes the Employment Relationship." Working paper no. 6900, National Bureau of Economic Research, Cambridge, Massachusetts.

Bies, Robert J., Thomas M. Tripp, and Margaret A. Neale. 1993. "Procedural Fairness and Profit-Seeking: The Perceived Legitimacy of Market Exploitation." *Journal of Behavioral Decision Making* 6(4): 243–256.

Bishop, Elizabeth, and David I. Levine. 1998. "Computer Mediated Communication as Employee Voice: A Case Study." *Industrial and Labor Relations Review* 52(2): 213–233.

Blackburn, McKinley, and David Neumark. 1992. "Unobserved Ability, Efficiency Wages, and Interindustry Wage Differentials." *Quarterly Journal of Economics* 107(4): 1421–1436.

Blanchflower, David G, Andrew J. Oswald, and Peter Sanfey. 1996. "Wages, Profits, and Rent-Sharing." *Quarterly Journal of Economics* 111: 227–251.

Blasi, Joseph, and Douglas Kruse. 1991. *The New Owners: The Mass Emergence of Employee Ownership in Public Companies and What It Means to American Business.* New York: Harper Collins.

Blau, Francine D., and Lawrence M. Kahn. 1997. "Swimming Upstream: Trends in the Gender Wage Differential in the 1980s." *Journal of Labor Economics* 15: 1–42.

Blau, Peter M. 1964. *Exchange and Power in Social Life.* New York: John Wiley.

Block, Richard H., and David Lagasse. 1997. "Making a Bonus Plan Work for You." *HR Magazine* 42: 126–129.

Boisjoly, Johanne, Greg J. Duncan, and Timothy Smeeding. 1998. "The Shifting Incidence of Involuntary Job Losses from 1968 to 1992." *Industrial Relations* 37(2): 207–231.

Bolton, Gary, and Axel Ockenfels. 2000. "ERC: A Theory of Equity, Reciprocity, and Competition." *American Economic Review* 90(1): 166–193.

Brockner, Joel. 1992. "Managing the Effects of Layoffs on Survivors." *California Management Review* 35(2): 9–28.

Brockner, Joel, Mary Konovsky, Rochelle Cooper-Schneider, Robert Folger, Christopher Martin, and Robert J. Bies. 1994. "Interactive Effects of Procedural Justice and Outcome Negativity on Victims and Survivors of Job Loss." *Academy of Management Journal* 37(2): 397–409.

Brown, Charles. 1980. "Equalizing Differences in Labor Markets." *Quarterly Journal of Economics* 94(1): 113–134.

Brown, Charles, and James Medoff. 1989. "The Employer Size-Wage Effect." *Journal of Political Economy* 97(5): 1027–1059.

Brown, Clair, Michael Reich, Lloyd Ulman, and Yoshifumi Nakata. 1997. *Work and Pay in the United States and Japan.* New York: Oxford University Press.

Cameron, Stephen, and Joseph Tracy. 1998. "Earnings Variability in the United States: An Investigation Using Matched-CPS Data." Photocopy, Federal Reserve Bank of New York, April.

Campbell, Carl, and Kunal Kamlani. 1997. "The Reasons for Wage Rigidity: Evidence from a Survey of Firms." *Quarterly Journal of Economics* 112(3): 759–789.

Cappelli, Peter. 1993. "Are Skill Requirements Rising? Evidence for Production and Clerical Workers." *Industrial and Labor Relations Review* 46(3): 515–530.

_____. 1995. "Rethinking Employment." *British Journal of Industrial Relations* 33: 563–602.

_____. 1999. *The New Deal at Work: Managing the Market-Driven Workforce.* Boston, Massachusetts: Harvard Business School Press.

Cappelli, Peter, and Keith Chauvin. 1991. "A Test of an Efficiency Model of Grievance Activity." *Industrial and Labor Relations Review* 45(1): 3–14.

Cappelli, Peter, and K.C. O'Shaughnessy. 1995. "Changes in Skill and Wage Structures in Corporate Headquarters, 1986–1992." Philadelphia: National Center on the Educational Quality of the Workforce (EQW).

Cappelli, Peter, Laurie Bassi, Harry Katz, David Knoke, Paul Osterman, and Michael Useem. 1997. *Change at Work.* New York: Oxford University.

Card, David. 1996. "Deregulation and Labor Earnings in the Airline Industry." Working paper no. 5687, National Bureau of Economic Research, Cambridge, Massachusetts.

Card, David, and Richard B. Freeman, eds. 1993. *Small Differences That Matter: Labor Markets and Income Maintenance in Canada and the United States.* Chicago: University of Chicago Press.

Carruth, Alan, and Andrew Oswald. 1989. *Pay Determination and Industrial Prosperity.* Oxford: Clarendon Press.

Cashman, Kevin, and Janet Feldman. 1995. "Reengineering the Employment Contract." *Executive Excellence* 12(2): 15–16.

Charness, Gary B. 1998. "Attribution and Reciprocity in a Simulated Labor Market: An Experimental Investigation." Working paper no. 283, Universitat Pompeu Fabra, Barcelona.

Charness, Gary, and David I. Levine. 2000. "When Are Layoffs Acceptable? Evidence from a Quasi-Experiment." *Industrial and Labor Relations Review* 53(3): 381–400.

_____. Forthcoming. "Changes in The Employment Contract." *Journal of Economic Behavior and Organization.*

Charness, Gary, and Matthew Rabin. 1999. "Social Preferences: Some Simple Tests and a Model." Photocopy, University of California, Berkeley.

Coase, Ronald. 1937. "The Nature of the Firm." *Econometrica* 4: 386–405.

Cowherd, Douglas, and David I. Levine. 1992. "Product Quality and Pay Equity between Low-Level Employees and Top Management: An Investigation of Distributive Justice Theory." *Administrative Science Quarterly* 37(2): 302–320.

Davis, Stephen J., John C. Haltiwanger, and Scott Schuh. 1996. *Job Creation and Destruction*. Cambridge, Massachusetts: MIT Press.

Davis, Steve J., and John Haltiwanger. 1991. "Wage Dispersion between and within U.S. Manufacturing Plants: 1963–86." *Brookings Papers on Economic Activity, Microeconomics* 115–200.

Dial, Jay, and Kevin J. Murphy. 1995. "Incentives, Downsizing, and Value Creation at General Dynamics." *Journal of Financial Economics* 37(3): 261–314.

Dickens, William. 1986. "Wages, Employment, and the Threat of Collective Action by Workers." Working paper no. 1856, National Bureau of Economic Research, Cambridge, Massachusetts, March.

Dickens, William, and Lawrence Katz. 1987. "Inter-Industry Wage Differences and Industry Characteristics." In *Unemployment and the Structure of Labor Markets*, Kevin Lang and Jonathan Leonard, eds. New York: Basil-Blackwell.

Dickens, William T., and Kevin Lang. 1985. "A Test of Dual Labor Market Theory?" *American Economic Review* 75(4): 792–805.

Diebold, Francis X., David Neumark, and Daniel Polsky. 1997. "Job Stability in the United States." *Journal of Labor Economics* 15(2): 206–233.

Doeringer, Peter B., and Michael Piore. 1971. *Internal Labor Markets and Manpower Analysis*. Lexington, Massachusetts: Heath.

Dow, Gregory K. 1993. "Why Capital Hires Labor: A Bargaining Perspective." *American Economic Review* 83(1): 118–134.

Duffy, Jim. 1999. "Cisco Wants to Help Host Your Applications." *Network World* 16: 111.

Dunlop, John. 1957. "The Task of Contemporary Wage Theory." In *The Theory of Wage Determination*. London: Macmillan.

Economist, The. 1999. "Leaders: The Trouble with Stock Options." 352(Aug. 7): 13–14.

Farber, Henry. 1993. "The Incidence and Cost of Job Loss: 1982–91." *Brookings Papers on Economic Activity, Microeconomics*: 73–119.

Farber, Henry S. 1995. "Are Lifetime Jobs Disappearing? Job Duration in the United States: 1973–1993." Working paper no. 5014, National Bureau of Economic Research, Cambridge, Massachusetts.

Farber, Henry S., John Haltiwanger, and Katherine G. Abraham. 1997. "The Changing Face of Job Loss in the United States, 1981–1995." *Brookings Papers on Economic Activity, Microeconomics*: 55–142.

Farh, Jiing-Lih, Philip M. Podsakoff, and Dennis W. Organ. 1990. "Accounting for Organizational Citizenship Behavior: Leader Fairness and Task Scope versus Satisfaction." *Journal of Management* 16(4): 705–721.

Feenstra, Robert. 1996. "NBER Trade Database, Disk 1: U.S. Imports, 1972–1994." Working paper no. 5515, National Bureau of Economic Research, Cambridge, Massachusetts.

Fehr, Ernst, and Klaus Schmidt. 1999. "A Theory of Fairness, Competition, and Cooperation." *Quarterly Journal of Economics* 114(3): 817–868.

Fehr, Ernst, Georg Kirchsteiger, and Arno Riedl. 1993. "Does Fairness Prevent Market Clearing? An Experimental Investigation." *Quarterly Journal of Economics* 108: 437–459.

Fehr, Ernst, Erich Kirchler, Andreas Weichbold, and Simon Gachter. 1998. "When Social Forces Overpower Competition: Gift-Exchange in Experimental Labor Markets." *Journal of Labor Economics* 16: 437–459.

Fortin, Nicole M., and Thomas Lemieux. 1997. "Institutional Change and Wage Inequality." *Journal of Economic Perspectives* 11: 75–96.

Foulkes, Fred. 1980. *Personnel Policies in Large Nonunion Companies.* Englewood Cliffs, New Jersey: Prentice Hall.

Freeman, Richard. 1980. "The Exit Voice Tradeoff in the Labor Market: Unionism, Job Tenure, Quits and Separations." *Quarterly Journal of Economics* 93(3): 643–672.

Frey, Bruno S., and Werner W. Pommerehne. 1993. "On the Fairness of Pricing—An Empirical Survey among the General Population." *Journal of Economic Behavior and Organization* 20(3): 295–307.

Gardner, Jennifer M. 1995. "Worker Displacement: A Decade of Change." *Monthly Labor Review* 118: 45–57.

Gibbs, Michael, and Wallace Hendricks. 1995. "Are Administrative Pay Systems a Veil? Evidence from within-Firm Data." Photocopy, University of Chicago.

Gilles, Paul L. 1999. "Alternatives for Stock Options." *HR Magazine* 44(1): 40–48.

Gorman, Raymond, and James B. Kehr. 1992. "Fairness as a Constraint on Profit-Seeking: Comment." *American Economic Review* 82(1): 355–358.

Gottschalk, Peter, and Robert Moffitt. 1994. "The Growth of Earnings Instability in the U.S. Labor Market." *Brookings Papers on Economic Activity* 2: 217–272.

Gouldner, Alvin. 1954. *Patterns of Industrial Bureaucracy.* New York: Free Press.

Greenberg, Eric Rolfe. 1992. "Upswing in Downsizings to Continue." *Management Review* 62(2): 5.

Greenberg, Eric Rolfe. 1998. "Downsizing and the Career Path." *HR Focus* 75: 2.

Groshen, Erica L. 1989. "Do Wage Differences among Employers Last?" Working paper no. 8906, Federal Reserve Bank of Cleveland, revised 1991.

_____. 1990. "Ability to Pay, Rent Capture, and Salaries in the Private Sector." In *Proceedings of the Fortieth Annual IRRA Meeting*, Madison, Wisconsin: Industrial Relations Research Association.

_____. 1991a. "Five Reasons Why Wages Vary among Employers." *Industrial Relations* 30(3): 50–381.

_____. 1991b. "Rising Inequality in a Salary Survey: Another Piece of the Puzzle." Working paper no. 9121, Federal Reserve Bank of Cleveland.

_____. 1991c. "Sources of Intra-Industry Wage Dispersion: How Much Do Employers Matter?" *Quarterly Journal of Economics* 106(4): 869–884.

_____. 1996. "American Employer Salary Surveys and Labor Economics Research: Issues and Contributions." *Annales d'Economie et de Statistique* 41/42: 413–442.

Groshen, Erica, and David I. Levine. 1998. "The Rise and Decline(?) of U.S. Internal Labor Markets." Research paper no. 9819, Federal Reserve Bank of New York, July; revised March 1999.

Groshen, Erica L., and Mark E. Schweitzer. 1996. *The Effects of Inflation on Wage Adjustments in Firm-Level Data: Grease or Sand?* Federal Reserve Bank of New York staff report.

Gustman, Alan, and Thomas Steinmeier. 1995. *Pension Incentives and Job Mobility*. Kalamazoo Michigan: The W.E. Upjohn Institute for Employment Research.

Hackett, Brian. 1996. *The New Deal in Employment Relationships*. Conference Board publication 1162, August.

Hackman, J. Richard, and Greg Oldham. 1980. *Work Redesign*. Reading, Massachusetts: Addison-Wesley.

Haisken-DeNew, John P., and Christoph M. Schmidt. 1997. "Interindustry and Interregion Differentials: Mechanics and Interpretation." *Review of Economics and Statistics* 79(3): 516–521.

Hall, Brian J., and Jeffrey B. Liebman. 1998. "Are CEOs Really Paid Like Bureaucrats?" *Quarterly Journal of Economics* 113(3): 653–691.

Haltiwanger, John, Julia Lane, and James Spletzer. 2000. "Wages, Productivity, and the Dynamic Interaction of Businesses and Workers." Working paper no. 7994, National Bureau of Economic Research, Cambridge, Massachusetts, November.

Hansen, Fay. 1998. "Currents in Compensation and Benefits." *Compensation and Benefits Review* 30: 6–13.

Hay Group (no date). "The Hay Guide Chart-Profile Method of Position Evaluation." New York.

Hellerstein, Judith K., David Neumark, and Kenneth R. Troske. 1999. "Wages, Productivity, and Worker Characteristics: Evidence from Plant-

Level Production Functions and Wage Equations." *Journal of Labor Economics* 17(3): 409–446.

Helper, Susan, David I. Levine, and Elliot Bendoly. Forthcoming. "Employee Involvement and Pay at U.S. and Canadian Auto Suppliers." *Journal of Economics, Management, and Strategy.*

Holzer, Harry. 1998. "Why Do Small Establishments Hire Fewer Black Employees?" *Journal of Human Resources* 33(4): 896–914.

Ichniowski, Casey, Thomas A. Kochan, David Levine, Craig Olson, and George Strauss. 1996. "What Works at Work: Overview and Assessment." *Industrial Relations* 35(3): 299–333.

Idson, Todd L., and Walter Y. Oi. 1999. "Firm Size and Wages." In *Handbook of Labor Economics,* Orley Ashenfelter and David Card, eds. Amsterdam: Elsevier.

Investor Relations Business. 1999. "Finding the Sweet Spot on Employee Stock Options." February 15: 1, 12.

IRS Employment Review. 1996. "Broadbanding Gains in Popularity." November (620): ET7.

———. 1997. "Growth in Job Evaluation Schemes." January (624): ET7.

Jacoby, Sanford M. 1999. "Are Career Jobs Headed for Extinction?" *California Management Review* 42(1): 123–145.

Jaeger, David A., and Ann Huff Stevens. 1999. "Is Job Stability in the United States Falling? Reconciling Trends in the Current Population Survey and Panel Study of Income Dynamics." *Journal of Labor Economics* 17(4, Part 2): S1–S28.

Juhn, Chinhui, Kevin M. Murphy, and Brooks Pierce. 1993. "Wage Inequality and the Rise in the Returns to Skill." *Journal of Political Economy* 101(3): 410–442.

Kahneman, Daniel, Jack Knetsch, and Richard Thaler. 1986. "Fairness as a Constraint on Profit-Seeking: Entitlements in the Market." *American Economic Review* 76: 728–741.

Kalleberg, Arne, and James Lincoln. 1988. "The Structure of Earnings Inequality in the United States and Japan." *American Journal of Sociology* 94(Supplement): S121–S153.

Kanter, Rosabeth Moss. 1987. "From Status to Contribution: Some Organizational Implications of the Changing Basis for Pay." *Personnel* 64: 12–37.

Katz, Lawrence. 1987. "Efficiency Wage Theories: A Partial Evaluation." In *NBER Macroeconomics Annual*, S. Fischer, ed. Cambridge, Massachusetts: MIT Press.

Katz, Lawrence F., and Alan Krueger. 1991. "Changes in the Structure of Wages in the Public and Private Sectors." *Journal of Labor Economics* 15(2): 206–233.

Kerr, Clark. 1954. *Labor Markets and Wage Determination: The Balkanization of Labor Markets and Other Essays.* Berkeley: University of California Press, pp. 21–37 ("The Balkanization of Labor Markets" was originally published in 1954).

Kiechel, Walter III. 1987. "Your New Employment Contract." *Fortune* 116: 109–110.

Killingsworth, Mark. 1990. *The Economics of Comparable Worth.* Kalamazoo, Michigan: W.E. Upjohn Institute for Employment Research.

Konovsky, Mary A., and S. Douglas Pugh. 1994. "Citizenship Behavior and Social Exchange." *Academy of Management Journal* 37: 656–669.

Kremer, Michael, and Eric Maskin. 1995. "Wage Inequality and Segregation by Skill." Working paper no. 5718, National Bureau of Economic Research, Cambridge, Massachusetts.

Krueger, Alan B., and Lawrence Summers. 1988. "Efficiency Wages and the Inter-Industry Wage Structure." *Econometrica* 56(2): 259–293.

Kruse, Douglas. 1992. "Supervision, Working Conditions, and the Employer Size-Wage Effect." *Industrial Relations* 31(2): 229–249.

Kruse, Douglas, and Joseph Blasi. 1998. "The New Employee/Employer Relationship." Prepared for the Aspen Institute's Domestic Strategy Group, Washington, D.C., August.

Labich, Kenneth. 1992. "The New Pay Game . . . and How You Measure Up." *Fortune* 126(8): 116–119.

Lawler, Edward E., Susan Mohrman, and Gerald Ledford. 1995. *Creating High-Performance Organizations.* San Francisco: Jossey-Bass.

_____. 1998. *Strategies for High-Performance Organizations.* San Francisco: Jossey-Bass.

Lawrence, Colin, and Robert Z. Lawrence. 1985. "Manufacturing Wage Dispersion: An End Game Interpretation." *Brookings Papers on Economic Activity* 1: 47–116.

Lazear, Edward. 1981. "Agency, Earnings Profiles, Productivity, and Hours Restrictions." *American Economic Review* 71: 606–620.

_____. 1992. "Agency, Earnings Profiles, Productivity, and Hours Restrictions." In *The Economic Value of Education: Studies in the Economics of Education*, Mark Blaug, ed. International Library of Critical Writings in Economics, vol. 17. Aldershot, U.K.: Elgar, pp. 226–240.

_____. 1995. "A Jobs-Based Analysis of Labor Markets." *American Economic Review* 85(2): 260–265.

Lazear, Edward, and Sherwin Rosen. 1981. "Rank-Order Tournaments as Optimum Labor Contracts." *Journal of Political Economy* 89: 841–864.

LeBlanc, Peter, and Paul Mulvey. 1998. "How American Workers See the Rewards of Work." *Compensation and Benefits Review* 30: 24–28.

Lee, Chris. 1987. "The New Employment Contract." *Training* 24(12): 45–56.

Leonard, Jonathan S. 1987. "Carrots and Sticks: Pay, Supervision and Turnover." *Journal of Labor Economics* 5: S136–S152.

_____. 1989. "Wage Structure and Dynamics in the Electronics Industry." *Industrial Relations* 28: 251–275.

_____. 1996. "Wage Disparities and Affirmative Action in the 1980s." *American Economic Review* 86(2): 285–289.

Lester, Richard A. 1948. *Company Wage Policies: A Survey of Patterns and Experience*. Princeton, New Jersey: Princeton University Press.

Leventhal, Gerald S. 1976. "The Distribution of Rewards and Resources in Groups and Organizations." In *Advances in Experimental Social Psychology*, L. Berkowitz and E. Walster, eds. New York: Academic Press, pp. 91–131.

Levine, David I. 1991a. "Job Characteristics and Wage Anomalies." Working paper OB/IR-56, Haas School of Business, University of California, Berkeley.

_____. 1991b. "Cohesiveness, Productivity, and Wage Dispersion." *Journal of Economic Behavior and Organization* 15: 237–255.

_____. 1992. "Can Wage Increases Pay for Themselves? Tests with a Production Function." *Economic Journal* 102: 1102–1115.

_____. 1993a. "What Do Wages Buy?" *Administrative Science Quarterly* 38(3): 462–483.

_____. 1993b. "Fairness, Markets, and Ability to Pay: Evidence from Compensation Executives." *American Economic Review* 83(5): 1241–1259.

_____. 1995. *Reinventing the Workplace*. Washington, D.C.: Brookings Institution.

_____. 1998. *Working in the Twenty-First Century*. Armonk, New York: M.E. Sharpe.

Levine, David I., and K.C. O'Shaughnessy. 1999. "The Ever-Increasing(?) Pace of Change." Photocopy, University of California, Berkeley.

Levine, David I., and Katherine Shaw. 2000. "The Quality of Incentives and the Incentives of Quality." In *The Quality Movement in America: Lessons for Theory and Research*, Robert Cole and Richard Scott, eds. New York: Russell Sage Foundation, pp. 367–386.

Lichty, D. Terrence. 1991. "Compensation Surveys." In *The Compensation Handbook,* 3rd ed., Milton L. Rock and Lance A. Berger, eds. New York: McGraw-Hill.

Lincoln, James, and Arne Kalleberg. 1990. *Culture, Control and Commitment.* New York: Cambridge University Press.

Lind, E. Allan, and Tom R. Tyler. 1988. *The Social Psychology of Procedural Justice*. New York: Plenum Press.

Lindbeck, Assar, and Dennis Snower. 1986. "Wage Setting, Unemployment and Insider-Outsider Relations." *American Economic Review* 76(2): 235–239.

_____. 1996. "Reorganization of Firms and Labor Market Inequality." *American Economic Review* 86(2): 315–321.

Lipset, Seymour Martin. 1990. *Continental Divide: The Values and Institutions of the United States and Canada*. New York: Routledge.

Lissy, William E., and Marlene L. Morgenstern. 1995. "Broadbanding Proves to Be Popular and Effective." *Compensation and Benefits Review* 27(3): 12.

Livernash, E. Robert. 1957. "The Internal Wage Structure." In *New Concepts in Wage Determination*, George Taylor and Frank Pierson, eds. New York: McGraw-Hill.

Luthans, Brett, and Steven Sommer. 1999. "The Impact of Downsizing on Workplace Attitudes." *Group and Organization Management* 24: 46–70.

MacKenzie, G.B., P.M. Podsakoff, and R. Fetter. 1991. "Organizational Citizenship Behavior and Objective Productivity as Determinants of Managerial Evaluations of Salespersons' Performance." *Organizational Behavior and Human Decision Processes* 50: 123–150.

Malcomson, James M. 1997. "Contracts, Hold-Up, and Labor Markets." *Journal of Economic Literature* 35(4): 1916–1957.

Manicatide, Mircea, and Virginia Pennell. 1992. "Key Developments in Compensation Management." *HR Focus* 69: 3–4.

Marginson, Paul, and Stephen Wood. 2000. "WERS98 Special Issue: Editors' Introduction." *British Journal of Industrial Relations* 38(4): 489–496.

Marglin, Steven. 1974. "What Do Bosses Do?" *Review of Radical Political Economy* 6(2): 33–60.

Martin, Justin. 1998. "Quieting the Concerns of Nervous Workers." *Fortune* (Oct 12): 191–192.

Medoff, James. 1993. *Middle-Aged and Out of Work: Growing Unemployment Due to Job Loss among Middle-Aged Americans*. Washington, D.C: National Study Center.

Milgrom, Paul R., and John Roberts. 1990. "Bargaining Costs, Influence Costs, and the Organization of Economic Activity." In *Perspectives on Positive Political Economy*, James E. Alt and Kenneth A. Shepsle, eds. New York: Cambridge University Press.

Milgrom, Paul, and John Roberts. 1992. *Economics, Organization, and Management*. New Jersey: Prentice Hall.

Moorman, Robert H. 1991. "Relationship between Organizational Justice and Organizational Citizenship Behaviors: Do Fairness Perceptions Influence Employee Citizenship?" *Journal of Applied Psychology* 76(6): 845–855.

Nalbantian, Haig R., and Andrew Schotter. 1997. "Productivity under Group Incentives: An Experimental Study." *The American Economic Review* 87(3): 314–341.

National Crosswalk Service Center. 1988. "General Description of Version 3 of the NOICC (National Occupational Information Coordinating Committee) Master Crosswalk Data Base." Iowa State Occupational Information Coordinating Committee, Des Moines, Iowa, May.

Neumark, David. 2000. *On the Job: Is Long-Term Employment a Thing of the Past?* New York: Russell Sage Foundation.

Neumark, David, Daniel Polsky, and Daniel Hansen. 2000. "Has Job Stability Declined Yet? New Evidence for the 1990s." In *On the Job: Is Long-Term Employment a Thing of the Past?* David Neumark, ed. New York: Russell Sage Foundation, pp. 70–110.

O'Dell, Carla, and Jerry McAdams. 1987. "The Revolution in Employee Rewards." *Management Review* 76: 30–33.

Organ, D.W. 1988. *Organizational Citizenship Behavior: The Good Soldier Syndrome*. Lexington, Massachusetts: D.C. Heath.

O'Shaughnessy, K.C., David I. Levine, and Peter Cappelli. 2001. "Changes in Managerial Pay Structures, 1986–1992 and Rising Returns to Skill." *Oxford Economic Papers* 53(3): 482–507.

Osterman Paul, ed. 1984. *Internal Labor Markets*. Cambridge, Massachusetts: MIT Press.

Osterman, Paul. 1994. "Supervision, Discretion, and Work Organization." *American Economic Review* 84: 380–384.

_____. 1995. "Skill, Training, and Work Organization in American Establishments." *Industrial Relations* 34: 125–146.

Parker, Mike. 1985. *Inside the Circle: A Union Guide to QWL*. Boston: South End Press.

Pfeffer, Jeffrey, and Yinon Cohen. 1984. "Determinants of Internal Labor Markets in Organizations." *Administrative Science Quarterly* 38(3): 382–407.

Pierce, Brooks. 1998. "Compensation Inequality." Photocopy, U.S. Bureau of Labor Statistics, April.

Podsakoff, Philip M., Michael Ahearne, and Scott B. MacKenzie. 1997. "Organizational Citizenship Behavior and the Quantity and Quality of Work Group Performance." *Journal of Applied Psychology* 82(2): 262–270.

Poe, Randall, and Carol Lee Courter. 1995. "Broadbanding . . . " *Across the Board* 31: 5–6.

Polsky, Daniel. 1998. "Change Consequences of Job Separation in the United States." *Industrial and Labor Relations Review* 52: 565–581.

Rabin, Matthew. 1993. "Incorporating Fairness into Game Theory and Economics." *American Economic Review* 83(5): 1281–1302.

Reinemer, Michael. 1995. "Work Happy." *American Demographics* 17: 26–30.

Reynolds, Lloyd G. 1951. *The Structure of Labor Markets*. New York: Harper and Brothers.

Rock, Robert H. 1998. "Hidden Costs of Stock Options." *Directors & Boards* 22(3): 4.

Rose, Stephen J. 1995. "Broken Promises: The Decline of Employment Stability in the 1980s." National Commission for Employment Policy Research, Washington, D.C., April.

Roth, Alvin E., Vesna Prasnikar, Masahiro Okuno-Fujiwara, and Shmuel Zamir. 1991. "Bargaining and Market Behavior in Jerusalem, Ljubljana, Pittsburgh, and Tokyo: An Experimental Study." *American Economic Review* 81(5): 1068–1095.

Rousseau, Denise M. 1995. *Psychological Contracts in Organizations: Understanding Written and Unwritten Agreements*. Thousand Oaks, California: Sage Publications.

Rousseau, Denise M., and R.J. Anton. 1988. "Fairness and Implied Contract Obligations in Job Terminations: A Policy-Capturing Study." *Human Performance* 1: 273–289.

_____. 1991. "Fairness and Implied Contract Obligations in Job Terminations: The Role of Contributions, Promises and Performance." *Journal of Organizational Behavior* 12: 287–299.

Salop, Joanne, and Steven Salop. 1976. "Self-Selection and Turnover in the Labor Market." *Quarterly Journal of Economics* 90: 619–627.

Sculley, John. 1987. *Odyssey: Pepsi to Apple*. New York: Harper and Rowe.

Segal, Lewis, and Daniel Sullivan. 1995. "The Temporary Labor Force." *Economic Perspectives* (Federal Reserve Bank of Chicago), 19: 2–19.

_____. 1997. "Temporary Services Employment Durations: Evidence from State UI Data." Working paper, Federal Reserve Bank of Chicago.

Shapiro, Carl, and Joseph Stiglitz. 1984. "Equilibrium Unemployment as a Worker Discipline Device." *American Economic Review* 74(3): 433–444.

Shore, Lynn McFarlane, and Lois E. Tetrick. 1994. "The Psychological Contract as an Explanatory Framework in the Employment Relation." In *Trends in Organizational Behavior*, Vol. 1, C.L. Cooper and D.M. Rousseau, eds. New York: John Wiley.

Siegel, Sidney, and N. John Castellan. 1988. *Nonparametric Statistics for the Behavioral Sciences*. New York: McGraw-Hill.

Simon, Herbert A. 1991. "Organizations and Markets." *Journal of Economic Perspectives* (Spring): 25–44.

Smith, Robert, and Ronald Ehrenberg. 1981. "Estimating Wage/Fringe Tradeoffs: Some Data Problems." Working paper no. 827, National Bureau of Economic Review, Cambridge, Massachusetts.

Snower, Dennis. 1998. "Causes of Changing Earnings Inequality." In *Income Inequality: Issues and Policy Options*, Federal Reserve Bank of Kansas City, pp. 69–134.

Stata. 1995. *Reference Manual: Release 4.0.* College Station, Texas: Stata Press.

Steel, Robert, and Joan Rentsch. 1997. "The Dispositional Model of Job Attitudes Revisited: Findings of a 10-Year Study." *Journal of Applied Psychology* 82: 873–879.

Stiles, Philip, Lynda Gratton, Catherine Truss, Veronica Hope-Hailey, and Patrick McGovern. 1997. "Performance Management and the Psychological Contract." *Human Resource Management Journal* 7: 57–66.

Summers, Timothy P., and William H. Hendrix. 1991. "Modeling the Role of Pay Equity Perceptions: A Field Study." *Journal of Occupational Psychology* 64: 145–157.

Swinnerton, Kenneth, and Howard Wial. 1996. "Is Job Stability Declining in the U.S. Economy? Reply to Diebold, Neumark, and Polsky." *Industrial and Labor Relations Review* 49(2): 352–355.

Tversky, Amos, and Daniel Kahneman. 1986. "Rational Choice and the Framing of Decisions." *Journal of Business* 59(4): S251–S278.

U.S. Bureau of Labor Statistics. "Metropolitan Area Employment and Unemployment: November 1998." Washington, D.C., available at ftp://146.142.423/pub/news.release/History/metro.12301998.news.

Valletta, Robert G. 2000. "Declining Job Security." In *On the Job: Is Long-Term Employment a Thing of the Past?*, David Neumark, ed. New York: Russell Sage Foundation, pp. 227–256.

Wagner, Frank H., and Michael Jones. 1994. "Broadbanding in Practice: Hard Facts and Real Data." *Journal of Compensation and Benefits* 10(1): 27–34.

Williamson, Oliver E. 1975. *Markets and Hierarchies*. New York: Free Press.

Womack, J.P., D.T. Jones, and D. Roos. 1990. *The Machine that Changed the World*. New York and Oxford: Rawson MacMillan.

The Authors

David I. Levine is an associate professor at the Haas School of Business at the University of California, Berkeley. He is also editor of the journal *Industrial Relations* and Associate Director of the Institute of Industrial Relations. Levine's research focuses on the causes and effect of compensation and on why good management is relatively rare. His published books include *Reinventing the Workplace* (Brookings, 1995), *Working in the Twenty-First Century* (M.E. Sharpe, 1998), and the edited volume *The American Workplace: Skills, Pay and Employee Involvement* (Cambridge University Press, 1999). He has a forthcoming book, *Carve-Outs in Workers' Compensation* (W.E. Upjohn Institute). Levine has taught at the Haas School since receiving his Ph.D. in economics from Harvard University in 1987. He has also held visiting positions at the Sloan School of Management at MIT, the U.S. Department of Labor, and the Council of Economic Advisers.

After 15 years in the Economics Department at the University of Wisconsin Milwaukee, Dale Belman recently moved to the School of Labor and Industrial Relations at Michigan State University, where he is an Associate Professor. He is also a research associate at the Economic Policy Institute and Associate Director of the University of Michigan Trucking Industry Program. His publications include articles in *Review of Economics and Statistics*, *Industrial and Labor Relations Review*, and *Empirical Economics*.

Gary Charness is an assistant professor in the Economics Department at the University of California, Santa Barbara. He has a Ph.D. in economics from the University of California, Berkeley. His papers have been published in numerous journals, including the *Quarterly Journal of Economics*. His research generally examines social influences on economic decision-making, bringing in ideas from other social sciences such as psychology and sociology. He has experience as an options trader, an importer, a real estate broker, and an arbitrator.

Erica L. Groshen is an Assistant Vice President in the Domestic Research Function at the Federal Reserve Bank of New York. She conducts research in wage rigidity and dispersion and in the role of employers in the labor market. Prior to joining the Bank in 1994, Dr. Groshen taught economics at Barnard College, Columbia University. She has also worked as a labor and regional economist for the Federal Reserve Bank of Cleveland. Dr. Groshen's other experience includes research on federal welfare reform and job-training programs for Abt Associates, Inc. and MPR, Inc. Dr. Groshen earned master's and doctoral degrees in economics from Harvard University.

K.C. O'Shaughnessy is an Associate Professor of Management at Western Michigan University. He has a B.S. from the University of Arizona, MBA from Indiana University, and Ph.D. from the Wharton School of the University of Pennsylvania. His research spans the gap between strategic management and human resource management. One of his particular interests is the effect of compensation choices on organizational performance. He has published in *Strategic Management Journal* and *Relationes Industrielles*, among others.

Cited Author Index

The italic letters *f*, *n*, *t* following a page number indicate that the cited name is within a figure, note, or table respectively, on that page.

Aaronsen, Daniel, 49, 233
Abowd, John A., 36, 233
Abowd, John M., 27, 92, 94, 233
Abraham, Katherine G., 1, 46, 61*n*2, 237
Academy of Management Executive, 15, 16, 233
Ahearne, Michael, 14, 244
Akerlof, George A., 13, 21, 25, 31, 165, 233
Allen, Steven, 46, 233
Allen, Timothy, 50, 233
Annable, James, 17, 38, 233
Anton, R.J., 143, 245
Aoki, Masahiko, 58, 233
Atrostic, B.K., 200, 233

Baily, Martin Neil, 25, 233
Baker, George, 12, 50, 58, 233, 234
Barnard, Chester Irving, 13, 234
Bassi, Laurie, 236
Batt, Rosemary, 49, 57, 234
Beaudry, Paul, 12, 234
Becker, Gary, 25, 143, 234
Belcher, D.W., 199, 234
Bellak, Alvin O., 112, 234
Belman, Dale, 30, 70, 84*n*1, 183, 234
Belous, Richard S., 47, 234
Belzer, Michael H., 36, 234
Bendoly, Elliot, 36, 240
Bertrand, Marianne, 18, 25, 29, 33, 34, 163, 214, 234, 246
Bies, Robert J., 142, 234, 235
Bishop, Elizabeth, 128*n*4, 142, 235
Blackburn, McKinley, 26, 235
Blanchflower, David G., 34, 163, 235
Blasi, Joseph, 1, 24, 53, 58, 59, 60*n*1, 200, 235, 241
Blau, Francine D., 174, 235
Blau, Peter M., 13, 235

Block, Richard H., 52, 235
Boisjoly, Johanne, 46, 235
Bolton, Gary, 175, 235
Brockner, Joel, 140, 141, 143, 168, 235
Brooks, Pierce, 244
Brown, Charles, 30, 31, 205, 226, 235
Brown, Clair, 12, 57, 235
Business Wire, 48

Cameron, Stephen, 175, 235
Campbell, Carl, 56, 236
Cappelli, Peter, 1, 11, 16, 32, 41, 48, 57, 60*n*1, 128*n*1, 156, 215, 236, 244
Card, David, 24, 36, 236
Carruth, Alan, 25, 34, 163, 236
Cashman, Kevin, 1, 236
Castellan, N. John, 139, 246
Charness, Gary B., 14, 150*n*1, 175, 236
Chauvin, Keith, 32, 236
Clark, Robert, 46, 233
Coase, Ronald, 25, 236
Cohen, Yinon, 244
Cooper-Schneider, Rochelle, 235
Courter, Carol Lee, 52, 245
Cowherd, Douglas, 21, 142, 236

Davis, Stephen J., 28, 59, 67, 92, 161, 174, 237
Dial, Jay, 143, 237
Dickens, William T., 19, 32, 33, 237
Diebold, Francis X., 46, 237
DiNardo, John, 12, 234
Doeringer, Peter B., 2, 9, 10–11, 17, 18, 57, 58, 107, 156, 237
Dow, Gregory K., 33, 237
Duffy, Jim, 59, 237
Duncan, Greg J., 46, 235
Dunlop, John, 10, 237

Economist, The, 55, 237
Ehrenberg, Ronald, 215, 246
Executive Excellence, 1

Farber, Henry S., 1, 46, 51, 60, 61*n*2,
    143, 237
Farh, Jiing-Lih, 14, 237
Feenstra, Robert, 213, 238
Fehr, Ernst, 14, 175, 238
Feldman, Janet, 1, 236
Ferris, N. Bruce, 199, 234
Fetter, R., 14, 243
Folger, Robert, 235
Fortin, Nicole M., 36, 175, 211, 238
Fortune, 1
Foulkes, Fred, 1, 16, 18, 50, 238
Freeman, Deena, 233
Freeman, Richard B., 24, 31, 236, 238
Frey, Bruno S., 150*n*2, 238

Gachter, Simon, 238
Gardner, Jennifer M., 46, 238
Gibbs, Michael, 12, 50, 58, 215, 234,
    238
Gilles, Paul L., 55, 176, 238
Gorman, Raymond, 23, 150*n*2, 178, 238
Gottschalk, Peter, 41, 175, 238
Gouldner, Alvin, 13, 238
Gratton, Lynda, 246
Greenberg, Eric Rolfe, 49, 238
Groshen, Erica L., 25, 26, 32, 34, 85, 90,
    91, 92, 93, 94, 97, 98, 101, 105,
    108*n*1, 163, 166, 183, 205, 234, 238,
    239
Gustman, Alan, 56, 239

Hackett, Brian, 1, 15, 50, 239
Hackman, J. Richard, 226, 239
Haisken-DeNew, John P., 113, 239
Hall, Brian J., 218, 239
Haltiwanger, John C., 1, 28, 46, 59,
    61*n*2, 67, 92, 161, 174, 237, 239
Hansen, Daniel, 1, 46, 244
Hansen, Fay, 53, 166, 239

Hay Group, 215, 239
Hellerstein, Judith K., 177, 239
Helper, Susan, 36, 240
Hendricks, Wallace, 215, 238
Hendrix, William H., 246
Holmstrom, Bengt, 12, 50, 58, 233, 234
Holzer, Harry, 75, 155, 240
Hope-Hailey, Veronica, 246

Ichniowski, Casey, 35, 58, 240
Idson, Todd L., 69, 240
Investor Relations Business, 55, 240
IRS Employment Review, 52, 240

Jacoby, Sanford M., 45, 60*n*1, 240
Jaeger, David A., 46, 61*n*2, 240
Jones, D.T., 57, 246
Jones, Michael, 52, 246
Juhn, Chinhui, 161, 172, 240

Kahn, Lawrence M., 174, 235
Kahneman, Daniel, 5*t*, 7, 15, 22, 129,
    132, 132*t*, 133, 134, 135–136, 135*t*,
    137*t*, 140, 150*n*2, 155, 159, 176, 227,
    240, 246
Kalleberg, Arne, 112, 126, 240, 242
Kamlani, Kunal, 56, 236
Kanter, Rosabeth Moss, 15, 16, 156, 240
Katz, Harry, 236
Katz, Lawrence F., 20, 32, 237, 240
Kehr, James B., 23, 150*n*2, 178, 238
Kerr, Clark, 2, 10, 241
Kiechel, Walter, III, 1, 241
Killingsworth, Mark, 30, 31, 241
Kirchler, Erich, 238
Kirschsteiger, Georg, 14, 238
Knetsch, Jack, 5*t*, 7, 15, 22, 129, 132,
    132*t*, 133, 134, 135–136, 135*t*, 137*t*,
    140, 150*n*2, 155, 159, 176, 227, 240
Knoke, David, 236
Kochan, Thomas A., 240
Konovsky, Mary A., 14, 235, 241
Kramarz, Francis, 27, 92, 94, 233
Kremer, Michael, 29, 93, 162, 241

Krueger, Alan B., 20, 26, 30, 32, 226, 240, 241
Kruse, Douglas, 1, 24, 53, 58, 59, 60n1, 200, 235, 241

Labich, Kenneth, 217, 241
Lagasse, David, 52, 235
Lane, Julia, 92, 239
Lang, Kevin, 19, 237
Lawler, Edward E., 36, 37, 53, 54t, 58, 199, 241
Lawrence, Colin, 42n3, 241
Lawrence, Robert Z., 42n3, 241
Lazear, Edward, 12, 25, 58, 241
LeBlanc, Peter, 49, 241
Ledford, Gerald, 36, 37, 53, 54t, 58, 199, 241
Lee, Chris, 1, 242
Lemieux, Thomas, 36, 175, 211, 233, 238
Leonard, Jonathan S., 22, 94, 242
Lester, Richard A., 10, 242
Leventhal, Gerald S., 14, 143, 242
Levine, David I., 11, 13, 14, 18, 21, 25, 29, 30, 31, 32, 36, 38, 58, 70, 84n1, 94, 108n1, 112, 128n1, 142, 150n1, 165, 167, 168, 178, 234, 235, 236, 239, 240, 242, 244
Lichty, D. Terrence, 199, 242
Liebman, Jeffrey B., 218, 239
Lincoln, James, 112, 126, 128n4, 240, 242
Lind, E. Allan, 14, 243
Lindbeck, Assar, 33, 35, 41, 164, 243
Lipset, Seymour Martin, 24, 42n3, 160, 243
Lissy, William E., 52, 243
Livernash, E. Robert, 10, 243
Luthans, Brett, 49, 243

MacKenzie, G.B., 14, 243
MacKenzie, Scott B., 244
Malcolmson, James M., 25, 61n3, 243
Manicatide, Mircea, 16, 156, 243

Marginson, Paul, 177, 243
Marglin, Steven, 33, 243
Margolis, David N., 27, 92, 94, 233
Martin, Christopher, 235
Martin, Justin, 55, 243
Maskin, Eric, 29, 93, 162, 241
McAdams, Jerry, 53, 244
McGovern, Patrick, 246
Medoff, James, 46, 205, 226, 235, 243
Milgrom, Paul R., 13, 25, 33, 163, 243
Moffitt, Robert, 41, 175, 238
Mohrman, Susan, 36, 37, 53, 54t, 58, 199, 241
Moorman, Robert H., 14, 244
Morgenstern, Marlene L., 52, 243
Mulvey, Paul, 49, 241
Murphy, Kevin J., 143, 237
Murphy, Kevin M., 161, 172, 240

Nakata, Yoshifumi, 235
Nalbantian, Haig R., 53, 244
National Crosswalk Service Center, 97, 244
Neale, Margaret A., 142, 234
Neumark, David, 1, 26, 46, 177, 235, 237, 239, 244

Ockenfels, Axel, 175, 235
O'Dell, Carla, 53, 244
Oi, Walter Y., 69, 240
Okuno-Fujiwara, Masahiro, 245
Oldham, Greg, 226, 239
Olson, Craig, 240
O'Neill, John, 199, 234
Organ, Dennis W., 14, 237, 244
O'Shaughnessy, K.C., 57, 128n1, 128n3, 167, 236, 242, 244
Osterman, Paul, 12, 57, 58, 236, 244
Oswald, Andrew J., 25, 34, 163, 235, 236

Parker, Mike, 35, 37, 41, 244
Pennell, Virginia, 16, 156, 243
Pfeffer, Jeffrey, 244

Pierce, Brooks, 161, 174, 200, 240, 244
Piore, Michael, 2, 9, 10–11, 17, 18, 57, 58, 107, 156, 237
Podsakoff, Philip M., 14, 237, 243, 244
Poe, Randall, 52, 245
Polsky, Daniel, 1, 46, 51, 237, 244, 245
Pommerehne, Werner W., 150n2, 238
Prasnikar, Vesna, 245
Pugh, S. Douglas, 14, 241

Rabin, Matthew, 14, 140, 175, 236, 245
Reich, Michael, 235
Reinemer, Michael, 49, 245
Reizenstein, Richard, 233
Rentsch, Joan, 50, 246
Rentz, Joseph, 233
Reynolds, Lloyd G., 33, 163, 245
Riedl, Arno, 14, 238
Roberts, John, 13, 25, 33, 163, 243
Rock, Robert H., 55, 176, 245
Roos, D., 57, 246
Rose, Andrew K., 31, 233
Rose, Stephen J., 51, 245
Rosen, Sherwin, 25, 241
Roth, Alvin E., 176, 245
Rousseau, Denise M., 13, 22, 23, 143, 178, 245

Salop, Joanne, 25, 245
Salop, Steven, 25, 245
Sanfey, Peter, 34, 163, 235
Schieber, Sylvester, 46, 233
Schmidt, Christoph M., 113, 239
Schmidt, Klaus, 175, 238
Schotter, Andrew, 53, 244
Schuh, Scott, 59, 67, 237
Schweitzer, Mark E., 105, 239
Sculley, John, 24, 245
Segal, Lewis, 47, 245
Shapiro, Carl, 25, 33, 245
Shaw, Katherine, 38, 242
Shore, Lynn McFarlane, 13, 245
Siegel, Sidney, 139, 246
Simon, Herbert A., 13, 246
Smeeding, Timothy, 46, 235

Smith, Robert, 215, 246
Snower, Dennis, 33, 35, 41, 164, 168, 243, 246
Sommer, Steven, 49, 243
Spletzer, James, 92, 239
Stata, 208, 246
Steel, Robert, 50, 246
Steinmeier, Thomas, 56, 239
Stevens, Ann Huff, 46, 61n2, 240
Stigler, George, 25, 234
Stiglitz, Joseph, 25, 33, 245
Stiles, Philip, 16, 156, 246
Strauss, George, 240
Sullivan, Daniel, 47, 49, 233, 245
Summers, Lawrence, 26, 30, 32, 226, 241
Summers, Timothy P., 246
Swinnerton, Kenneth, 46, 246

Tetrick, Lois E., 15, 245
Thaler, Richard, 5t, 7, 15, 22, 129, 132, 132t, 133, 134, 135–136, 135t, 137t, 140, 150n2, 155, 159, 176, 227, 240
Tracy, Joseph, 175, 235
Training, 1
Tripp, Thomas M., 142, 234
Troske, Kenneth R., 177, 239
Truss, Catherine, 246
Tversky, Amnos, 176, 246
Tyler, Tom R., 14, 243

Ulman, Lloyd, 235
U.S. Bureau of Labor Statistics, 43n7, 84n5, 246
U.S. Department of Labor, 161
Useem, Michael, 236

Valletta, Robert G., 18, 33, 163, 200n1, 246

Wagner, Frank H., 52, 246
Weichbold, Andreas, 238
Wial, Howard, 46, 246
Williamson, Oliver E., 13, 18, 25, 33, 163, 246

Womack, J.P., 57, 246
Wood, Stephen, 177, 243

Yellen, Janet L., 13, 21, 31, 165, 233

Zamir, Shmuel, 245

Subject Index

The italic letters *f*, *n*, *t* following a page number indicate that the cited name is within a figure, note, or table respectively, on that page.

Ability to pay (employers')
  deregulation and, 35, 36
  predictor of wage levels, 163–164
  wage determination and, 33–34, 175
Accountability factor
  definition of, 215
  measure of, 33
  as wage determinant, 118
  See also Job characteristics
Affirmative action, 171
Age. *See* Employee characteristics
American Compensation Association
  survey, 52
American Management Association
  survey, 49
Aon Consulting Group, 49
Apple, 151*n*4
Autonomy. *See* Job characteristics
AWS. *See* U.S. Bureau of Labor
  Statistics Area Wage Surveys

Bargaining power, employee, 35–36,
  37–38, 164–165
Bargaining theories. *See* Rent-sharing
  theories
BLS Industry and Area Wage Surveys,
  101, 166
Broadbanding, 52
Buck Consultants, 52

Canada, 42*n*3
  layoffs, perceived fairness of,
    144–145, 145–147, 146*t*, 147*t*,
    148, 149*t*, 150, 231–232
  pay cuts, perceived fairness of,
    134–136, 135*t*, 137*t*, 138,
    155–156, 159–160
Career length. *See* Tenure
Career paths, modern, 48

Center for Effective Organization
  (University of Southern
  California), 53, 54*t*, 55
CEO bonuses, impact on perceived
  fairness of layoffs, 142–143, 148,
  149*t*
Cisco Systems, 59
Civil Rights Act, Title VII, threat of
  litigation under, 22
Cleveland Community Salary Survey
  (CSS), 3, 5–6, 5*t*, 199–200
  Compustat comparison, 207–208,
    208*t*, 209
  Current Population Surveys
    comparison, 87, 91, 205, 206*t*,
    207, 209
  data characteristics of, 85–87,
    88*t*–89*t*, 177, 201*t*–203*t*
  measure of factors determining wage
    variation, 87, 89–91
  representative strength of, 205, 206*t*,
    207–209
  U.S. Bureau of Labor Statistics Area
    Wage Surveys comparison, 207,
    209
  wage structures impact of, 208–209
Compensating differences, theory of, 4,
  30–32, 163
Compustat
  Cleveland Community Salary Survey
    comparison,
      207–208, 208*t*, 209
  Hay data set comparison, 219
Coopers and Lybrand survey, 53
CPS. *See* Current Population Surveys
CSS. *See* Cleveland Community Salary
  Survey
Current Population Surveys (CPS), 3,
  5–6, 5*t*, 175

Current Population Survey (cont.)
Cleveland Community Salary Survey
comparison, 87, 91, 205, 206*t*,
207, 209
Longitudinal Research Datafile
comparison, 92
Pension and Benefits supplements,
183–184, 185*t*–197*t*

DEC (corporation), 151*n*4
Declining rigidities hypothesis, 17–18,
21, 173*t*–174*t*, 174–175
Defined-contribution plans, 56
Deregulation, 35, 36–37
wage structures impact of, 164,
211–213, 212*t*
Dictionary of Occupational Titles (U.S.
Department of Labor), 161
Displacement penalty, 51
Downsizing
employee loyalty and, 49–50
job security and, 57
See also Layoffs

EDS (corporation), 59
Education
as wage determinant, 119*t*, 121*t*, 125
See also Employee characteristics
Education, returns to, 161
convergence between large and small
firms, 19–20, 72, 77, 156–157
occupational wage variation and,
97–98
Efficiency wage theory, 4, 27, 32–33,
35–36, 165–166
Employee attitudes, 48–50
See also Fairness, perceptions of
Employee bargaining power. *See*
Bargaining power, employee
Employee characteristics
convergence between large and small
firms, 74–75, 193*t*–194*t*
impact on perceived fairness of
layoffs, 139, 143–144, 148, 149*t*

as wage determinants, 119*t*, 121*t*,
125
See also Human capital theory
Employee characteristics, returns to, 30
convergence within regions, 81–83,
83*t*
large *vs.* small firms, 73, 154
Employee involvement, impact on
employee bargaining power,
35–36, 164–165
Employee stock ownership programs
(ESOPs), 53, 54*t*, 55, 176
Employer wage effects
efficiency wage theory and, 165
human capital theory and, 27, 111,
161–162
persistence of, 93–94, 103–104, 104*f*,
158
trend in, 95*f*, 98–99
trend in persistence of, 105, 106*f*,
107, 108
wage variation and, 92, 154–155,
174, 176
Employment, distribution by firm size,
67, 67*t*–69*t*, 69
Employment contract, 2, 15–16,
167–168
comparison to new employment
contract, 1, 3–4, 129
perceived fairness of, 22–24
See also New employment contract
ESOPs. *See* Employee stock ownership
programs
Establishment effects. *See* Plant wage
effects
Exchange rate shock, 34
External labor markets
relation to internal labor markets,
50–51
See also Local labor markets

Fairness, perceptions of
downsizing, 50
employment contract and, 22–24

individual characteristics' effect on,
177–178
internal labor markets, 13–15
layoffs, 140–145, 145–147, 146t,
147t, 148, 149t, 150, 231–232
new employment contract, 23–24
occupation effect on, 139
pay cuts, 131t–132t, 132–135,
134–136, 135t, 137t, 138
productivity and, 13–14, 21–22
wage determination, 175–176
Fairness Survey, 5–6, 5t
methodology of, 138–139
protocols of, 129–130
questionnaire, 227–229
Federal government, nominal wages of,
20
Federal Reserve Bank of Cleveland, 85,
87, 199
Firm effects. *See* Employer wage effects

Gain sharing, 53, 54t, 55
Ganz-Wiley, 48
Gender
internal labor markets and, 22
See also Employee characteristics
General human capital theory. *See*
Human capital theory
General Social Survey, 49
Globalization, 35, 36–37
wage structures impact of, 164,
213–214, 214t

Hay Associates, 48, 111–112, 216–217
Hay points, 215
predictor of wages within firms,
115–116, 116f, 126, 128
returns to, 161
wage determination by use of, 128n2
Hay Survey, 3, 5–6, 5t, 52, 177, 218,
220t–223t
representative strength of, 219
skill and responsibility measure, 33,
111–112, 215–217

wage variation, 92
See also Hay points
Health insurance plans, 56
Hewitt Associates, 52, 55
High-performance work systems, 57–59
Hoarding labor, 141, 142
perceived fairness of, 147
Human capital theory, 4, 26–30
employer wage effects, 27, 111,
161–162
returns to skills, 172, 173t–174t, 174
sorting and, 29, 155, 161–162
wage determination and, 33, 179–182
wage structures and, 28–29
See also Employee characteristics;
Job characteristics

IBM, 1, 151n4
Incentive pay, 54t, 55
Incentive theories, 4, 38, 40, 166–167
Indiana
wage determination in, 119t–120t,
120, 121t–125t, 125–126
Indiana/Japan data set, 5–6, 5t, 225–226
Industrial Society, 52
Information Access Company, 151n4
Informix, 151n4
Insider-outsider theories. *See* Rent-
sharing theories
Interim Services, 49
Internal labor markets, 10–12, 25, 41, 45
Civil Rights Act litigation threat, 22
employee attitudes and, 48–50
employee benefits, 56–57
employer size and, 18–21
fair agreement contract of, 13–15
high-performance work systems
adoption within, 57–59
Japanese vs. U.S., 12
job ladders, 11, 57, 58
new employment contract threat to,
42n5
pay practices within, 50–53, 54t,
55–56

Internal labor markets (cont.)
    ports of entry, 2, 11, 58
    relation to external labor markets,
        50–51
    relation to local labor markets,
        20–21, 154, 157–158
    sectoral employment shifts
        discouraging, 59
    tenure and, 46–48
    theories vs. results, 173*t*–174*t*
    theory predictions, 153–154
    wage determination within, 2, 9, 11,
        34, 52
    wage variation within, 56, 175
Internal labor markets, economic
        theories of, 25–40, 39*t*–40*t*
    compensating differences theory,
        30–32
    efficiency wage theory, 32–33
    human capital theory, 26–30
    incentive theories, 38, 40
    rent-sharing theories, 33–38
Internal labor markets, institutionalist
        theories of changing, 17–24
    declining rigidities, 17–18, 21,
        173*t*–174*t*, 174–175
    employer size, 18–21
    perceptions of fairness, 21–24
Internal wage structure effects
    persistence of, 94, 104, 104*f*
    trend in, 95*f*, 99–100
    trend in persistence of, 107–108,
        107*f*

Japan
    internal labor markets, 12, 47
    wage determination in, 119*t*–120*t*,
        120, 121*t*–125*t*, 125–126
Japanese management practices. *See*
        High-performance work systems
JDI. *See* Job Description Inventory
Job characteristics
    as wage determinants, 120,
        121*t*–125*t*, 125–126
    See also Human capital theory

Job Description Inventory (JDI), 226
Job displacement, 46–47, 47–48
Job evaluation process
    by Hay Associates, 216
    wage determination and, 11, 52, 86
Job ladders, internal labor markets, 11,
        57, 58
Job length. *See* Tenure
Job security
    internal labor markets, 11–12
    perceived, 50
Job title, as wage determinant, 20,
        51–52, 119*t*, 121*t*

Know-how factor, 33, 215
    as wage determinant, 118
    See also Job characteristics
Kodak, 1

Layoffs, 140, 141–142, 145–146
    procedural justice and, 142–143
    See also Downsizing
Layoffs, perceived fairness of
    Canada vs. Silicon Valley, 144–145,
        145–147, 146*t*, 147*t*, 148, 149*t*,
        150, 231–232
    CEO bonuses and, 142–143, 148,
        149*t*
    justifications, effect of, 140–145
    managerial implications, 168–169
    source of shock and, 146*t*
    union leadership implications,
        170–171
Levi Strauss, 55
Local labor markets, 20–21, 154,
        157–158
    See also External labor markets
Longitudinal Research Datafile, 92
Louis Harris and Associates, 49
Luntz Research Company, 56

Manufacturing sector, 68*t*, 77
    employment decline, 59, 75
    growth in temporary workers, 47
    internal labor markets of, 10–11

size-wage elasticity, 69
wage variation and, 99, 161
Mayflower Group, 48
Medicare. *See* Social insurance

National Center for Employee
Ownership, 53
National Employer survey, 59
National Longitudinal Survey of Youth
(NLSY), 175
Netscape, 151*n*4
New employment contract, 1, 16, 159,
167
Canada vs. U.S., 24
comparison to old employment
contract, 1, 3–4, 129
employee attitudes to, 48–50
managerial implications, 24,
168–169
perceived fairness of, 23–24
public policy implications, 171–172
threat to internal labor markets, 42*n*5
union leadership implications, 170
See also Employment contract
NLSY. *See* National Longitudinal
Survey of Youth
Nonmonetary recognition awards, 54*t*

Occupation
impact on perceived fairness of
layoffs, 139
See also Job characteristics
Occupation-employer covariance
wage variation and, 100–101, 100*f*
Occupation wage effects
persistence of, 93, 103, 104*f*
trend in, 95*f*, 96*t*, 97
trend in persistence of, 105, 106*f*, 108
Occupational wage variation, 97–98
Organizational change, 37–38, 164–165
Organizational citizenship behavior, 14
Organizational Revolution, 35–36
Outsourcing
high- and low-wage industries,
76–77, 76*t*

wage structures and, 21–22, 165–166
See also Sorting

Panel Study of Income Dynamics
(PSID), 175
Pay cuts, perceived fairness of, 22–24,
131*t*–132*t*, 132–135, 155–156
Canada vs. Silicon Valley, 134–136,
135*t*, 137*t*, 138, 159–160
Pay cuts, product-market competition
and, 42–43*n*6
Pay incentives
wage variation and, 38, 40, 101–103,
102*t*, 108–109*n*3, 117*t*, 166–167
Pension coverage, 84*n*4
Performance bonuses. *See* Variable
individual pay
Plant wage effects, 126, 127*f*
Porsche, 57
Ports of entry, internal labor markets, 2,
11, 58
Procedural justice
impact on employee attitude, 50
layoffs and, 142–143
theories of, 14–15
Product-market competition, effect on
wages, 42–43*n*6, 164, 213–214,
214*t*
Productivity
incentives for, 38, 40
perceptions of fairness and, 13–14,
21–22
Profit sharing, 53, 54*t*, 55, 176
PSID. *See* Panel Study of Income
Dynamics
*Psychological Contracts in
Organizations* (Rousseau), 23
Public policy, new employment contract
implications for, 171–172

Quebec (Canada), 42*n*3
See also Canada
Quit rates, relation to wages, 31

Race
    size-wage effect and, 75, 161
    sorting and, 22, 155
    as wage determinant, 119t, 121t
    See also Employee characteristics
Reciprocity, 174–175
    managerial implications of, 168
    productivity and, 14
    union leadership implications, 170
Rent-sharing theories, 4, 33–38,
        163–165
Returns
    convergence between large and small
        firms, 71–73, 156–157, 157f,
        190t–191t
    See also specific returns
Rolling sample technique, 93

Shell Oil Co./Peter Hart Research
        survey, 49
Sibson and Co., 49
Silicon Valley (California), 24
    layoffs, perceived fairness of,
        144–145, 145–147, 146t, 147t,
        148, 149t, 150, 231–232
    pay cuts, perceived fairness of,
        134–136, 135t, 137t, 138,
        159–160
Size-wage effect, 84n2
    convergence within regions, 78–83
    decline of, 19–20, 69–70, 70t, 72–73
    decomposition of sources of changes
        in, 71–78, 71t
    employee characteristics
        convergence between large and
        small firms, 74–75
    methods of decomposition of
        changes in, 63–66
    organizational change and, 37–38,
        164–165
    pension coverage and, 84n4
    race and, 75, 161
    returns for characteristics common at
        large firms, 77–78, 194t–195t
    sorting and, 156–157, 157f, 165

Size-wage gap. *See* Size-wage effect
Skills
    measures of, 26–27, 33, 111–112,
        215–217
    sorting of, 155, 158
    See also Employee characteristics;
        Job characteristics
Skills, returns to, 4, 6–7, 161–162
    convergence between large and small
        firms, 73
    human capital theory and, 172,
        173t–174t, 174
Social insurance, 171, 172
    expected value of, 56–57
Social Security. *See* Social insurance
Sorting
    human capital theory and, 29, 155,
        161–162
    race and, 22, 155
    size-wage effect, 156–157, 157f, 165
    of skills, 155, 158
    See also Outsourcing
S.R.A. Corporation, 48
Starbucks, 55
Sybase, 151n4

Technological change, bias toward the
        highly skilled, 30
Temporary workers, employment
        growth, 47, 59
Tenure, 60, 61n2
    convergence between large and small
        firms, 74
    internal labor markets, 46–48
    as wage determinant, 119t, 121t
    wage rigidity and, 42n1
    See also Employee characteristics
Tenure, returns to, 77
    convergence between large and small
        firms, 19–20, 156
Towers Perrin, 48, 49

Unemployment insurance. *See* Social
        insurance
Union avoidance, 19, 33, 35

Union membership
    decline in, 74
    new employment contract
        implications on, 170
    returns to, 77
    wage variation and, 99
U.S. Bureau of Labor Statistics Area
    Wage Surveys (AWS), 207, 209
U.S.-Canadian attitude gap, managerial
    implications, 169
U.S. Department of Defense, 50
United Steel Workers of America,
    nominal wages of, 20

Variable group-based pay, 38, 40, 53,
    54t, 55
Variable individual pay, 38, 40, 52, 54t
Vocational preparation, returns to,
    97–98, 161

Wage determination
    accountability factor, 118
    employee characteristics, 119t, 121t,
        125
    employers' ability to pay, 33–34, 175
    factors in, 119t–120t, 121t–125t,
        125–126
    human capital theory, 33, 179–182
    internal labor markets, 2, 9, 11, 34,
        52
    job characteristics, 120, 121t–125t,
        125–126
    job evaluation process, 52, 86
    job title, 20, 51–52, 119t, 121t
    occupational wage surveys, 11, 18
    perceptions of fairness and, 175–176
    performance, 51–52
    relationship between initial and
        future wages, 61n3
Wage inequality, 6–7
Wage inequality, internal
    outsourcing and, 21–22
Wage levels
    convergence between large and small
        firms, 19, 156

convergence within regions, 78–81,
    80t, 81t
employers' ability to pay as predictor
    of, 163–164
globalization effect on, 213–214,
    214t
product-market competition effect
    on, 164, 213–214, 214t
See also Wage variation
Wage patterns, changes to
    decomposition of sources of, 71–78,
        185t–189t
Wage reductions. See Pay cuts
Wage structures
    Cleveland Community Salary Survey
        impact on, 208–209
    convergence between large and small
        firms, 19–20
    convergence within regions, 78–83
    deregulation effect on, 164, 211–213,
        212t
    determination of, 9, 11
    globalization effect on, 164,
        213–214, 214t
    human capital theory and, 28–29
    outsourcing, 21–22, 165–166
    persistence of, 155, 158
    product-market competition impact
        on, 213–214, 214t
    rent-sharing theories of, 163
    See also Wage variation
Wage surveys, occupational, 11
Wage variation
    Current Population Surveys vs.
        Longitudinal Research Datafile,
        92
    employer wage effects, 92, 154–155,
        174, 176
    internal labor markets, 56, 175
    large vs. small firms, 154
    manufacturing sector, 99, 161
    measure of factors determining, 87,
        89–93
    measure of trends in persistence of
        factors determining, 93–94

Wage variation (cont.)
    occupation-employer covariance and,
        100–101, 100*f*
    pay incentives and, 38, 40, 101–103,
        102*t*, 108–109*n*3, 117*t*, 166–167
    persistence of factors determining,
        103–104, 104*f*
    skills and, 113, 114*t*, 115–116, 117*t*,
        118
    trends in factors determining, 91–93,
        95, 95*f*, 96*t*, 97–103, 98*f*, 100*f*,
        102*t*
    trends in persistence of factors
        determining, 105, 106*f*, 107–108,
        107*f*
    See also Wage levels; Wage
        structures
Wage variation, analysis of
  household vs. salary surveys, 85
Wal-Mart, 59
Watson Wyatt, 49
Welde, Ken, 219*n*2
Wilcoxon-Mann-Whitney rank-sum test,
    139
William A. Mercer, 52
Workplace Employee Relations Survey
    (United Kingdom), 177

About the Institute

The W.E. Upjohn Institute for Employment Research is a nonprofit research organization devoted to finding and promoting solutions to employment-related problems at the national, state, and local levels. It is an activity of the W.E. Upjohn Unemployment Trustee Corporation, which was established in 1932 to administer a fund set aside by the late Dr. W.E. Upjohn, founder of The Upjohn Company, to seek ways to counteract the loss of employment income during economic downturns.

The Institute is funded largely by income from the W.E. Upjohn Unemployment Trust, supplemented by outside grants, contracts, and sales of publications. Activities of the Institute comprise the following elements: 1) a research program conducted by a resident staff of professional social scientists; 2) a competitive grant program, which expands and complements the internal research program by providing financial support to researchers outside the Institute; 3) a publications program, which provides the major vehicle for disseminating the research of staff and grantees, as well as other selected works in the field; and 4) an Employment Management Services division, which manages most of the publicly funded employment and training programs in the local area.

The broad objectives of the Institute's research, grant, and publication programs are to 1) promote scholarship and experimentation on issues of public and private employment and unemployment policy, and 2) make knowledge and scholarship relevant and useful to policymakers in their pursuit of solutions to employment and unemployment problems.

Current areas of concentration for these programs include causes, consequences, and measures to alleviate unemployment; social insurance and income maintenance programs; compensation; workforce quality; work arrangements; family labor issues; labor-management relations; and regional economic development and local labor markets.